THE AUSTRALIAN BOOK OF TRUE CRIME

THE AUSTRALIAN BOOK OF TRUE CRIME

LARRY WRITER

PIER 9

CONTENTS

CHAPTER 1

THE GRAEME THORNE KIDNAPPING

Stephen Bradley: Kidnapper and murderer

1960

In 1960, £100,000 would buy, more or less, what $4 million does today. Imagine, then, the jubilation in the Bondi, Sydney, household of the Thorne family when their ticket won them first prize in Opera House Lottery No. 10. In those days, beaming lottery winners were a feel-good staple of newspapers' front pages, and when news broke of the massive win reporters were despatched to the Thornes' flat. On 1 June, the *Daily Mirror* ran a large shot of a jubilant Mrs Freda Thorne cradling daughter Belinda and smiling broadly at her good fortune. Husband Bazil and son Graeme were out of frame but no less a part of the celebrations.

Five weeks later, the media was back. But this time the smiles had been replaced by tears of unimaginable anguish.

At 8.20 am on Thursday, 7 July, a fair, mild midwinter day, 8-year-old Graeme Thorne, as he did every morning, kissed his mum goodbye and left home to walk the 200 metres to the nearby corner of Wellington and O'Brien Streets where, as usual, he was to be collected by family friend Phyllis Smith and driven to his preparatory school at Scots College in Bellevue Hill. When Smith arrived at the corner at 8.30 Graeme was not there. Puzzled, she drove to Scots and asked teachers if the boy had already arrived. He hadn't. Smith immediately returned to the Thornes' home and told Freda that Graeme was missing.

Freda telephoned her husband, who was in the country on business, with the alarming news. Bazil Thorne told her he would return home immediately. And then, because her son, a responsible little boy who enjoyed school, was most unlikely to have wandered off on his own volition, Freda alerted police. Officers canvassed all homes in the immediate area. No one had seen Graeme that day.

Meanwhile, Sergeant Larry Shea sat with Freda to comfort her and talk to her about Graeme in a bid to elicit information that could help in the search.

At 10.30 am, the telephone rang and a male voice, with what Freda described as 'a slight foreign accent', asked, 'Is that Mrs Thorne?' When she replied that it was, the caller said, 'Is your husband there? Put him on.' Freda handed the phone to Sergeant Shea who, suspecting the call had something to do with Graeme's disappearance, made the instantaneous decision to pose as the boy's father, and said, 'This is Mr Thorne here.' Continued the man, 'I've got your boy. I want £25,000 by 5 pm or I'll feed him to the sharks.' 'Where would I find that kind of money?' The caller, voice rising: 'You've got it … you've got it. *Yes, you have!* I'll contact you later.' Click.

Shea told Freda, as gently as he could, what the mystery man had said, and called headquarters. Within minutes the search for Graeme Thorne had turned state-wide, occupying every available police officer and augmented by civilian volunteers. A photograph of Graeme, a small, open-faced boy in a horizontal-striped T-shirt, his hair brilliantined, side-parted and swept back – was broadcast on television and published in large format on the front page of newspapers. Detectives – all, from the photographs of the day, with cigarette smoke-lined faces, short back and sides haircuts under soft felt hats, and seemingly in their sixties and seventies – converged on the Edward Street flat to further interview the distraught Freda and Bazil, who had only just reached home. They also wanted to be there if the kidnapper telephoned again later, as he had indicated he would.

At 9.47 that night the phone rang. Detective Sergeant David Valentine, who had relieved Shea, answered it. A male voice with what, concurred Valentine with Freda Thorne, seemed like a European accent said, 'Is that you, Mr Thorne?' Valentine said it was. The man asked, 'Have you got the money?' 'Yes,' said Valentine. Continued the caller, 'Put it in two paper bags.' Valentine: 'Wait a minute. I want to take your instructions down. I don't want to make a mistake.' At that, thought Valentine, the man lost his nerve, for he suddenly sounded agitated, mumbled something the policeman found unintelligible and hung up.

The Thornes, by now in a state of near-collapse, embraced loved ones and their minister, the Reverend Clive Goodwin, who offered a consolatory embrace and religious counsel.

Over the course of the day, the information was gleaned from interviews with the Thornes and their neighbours that on or around 14 June, three weeks before the abduction, a stranger claiming to be a private investigator had called at the block of flats asking questions. He was remembered as a thick-set man in his thirties or forties, dark brown hair longish at the back, sallow complexion, bushy black brows, who spoke with an accent. The visitor wore light-coloured trousers, an open-necked shirt with a cravat tucked inside, and a light brown tweed sports coat, and seemed to be on edge. He had knocked on the Thornes' door and asked Freda if she knew a Mr Bognor. She said she did not, but perhaps the people in the flat above did, and why didn't he try there. He did, but this time the man wanted to know if the occupant, whose name was Dorothy Lord, knew a Mr Bailey or Balley.

Other locals had noticed the fellow around the area at various times in June leading up to the disappearance of Graeme Thorne. He was spotted sitting on a park seat across the road from the Thornes' block of flats, and generally lurking in Thorne's neighbourhood and around Scots College where he had approached two 7-year-olds and asked, 'Do you know Graeme Thorne?'

A number of locals also reported an unfamiliar iridescent blue 1955 Ford Customline car cruising the vicinity, and parked in the Thorne's Street.

After she closed the door on the man and sent him upstairs to continue his enquiries, Freda Thorne told police, she had thought no more about the visit until her son disappeared, but now it took on sinister significance. A police artist's likeness of the 'investigator', by now the prime suspect, was published in the press.

The realisation dawned on the police, and on ministers and advisers in the NSW Government, that if in fact this was an abduction, as now seemed certain, it was the first kidnapping of a child for ransom ever known in Australia. A task force was established to probe whether the snatching of Graeme Thorne could be the work of a European, Asian or American criminal. The *modus operandi* of Bruno Hauptman, who had kidnapped and murdered the baby of American aviator Charles A. Lindbergh in 1932, was studied, as were, the public was assured, a number of recent film, radio and television dramas that featured a kidnapping.

In the days after the vanishing, panic gripped Sydney. Parents accompanied their children to school or, better yet, kept them at home. Any stranger showing up in a neighbourhood was met with scowls and muttered threats. Tracker dogs with police in tow scoured parks, river banks and deserted areas. Helicopters and light aircraft swooped, and there seemed to be a police car, transmitter crackling, on every street. Radio and television stations interrupted their programs to breathlessly apprise listeners and viewers of every development. Newspapers devoted the front page, and three or four more inside, to the hunt for Graeme Thorne. There were the usual cruel hoaxers whose claims sent the Thornes' hopes soaring until they were revealed as false and plunged the family into despair. One particularly reprehensible character, a photographer named Alfred Vercoe, of Beresford, near Newcastle, contacted Bazil Thorne and claimed to be holding Graeme. He organised for Bazil to drop off the £25,000 ransom at an appointed place and time. However, not Bazil but a squad of detectives was waiting at the rendezvous. There is little reason to doubt the later claim by Vercoe's solicitor that Vercoe was far from the most popular inmate of the Newcastle holding cells, nor to doubt that he was very roughly treated by police while in custody.

Even the denizens of Sydney's underworld lent a hand, growling that they were on the lookout for the kidnapper – and woe betide him if he fell into their hands. One anonymous criminal, with a long record of assault, battery and theft, revealed as much about the xenophobic Australian mindset in those days as his grisly plans for the kidnapper when he confided to the *Daily Mirror*, 'I'm shocked that anyone would start snatching kiddies in Australia. I know a dozen men who would tear him to pieces if they got their hands on him. There are some pretty willing boys and bad crims among the team, but each one has some sort of idea of a fair go. I'll bet a pound to a peanut it's not an Australian knockabout man responsible for this. I've heard jobs planned in gaol, pubs and beer houses over the past twenty years but never heard it suggested that anyone take on kidnapping. I'll be proud to be called a "copper" if I can help in any way to find this little kid.'

Kate Leigh, murderess, queen of sly grog and former razor-gang boss, weighed in too: 'I've got one of the biggest butcher's knives in Sydney and it would give me the greatest pleasure to use it on the mongrels. I hope I hear something that will put me on their trail. By the time I finish with them, they'll make a good meal for the dogs' home.'

The day after Graeme Thorne disappeared, his empty schoolbag was found in scrub at Bantry Bay near Frenchs Forest on Sydney's North Shore, and three days later the contents of the bag – Graeme's cap, raincoat, a schoolbook and a plastic lunchbox with a peeled apple inside – were found in thick bush a kilometre away. But a painstaking search of the region by police and tracker dogs, including its many sandstone caves, in the teeming rain and fog that was engulfing Sydney that day, was fruitless.

Bazil Thorne made an impassioned televised plea, the first use of the medium in Australia for such a purpose: 'To whoever is holding my son: I am ready to pay you the money you are demanding for his safe return. I will pay you in cash at any place and at any time you specify. You may contact me at my home. You will not be betrayed. Bazil Thorne.'

The newspapers printed the plea and ran German, Italian and Greek versions. There was no response and on 13 July the Thornes tried again: 'We, the mother and father of Graeme Thorne, earnestly request you to return our son to us at the earliest possible moment. We plead with you to at least let Graeme contact us. We again emphasise we are prepared to pay the sum of £25,000 asked for and wish to do all we can to make that easy. We are writing this letter in the presence of the Reverend Clive Goodwin of St Mark's Church of England, Darling Point, who christened Graeme and his sister and is willing to help us and you in every way possible. Freda Thorne and Bazil Thorne.' Again, silence.

On 23 July, a pale, thin, desperately sad-eyed Freda appeared on television. She addressed her son through her tears, her voice catching: 'Keep your chin up, darling. We are doing all in our power to get you back. If you are out there, Graeme, if you can see me, keep your chin up, darling. We are thinking of you every minute.' Her next words were addressed to the kidnapper, reiterating that the ransom would be paid in full.

As July turned to August, most Australians, police and public alike, now feared that Graeme Thorne would not be found alive. Yet when his body was discovered on 16 August, nothing could alleviate the shock and fury. Children playing cowboys and Indians in a vacant lot in Grandview Street, Seaforth, found the body under a rock shelf. Graeme was wrapped in a cheap blue tartan rug with a tassel missing from its fringe. There was a wound and bruising on the left back of his head, and beneath the wound his skull was fractured. There were abrasions on his neck. A scarf was knotted around his chin. His feet were tied with coarse twine. He still wore his school uniform – shirt, jumper, pants, shoes and socks, and blazer. The street was closed off to the public and a thorough search conducted for clues to the killer's identity. The rug in which Graeme's body was wrapped was taken to the police laboratory for analysis.

Bazil Thorne performed one of the most terrible duties any parent can when he identified his son's body at the City Morgue.

At Scots College and in churches across the city, there were prayers for the little lost boy. The Thornes were sedated to blunt their grief. Graeme was buried on 19 August to the sounds of the weeping of his loved ones and classmates and a lament played by the Scots College Pipe Band.

An autopsy had shown that Graeme had died from his head injury or from asphyxiation, or both. Not only that, but his stomach contents, the condition of his clothing and the growth of fungus on his shoes indicated that he had been killed within 24 hours of being abducted and that his body had lain undisturbed under the rock shelf in the vacant lot for a month and a half until it was stumbled upon by the children. Neither Graeme's tie nor his blazer buttons had been undone after they were tied and buttoned by his mother just before he left home that morning of 7 July. His pocket handkerchief was unused.

The rug was found to have been manufactured by the Onkaparinga company in South Australia between May 1955 and January 1957. It was festooned with hairs: reddish animal hairs like those of a Pekingese dog, and dark brown human hairs, blonde-brown hairs 23 cm long, and blonde hairs rinsed with henna. Foliage from two types of ornamental garden cypress, *Chamaecyparis pisifera* and *Cupressus glabra*, was also found in the rug. Particles of dirt and of lime-stock mortar, like that used in the construction of the foundations of a house, were found in the blanket, and on the boy's clothes and shoes.

With the evidence accumulated so far, police were now able to report that Graeme Thorne was probably battered or choked to death by a stocky, dark-haired man with a foreign accent on or close to the day of his abduction; that his body had lain under a house with lime-stock mortar foundations, and that in the garden of the house were two particular plants. Police searched all the homes in Seaforth and surrounding suburbs for the plants and the mortar.

Then, a break. A local postman who, serendipitously, was an amateur botanist, knew of one house where specimens of both *Chamaecyparis pisifera* and *Cupressus glabra* were thriving. It was in Moore Street, Clontarf, only a couple of kilometres from Seaforth, and its former inhabitants were the Bradley family – Stephen, his wife Magda and their three children.

The postman, who also seemed to possess an encyclopaedic knowledge of the local residents' movements and whereabouts, added that the Bradleys had quit the house sometime early in August and taken up residence in a holiday flat in Osborne Street, Manly, and, furthermore, that they had left Australia a week ago and were travelling to the United Kingdom on board the P&O liner *Himalaya*.

When the investigators checked out Stephen Leslie Bradley they realised that they had already interviewed him at his employers, Nutt & Muddle, the poker machine manufacturing company, in Rushcutters Bay on 24 August, after neighbours had reported him as someone who drove an iridescent blue 1955 Ford Customline and spoke with a foreign accent.

Bradley, their notes reminded them, had been plausible that day and raised no suspicions with the interviewing officers. He coolly explained that on 7 July, the day of Graeme Thorne's abduction, he had moved house from Moore Street, Clontarf, to a flat in Osborne Street, Manly, while his family had left at 10 that morning in a taxi bound for Sydney Airport to catch a flight to Hayman Island in Queensland, where they would holiday. His Customline car, he said, had remained in the Moore Street garage all day, except when he had driven to the local hardware shop in Balgowlah where he had purchased some tie-wire for packing cases. The removalists, he went on, had arrived at around 11 am and removed all the furniture to Manly by 2 pm. Apart from his trip to the hardware store, Bradley said, he had been at the house the entire morning. Certainly he was nowhere near Bondi at 8.30 am.

The Bradleys, police learned after Stephen Bradley became their prime suspect, had told friends and acquaintances that they were going to live in England because Magda, an unsuccessful composer of popular songs, thought she would have a greater chance of selling them in London where there were so many more music publishers. Those who knew them said the Bradleys were friendly people, popular with neighbours and workmates, not extraordinary in any way. They had three children from previous marriages. Rupert, 13, and the deaf-since-birth Robert, 15, were Magda's children, and Helen, 7, was Stephen's daughter. Steve and Magda Bradley gave every appearance of being devoted parents. He, who they understood had been born in Budapest, Hungary, but was a naturalised Australian, was a quiet bloke, while she, a tiny woman who wore heavy makeup and was proud of her long blonde hair, was more garrulous, with her favourite topics of conversation being children and clothes. On her arm, remembered one acquaintance, was a tattoo, a Nazi-inflicted memento of her incarceration in Auschwitz during World War II.

The authorities swarmed all over the house in Moore Street. They took to the laboratory cuttings from the plants and lime-stock mortar fragments from under the house by the garage. Now that they had the Customline's registration number – AYO 382 – they were able to locate it at a car salesyard in Granville to whose proprietor Bradley had sold the vehicle days before he left Australia on the *Himalaya*. Hairs, human and canine, just like those found on the Onkaparinga blanket, were located on the floor and seats of the car and caked thick in a dog's brush in the boot. Also in the boot was foliage similar to that in the blanket. A visitor to the Bradleys' house after they vacated it had found a 35mm negative in the garden. He gave it to police. In the picture one of the Bradley children was sitting on a tartan rug, exactly like the one that wrapped Graeme Thorne's body. Then searchers found a tassel from a blue rug, the very tassel that was missing from the fringe of the blanket.

There was more. The Bradleys had left their Pekingese dog, Cherry, at a Sydney veterinary clinic – its hairs were similar to those in the rug. Pieces of twine found in the Moore Street house were identical to that used to bind the boy's feet. The soil and lime-mortar particles under the Bradleys' home and in the garage matched that found in the blanket and on Graeme's shoes and clothes.

Estate agent Markus Bernhardt came forward to report that just before the abduction he had shown Stephen Bradley around the house next door to the vacant lot in Grandview Street where Graeme's body was found. The yard, said the agent, offered a perfect view of the vacant lot.

The Everest of accumulating evidence that Stephen Bradley was the kidnapper and murderer of Graeme Thorne was all circumstantial – remember, these were the days before DNA analysis – but compelling.

Next, police showed photographs of Stephen Bradley to Freda Thorne and the people in the flat above theirs. Each readily identified him as the 'private investigator' who had knocked on their door around 14 June. 'That is the man who called at my home,' said Freda.

A warrant was issued for Stephen Bradley's arrest. On 9 October, detectives Jack Bateman and Brian Doyle were despatched to Colombo, the capital of Ceylon (now Sri Lanka), where the *Himalaya* was about to berth en route to the United Kingdom. Their mission: bring him back.

Istavan Baranyay migrated from Italy to Melbourne in 1950. Like most of his countrymen, he had suffered in the war, narrowly escaping being murdered by the Nazis. Australia seemed to him, as it struck other refugees, to be a place of unbridled opportunity, a land of happiness and sunshine. To help him fit in with the locals, he changed his name by deed poll to Stephen Leslie Bradley. Although he boasted of having been a respected doctor and engineer back in Europe (claims never substantiated), his usual lines of work in his adopted country were as a mechanic, a labourer, an electroplater, a real estate agent paid on commission, and a hotel manager. He wed Eva Laszlo in Melbourne in 1952 and they had a daughter, Helen. Three years after their wedding, Eva was killed in a car crash, leaving Stephen to raise Helen alone. In 1958, the impoverished widower married Magda Wittman, who had recently divorced and retained custody of sons Peter and Robert. The newly blended family moved to Bondi before they purchased the home in Moore Street, Clontarf. (After Bradley became the most notorious man in the land, Eva Laszlo's father, Dr Franz Laszlo, took legal steps to remove Helen from Magda's custody, and the girl returned to live with the Laszlo family in Melbourne.)

On 10 October, Bradley was with his family buying ebony elephants from boatmen who had pulled their vessels alongside the *Himalaya* where it was berthed in Colombo. He was handed a note by a ship's messenger: He was required in Captain Slinn's quarters at once. Did his heart sink? He must have known right then that it was all over. Local policemen detained him until Bateman and Doyle arrived to charge him with the kidnapping and murder of Graeme Thorne.

More than a month of diplomatic argy-bargy ensued while extradition details were nutted out with a Ceylonese government loath to cooperate with Australia, a member of the British Empire from which Ceylon had recently and acrimoniously extricated itself. Meanwhile Bradley languished in a cell with views of Colombo's picturesque and bustling harbour while Magda continued on to London with the children on the *Himalaya*. When told that Stephen was charged with the kidnapping and murder of Graeme Thorne, she gasped, 'I spent a year in a Nazi concentration camp but this is a worse shock. Steve is a marvellous husband and good father. He is not capable of doing anything wrong. I'll always love him for his kindness and thoughtfulness. He will clear himself on any charge ... There must be a misunderstanding. This must all be a bad dream.'

But it wasn't. And on the flight back to Australia on 18 November, handcuffed to a seatbelt beside detectives Bateman and Doyle, and later when interrogated further in Sydney, Bradley confessed. 'I've done this thing with the Thorne boy,' he began. 'What will happen to me?' And then it all came out ...

Bradley's handwritten confession was tendered to the court during Graeme Thorne's inquest. He wrote:

> I have red in the newspaper that Mr Thorne won the first prize in the Operahouse Lottery. I decided that I would kidnap his son, and I knew there address from the Newspaper, and I have got their phone number from the telephone exchange. I went to the house to see them, I have asked for someone but cannot remember what name. Mrs Thorne said she did not know that name and she told me to enquier in the flat upstairs. I went upstairs and I seen the woman there. I have done this because I thoht that the Thornes will check up. I went out and watched the Thorne boy leaving the house and seen him for about three mornings and I have seen where he went. And one morning I have followed him to the school at Bellevue Hill. One or two mornings I have seen a woman pick him up, and

> take him to School. On the day we moved from Clontarf I went to [the Thorne's street]. I parked the car in a street, I don't know the name of the street. It is off Wellington Street, I have got out from the car and I waited on the cornor untill the boy walked down to the car. I have told the boy that I am to take him to the School. He sed why, where is the Lady. I sed she is sick and can not come today. Then they boy got in the car, and I drove him around for a while, and over harbour bridge. I went to a public phone box near the spit bridge and I rang the Thornes. I talked to Mrs Thorn and to a man who sed he was the boys father. I have asked for £25,000 from the boys mother and father. I told them that if I don't get the money I feed him to the Sharks and I have told them I ring later. I took the boy in the car home to Clontarf and I put the car in my Garage. I told the boy to get out of the car to come and see another boy. When he got out of the car I have put a scarf over his mouth, and put him in the boot of the car, and slammed the boot. I went in my house and the furniture removalist came, a few minutes after. When it was nearly dark, I went to the car and found the boy was dead. That night I tied the boy up with string and put him in my rug. I put the boy in the boot of the Ford car again, and then I throw his case and cap near Bantry Bay, and I put the boy on a vacant lotment near the house I went to see with a estate agent, to buy it sometime before.

Detectives Bateman and Doyle said Bradley had told them how he had kidnapped Graeme Thorne because '[he] wanted money' and he thought he could get it in the form of a ransom from Bazil Thorne, who everyone who read a newspaper knew was wealthy because of his lottery win. Bradley claimed he had not meant for the boy to die. He had taken Graeme in the boot of the car to his home in Clontarf before the removalists arrived. 'There is the garage. I don't want to go in there,' the accused man said when he took detectives on a run-around of the various scenes of his crime. 'That's where I done it.' Said Doyle, 'The boy had a fractured skull. Did you hit him with something?' Bradley answered, 'No, I never hit the boy. I think he hurt his skull on the spare tyre.' When Doyle asked Bradley, 'What did you use the scarf for?', Bradley replied, 'I put it in his mouth to stop the noise of his calling out – not on his neck as the newspapers say.'

Hairs from Bradley's hairbrush in his luggage from the *Himalaya* matched the dark hairs found in the rug.

When the police said they would place Bradley in a line-up to see whether the Thornes could recognise him, Bradley had spluttered, 'Please don't line me up. I am the one who has done this thing. Do not bring the people to see me. There is no need.' Nevertheless, Bradley was placed among a group of men and Freda Thorne was brought to see if she could identify him as the one who had passed himself off as a private eye in mid June. If he was that man, she was to place her hand on his shoulder. The grief-stricken mother looked at him, said he was the one, but refused to touch the man who had slain her son.

By the time of his murder trial, which began in Sydney's Central Criminal Court on 23 March 1961, Bradley had had a re-think. He retracted his confession and pleaded not guilty to kidnapping and murdering Graeme Thorne. Before Judge Clancy and a packed and seething gallery, which included the old gangster Kate Leigh, the one with the butcher's knife, as usual dressed in a wide hat and fur coat and catcalling relentlessly despite warnings from the Bench to desist, Bradley claimed that he had been verballed by the detectives. They had frightened him into confessing to killing Graeme Thorne by telling him his wife and children would be persecuted and that he himself would be 'taken care of' by violent police officers ('a gang of wolves,' he averred) if he did not. Detectives Doyle and Bateman denied this in the face of spirited questioning by defence counsel Fred Vizzard.

The prosecution introduced Dr John Laing, who testified that Graeme had died violently after being struck on the head with tremendous force, throttled, or both. Bradley's explanation for the boy's death, that he must somehow have accidentally hit his head on the spare tyre, was dismissed as ridiculous. At that, Freda Thorne wept, and her husband looked stricken. She wept once more when Bradley's telephone threat to feed Graeme to the sharks was aired.

Cherry, the Pekingese dog, made a surprise appearance in court from beyond the grave. The dog had died some weeks past, but knowing the matching of its hair with some of the strands found on the blanket was vital to the prosecution, the Crown had had Cherry preserved by a taxidermist. At the relevant time, when government microbiologist Dr Cameron Cramp was called to the stand, the dog's body, wrapped in brown paper, was brought to the courtroom and exhibited. One wit in the public gallery hollered that he hoped Cherry would be spared cross-examination.

Further experts were called to state that there was 'no difference' between the foliage, twine, mortar fragments and soil samples found in the blanket and on Graeme's clothes and collected by investigators at the Bradleys' home and in their car.

Throughout, Stephen Bradley sat impassively, his face betraying no emotion no matter how pathetic or gruesome the evidence aired.

At that moment, Bradley was the most despised person in Australia. He ticked many boxes. Killing a child ranks as the most heinous of crimes and, trial or no trial, most people believed he had done just that. He was a foreigner. He was unrepentant. He was swarthy and squat and bore a close resemblance to the American bad man Al Capone. And rare was the Australian who did not find his threat, after he kidnapped Graeme Thorne, to 'feed him to the sharks', particularly repellent. Perhaps, to Bradley, it was a simple figure of speech he'd heard used in some kidnap flick and he had no sense of the visceral horror such an image evokes in Australians. But in using those callous words Bradley had stamped himself, in the eyes of millions, as a black-hearted villain undeserving of mercy.

Most people followed the daily proceedings assiduously in the media, and the case was the subject of choice around breakfast tables, in workplace lunch rooms and at dinner parties.

Each day of the trial, ordinary folk, celebrities, sports stars, politicians and even a team of Tasmanian women softballers (who were refused entry until they went to their hotel and changed their slacks for skirts) began queuing outside the court at sunrise, hoping to get a seat when the doors opened at nine. The *Daily Mirror* sent reporter William Olson along to interview some of the punters for a side feature. One 'court regular' laid down the law to him about what was and was not acceptable to the judge: 'While court's in session, don't pull your trousers up around your knees, don't eat, don't smoke and don't read. The judge don't like it, and if you do any of them things, they'll pull you up and make a fool of you in front of the whole place.'

Bradley was called to the stand on 27 March. He reiterated that his earlier confession had been forced from him by Doyle and Bateman. In a clear, strong voice he swore he had neither kidnapped nor killed Graeme Thorne, and that he had never been to the street where the Thornes lived. On the day of the murder, he was at home organising the removal of his goods to the Manly flat. 'Sirs,' he said, 'I have nothing to do with the taking of the little boy.' He added that he did not believe he could receive a fair trial because as a 'new Australian' he was the victim of 'powerful emotions' and 'prejudice'.

To establish a motive, the prosecution quizzed Bradley on his finances. It transpired that the Bradleys were in financial strife. Stephen, though claiming to be a qualified engineer, could land only menial factory jobs. Magda could sell no songs. Nine pounds out of the £25 Bradley made each week at Nutt & Muddle went to their mortgage. That left only £16 to live on. Yet they borrowed the funds to take holidays, they had two cars – the Customline and a yellow Goggomobil – and Magda and the children wore new and stylish clothes. The £3,500 Magda brought to the marriage two years before was fast diminishing. Prosecutor W.J. Knight reminded the court that Bradley had told police in his confession that he had done it 'for money'.

Magda's appearance on the stand literally triggered a riot. A group of around thirty women stormed into the courtroom, desperate to see the woman who lived with the fiend Bradley give her evidence. A number fell to the ground in the crush and were trampled. Scuffles broke out and police trying to restore order were attacked. Packed lunches and shopping bags were strewn all over the floor. A court clerk tutted that in all his days he had never seen anything like this 'disgusting bargain sale stampede'.

When order was restored and the rioters evicted, Magda Bradley began her evidence. She denied that her husband had abducted and murdered Graeme Thorne and indignantly refuted a suggestion that she was an accomplice. No, the trip to England on the *Himalaya* was not an attempt to flee Australia; they were going because her work prospects were better there and she felt her deaf son would receive better treatment in London. The scarf tied around the boy's chin was not her husband's. At every accusation by the prosecution, she replied calmly and implacably, 'No, sir. You are wrong' or 'I am sorry, sir, it is just a coincidence.'

Summing up for the defence, lawyer Vizzard ridiculed the evidence against his client as 'circumstantial' and made particular mention of the uselessness of the police's line-up identifications because photographs of Bradley had been published in the newspapers on the day of his arrest in Colombo.

The day of the verdict, 29 March, a crowd began queuing outside the court at 1.30 am. Fortified by sandwiches and thermos tea, they nattered about the jury's impending decision. No one countenanced the possibility that Bradley would get off.

After retiring for three hours and 22 minutes, the jury returned at 8.10 pm. The court, and the nation tuned in to its radios and televisions, learned that Bradley had been found guilty of the murder of Graeme Thorne. The evidence arrayed against him was too incriminating, and the jurors were particularly swayed by Dr Reid's testimony that Graeme died because he had been hit on the head with great force, thus catching Bradley in a seeming lie.

In sentencing Bradley, Judge Clancy believed that Bradley's written confession had the ring of truth – the language he had used was not that of a man being forced to confess under duress – and ordered him to serve the rest of his days in prison. Bradley had shown no emotion throughout the trial, and he showed none now.

Freda and Bazil Thorne stood stony-faced, drawn, diminished by their ordeal as the verdict was announced. Yes, justice had been served, but all they really wanted was to have their darling son back. And that, of course, could never happen.

At the words 'life imprisonment', the public gallery erupted into cheers and furious cries of 'Hang the bastard!'. Kate Leigh had a more fitting, more picturesque punishment in mind. 'Feed *'im* to the sharks!' she bellowed.

Magda Bradley vowed to fight on to clear Stephen's name – 'I'll never stop trying to prove his innocence!' – but soon after the trial she took her sons to London to set up a new home, in 1965 returning quietly to Australia to divorce her husband. After that she faded into obscurity, although it is believed she remarried.

Did Magda know of Stephen Bradley's plot to kidnap Graeme Thorne? People wondered – as they would wonder of the wife of Granny Killer John Wayne Glover two decades later – how could any wife *not* know? Was it a coincidence that Magda and the children flew to Hayman Island on the very day of the abduction? Was the voyage to England a frantic attempt to flee retribution or a genuine bid for a new life? Whatever, there was never a shred of proof that Magda Bradley was an accomplice to her husband's crime. Certainly her husband never implicated her in any way.

Early on, Bradley struggled in prison. He was scorned and occasionally attacked by fellow prisoners at Sydney's Long Bay Gaol. In time, however, his mild nature and stoic geniality in the face of abuse won him a kind of acceptance among fellow prisoners and gaol staff, and a quieter, less put-upon life. If never exactly Mr Popularity, he was left pretty much alone. After a couple of years in Long Bay he was moved to Goulburn Gaol, where he proved a model prisoner. He taught himself to play musical instruments and conducted the prison orchestra. He also became a dab hand at table tennis. But on 6 October 1968, after a strenuous game, he suffered a massive heart attack and was dead within twenty minutes. He was forty-two years old.

In 1978, Bradley claimed another victim. Bazil Thorne, still grieving for Graeme, died suddenly and far too young. By then, the names and addresses of lottery winners were no longer published in the press.

CHAPTER 2

THE VAMPIRE KILLER

Tracey Wigginton: Murderer
1989

It had been a long and boozy Friday night for Eddie Baldock. It was 20 October 1989, and after a hard week's work he had imbibed a skinful with his council-worker mates at the Caledonia Club in Brisbane's Kangaroo Point. The friends' laughter had been loud – jokes seem funnier after a few beers. Around midnight Eddie staggered out into the warm subtropical night to consider how he was going to make it home to his wife and five children. The 47-year-old knockabout, described by his wife as 'a lovely, gentle man, a loving husband and devoted grandfather', was drunk, too drunk to stand, so he clung to a lamp-post in River Terrace, fuzzily hoping that a taxi would materialise and whisk him home to the warmth of his bed, where he would sleep off his hangover and, the next day being Saturday, not have to get up till late.

But what loomed out of the night was not a taxi. It was the green Holden Commodore of Tracey Avril Wigginton, who had been cruising the streets of Brisbane with three other women, looking for someone to kill.

Wigginton, then 24, her lover of one week Lisa Ptaschinski, also 24, Kim Jervis, 23, and Tracey Waugh, 23, had spent the evening drinking, too. Their tipple had been cheap champagne at a Fortitude Valley lesbian nightspot called Club Lewmors.

Wigginton, the others claimed to believe, was a vampire who had hatched a plot to kill someone, anyone, and drink his blood. They had spent the last half hour prowling Brisbane, car radio blasting out Prince's 'Batdance', looking for a victim. When Wigginton saw the small, balding, pot-bellied Baldock lurching about at the side of the road, she decided he would be the one.

The women's car stopped. Wigginton asked Baldock if he wanted to have sex with her. He slurringly replied that he did. 'Then get in the car,' she said. With Baldock aboard, they now drove to Orleigh Park on the Brisbane River at West End.

Wigginton and her befuddled and unwitting prey, with Ptaschinski bringing up the rear, disappeared into the bush. Next to the wall of a large shed at the South Brisbane Sailing Club, right on the water, Baldock undressed, save for his socks. Wigginton then stabbed him repeatedly – twenty-seven times in the back, side, throat and chest – with such ferocity that his head was nearly severed and 75 per cent of his blood coursed from his body.

Later, in court, Tracey Waugh testified that when Wigginton returned to the car after having spent some time alone with Baldock's corpse her breath stank of blood.

Not everyone who has a hard upbringing becomes a killer, let alone, as Ptaschinski and her friends claimed of Wigginton, a vampire. But considering her formative years, it's not easy to imagine life turning out well for Tracey Wigginton.

When George Wigginton, wealthy proprietor of a Rockhampton transport company, and his wife, Avril, learned that they were unable to have children, they took three foster children – Rhonda in 1942, Dorelle in 1950, and Michelle a few years later – into their palatial home. George and Avril were respected members of the community, to all appearances attractive, generous people, and their decision to provide a good home for the children seemed to be yet another example of their altruism. Yet behind closed doors the Wiggintons, it seemed, had hearts of darkness.

Years later, it was alleged in court that the elderly couple whipped their foster daughters with electrical cords and a chain, and that George sexually abused them. If George's purported actions were not enough to instil in the girls a hatred of men, Avril would drum into them, 'When you grow up, men will do horrible things to you. All they'll want you for is sex.'

Rhonda left the home of her foster parents to marry and in 1965, when she was twenty-one, gave birth to Tracey. But the marriage failed, and she and Tracey, with nowhere else to go, moved back with the Wiggintons. A year or two later, Rhonda married again. She set up house with her second husband, but left 4-year-old Tracey with George and Avril, who officially adopted her.

Her 'grandfather', Tracey Wigginton later claimed, sexually abused her from early childhood until she was eleven or twelve years old, although for some reason she was spared the beatings meted out to her mother and foster-aunts. Indeed, the Wiggintons sent her to good schools and financed dance, music and elocution lessons. They took her to church. The young Tracey was recalled by one close family friend as 'loving, caring and considerate, fond of animals, a devout Catholic and a gifted artist'.

But – no surprise – torn between cruelty and kindness, Tracey Wigginton grew into a mixed-up, conflicted young girl. She continued to be an ardent churchgoer, singing and praying with gusto every Sunday, but she also embraced the occult very young. Wigginton today denies it, but friends of the time have reported her reading tarot cards and attending séances. They say she told them she could converse with the dead. They say she was for a time a member of a Satanic cult that sacrificed animals, cutting them and draining them of their blood.

After George and Avril Wigginton died in 1979 and 1981 respectively, the 16-year-old Wigginton took $75 000 of her inheritance and went to live with a friend of her mother's in Rockhampton, North Queensland. She attended the Sisters of Mercy Range College, where she became, said a former teacher, notorious for her odd behaviour, antisocial ways and bad temper. 'She was big and handsome but the girls didn't like her. They shunned her. The poor girl had everything stacked against her.' She habitually got into physical fights with schoolmates, friends and relatives.

After school Wigginton attended Rockhampton TAFE where, ironically for one by then widely known and feared for her poisonous disposition, she began a hospitality course. She became pregnant to the husband of a family friend, and travelled to Tweed Heads to have an abortion.

Wigginton was a tall and strapping young woman, gay and proud of it. She had a masculine voice and mesmeric dark brown eyes that, a detective would later say, with a shudder, 'looked right through you'.

Her propensity for cruelty had by now become pronounced. She hurt people, and she hurt animals, variously breaking a cat's back, throttling a budgerigar and pulling the legs from insects. Once, after an argument with her foster-aunt Dorelle, Wigginton broke into her home and daubed the walls with swastikas and obscenities. She heaped sand into the washing machine, slashed pillows and cushions, emptied the contents of a freezer over the floor and scratched and spray-painted obscenities all over Dorelle's car.

Calling herself 'Bobby' because, apparently, her head bobbed when she walked, she cloaked herself in the mantle of a hard-bitten, gutter-mouthed lesbian outlaw. A bizarre anomaly among the palm trees and aloha shirts of North Queensland, Wigginton dressed in black with silver-studded leather collar and wristlets, black leather gloves with the fingers cut off and the knuckles studded, and a black leather jacket with silver chains. She carried a knife in her mid-calf length black leather boots. She had tattoos: the eye of Horus (along with the occult, Egyptology was a passion) on the back of one hand and her star sign, Leo, on the other; a black rose on her right bicep; Merlin the magician on her left. She dyed her buzz-cut hair jet black and rode a huge and noisy motorbike, her lover of the moment riding pillion. In a stoush she could hold her own with most men. A friend remembered a male biker insulting Wigginton and Wigginton beating him so badly with her fists and then her motorcycle helmet that he ran off. 'She wasn't frightened of anyone.' Always a gifted illustrator, she obsessively drew symbols of the occult: bats, mummies, vampires, gravestones, weaponry.

From her late teens to her early twenties, Wigginton drifted in and out of a number of lesbian relationships and lived a nomadic existence from Brisbane to Cairns, where she worked occasionally as a definitely-not-to-be-trifled-with bouncer in a lesbian bar. She reportedly married a woman named Sunshine in a Hare Krishna ceremony. The couple decided to be parents, and Wigginton agreed to become pregnant to an acquaintance. She succeeded in becoming pregnant, but the baby did not survive.

After this episode she fell frantically in love with a woman who insisted, to her despair, on continuing relationships with other lovers. Her lover's blatant infidelity plunged Wigginton into black, reclusive moods when she would lie for hours curled in the foetal position, eyes staring, face set in a sullen funk, fondling a knife. This was Wigginton's deadly state of mind when she began an affair with Lisa Ptaschinski after they had hooked up in Lewmors lesbian bar in Fortitude Valley in October 1989. Chillingly, the night they met was Friday the 13th, and there was a full moon. Between them there was, said Ptaschinski – a pensioner who had been admitted to hospitals more than eighty times in five years for drug overdoses and self-mutilation injuries – an instant, strong attachment. She had never met anyone like Wigginton. 'It's normally very unusual for anyone to push me around,' Ptaschinski later told a psychiatrist. '[Tracey] dominated me more than anyone ever has in my life.'

The two leapt headlong into a tempestuous sexual and emotional relationship. Ptaschinski would later say that her lover told her she was a vampire who was involved in Satanic worship and witchcraft; that she did not eat solid food but drank the blood of pigs and cows which she bought from butchers; that she avoided sunlight and shied from mirrors, and possessed supernatural powers. Ptaschinski also said that Wigginton had ominously informed her that if she did not get blood when she needed it, she would fly into a rage.

Lisa Ptaschinski said she was so besotted with Wigginton that 'to keep in her good books' she agreed when Wigginton demanded that she let her drink her blood – and on four occasions she had wrapped a tourniquet around her forearm, pumped up a vein and sliced it with a blade and allowed Wigginton to suck at the wound.

The dreadfully lacerated, blood-drained body of Eddie Baldock was found on the morning of 21 October. Police found in one of his shoes a Commonwealth Bank ATM keycard. It belonged to one Tracey Wigginton.

Brought in for interrogation, Wigginton aggressively denied killing Baldock. She remained defiant, said police, until they told her that Lisa Ptaschinski had turned herself in and was cooperating with them. Only when she realised it was useless to do otherwise did she confess. Even then, said Detective Senior Constable Nick Austin of the homicide squad, 'She showed no remorse whatever ... a very calculating woman ... a typical psychopathic personality.'

Jervis, a photo-processor, and her unemployed lover, Waugh, gave themselves up to police the following day and joined Wigginton and Ptaschinski in the cells.

In a signed statement, Ptaschinski said Wigginton had acted alone in slaying the council worker. The two couples, she and Wigginton, and Jervis and Waugh, Ptaschinski told officers as the videocamera ran, had rendezvoused in Jervis's flat in suburban Clayfield on 18 October and decided that two days later, on Friday night, they would stalk and kill a victim so Wigginton, who was a vampire, could drink his blood. Waugh and Ptaschinski were to pose as prostitutes and inveigle someone they plucked off the street to a quiet area, where Ptaschinski would hit their victim over the head and knock him out. Wigginton would then murder the unfortunate man and drink his blood.

Through the appointed evening, continued Ptaschinski in her statement, the women had bolstered their courage with cheap champagne at Club Lewmors. ('I can't sleep at night,' Bettina Lewis, proprietor of Lewmors, would later say, 'knowing those creeps drank in my club.') Around 11.30 pm, the quartet had left together and trawled the Botanic Gardens and New Farm Park in Wigginton's Commodore looking for a victim. Unsuccessful in those locations, they drove to Kangaroo Point and spotted Eddie Baldock.

Ptaschinski told police that Wigginton and Baldock had gone off together, leaving her and the others in the car, but Wigginton had returned and asked Ptaschinski to come too because she believed Baldock was too strong to overpower on her own. 'I need help,' she had growled, 'the bastard's too strong.' Wigginton wanted Ptaschinski to stab Baldock from behind to disable him, and for this purpose Jervis had given Ptaschinski her 'ninja butterfly knife'.

Wigginton and Ptaschinski, who'd thoughtfully changed her white top for a black T-shirt, came across Baldock sitting woozy and naked on the river bank. Ptaschinski stood behind him but could not bring herself to stab him. Wigginton, in a fury of recrimination, had snatched the knife from her and fallen upon Baldock, stabbing him again and again with the ninja knife and a pocketknife of her own, like 'a shark in a feeding frenzy'. Appalled by what she had seen, Ptaschinski returned to the car. Wigginton came back fifteen minutes later, having washed the blood from her body and the knives in the Brisbane River. 'Have you fed?' Ptaschinski said she had asked, and Wigginton assured her that she had.

In her statement, Kim Jervis tearfully told the officers that on 18 October, when Wigginton had suggested killing someone at random so she could drink his blood, 'I thought it was a bit of a joke, I thought it would be talk, not action. That was the biggest mistake of my life.' On the night of the murder, as they prowled for their victim, Wigginton had ordered Jervis to watch as she drank his blood, saying, according to Jervis, 'I want to scare you, to frighten the living hell out of you. [But] if anyone touches me while I'm doing it I'm liable to rip your arm off.'

In the end, Jervis had witnessed neither the murder nor the blood drinking, but it occurred to her that when Wigginton returned to the car she seemed as sated as someone 'who had just eaten a three-course meal'.

Tracey Waugh told police that after agreeing at first to be part of Wigginton's murderous plan, she and Jervis had had second thoughts: 'I knew it wasn't right. It was wrong.' She hadn't wanted to leave the bar with Wigginton and Ptaschinski that fateful night but 'Tracey ... she just sort of, I don't know, mindpower I guess, used her mind to make us think it was all right, nothing was going to go wrong.' Yes, she had been scared to accompany Wigginton but more scared of what Wigginton would do to her if she opted out at that late stage. She recalled that after the murder she could smell blood on Wigginton's breath.

All four women were charged with Baldock's murder and on 1 February 1990 were committed for trial in Brisbane's Supreme Court.

Wigginton, however, after the state's Mental Health Tribunal declared her mentally fit to stand trial, confessed her guilt. In January 1991, two months before the trial was to commence, after a nine-minute hearing she was jailed for life.

Some psychiatrists disagreed with the Tribunal's finding. Eminent mental health professionals Dr James Clarke, a clinical psychologist and hypnosis expert, and psychiatrist Dr James Quinn, both of whom examined Wigginton at length, felt strongly that she suffered multiple personality disorder. During hypnosis sessions, they reported, Wigginton 'flitted in and out of' four distinct personalities: 'Bobby', contemptuous, cynical and callous; 'Big Tracey', anxious and depressed, who was distressed by the murder; the sweet-natured and childlike 'Little Tracey'; and 'The Observer', detached, calm and rational. They believed that the sexual abuse and rejection that Wigginton said she had suffered as a child could have contributed to her mental condition.

In the transcript of a mid-1990 interview, Wigginton, who has been hypnotised by Dr Clarke and is speaking in the persona of 'Big Tracey', says that 'Bobby' was a mean person. Dr Clarke asks who stabbed Baldock in the neck. Suddenly, shockingly, Wigginton's voice drops to a throaty growl as she snaps, 'It was me.'

Dr Clarke: 'Who are you?'

Wigginton: 'Bobby.'

Dr Clarke: 'Why did you stab him? You can hear the chunky sound of the knife hitting the flesh. Why are you doing it, Bobby?'

Wigginton: 'Angry.'

Dr Clarke: 'Why are you angry?'

Wigginton: 'Everything ... I'm angry at all of them ... I was killing many, many people. Everyone who has ever hurt me.'

Dr Clarke asks Wigginton what she felt when she saw Baldock drunk in the street that night. Again, the guttural voice: 'I want him.' The psychologist would tell the Mental Health Tribunal that Wigginton's voice at that point 'dropped several octaves to a basso profundo. It literally moved me in my seat'.

Wigginton, again under hypnosis, tells Dr Clarke that 'Bobby was intrigued by the occult' and that she was 'a tornado who might kill again'.

'The Observer', Wigginton's 'good' personality, suggested Dr Clarke, may have planted the keycard in Baldock's shoe so that 'Bobby' would be apprehended and unable to kill again.

In another interview, this time not under hypnosis, Wigginton talks rationally, ruefully, about killing Eddie Baldock: 'Thinking about the concept that these hands killed somebody is impossible for me to comprehend. I have to dissociate myself to think about the killing or it freaks me out. I start shaking and crying. It's taken me ten and a half months to be able to say I murdered someone and accept it as true. I can see the knives, the blood, the body, I can see me standing over him and the most horrific of all, me striking [the knife] into his chest. I can remember the sounds, like someone gargling in the morning – a bloody gargle.' She is glad she has been caught, she adds, because in prison she will not be able to commit such an act again.

Dr Clarke said he was convinced that Wigginton was not faking her various personae.

At their trial in February 1991, Ptaschinski, Jervis and Waugh all pleaded not guilty to killing Baldock. Their grisly testimony, as they described how Wigginton butchered Baldock, made the so-called 'Lesbian Vampire Killing' one of Australia's most notorious crimes and led prosecutor Adrian Gunderlach to call it, with considerable understatement, 'an extraordinary case with some bizarre features'. The nation was horrified and incredulous.

The prosecution refuted the defence's assertion that Ptaschinski, Jervis and Waugh had been cowardly and hapless but essentially innocent onlookers under the 'spell' of Wigginton. Prosecutor Gunderlach said that each woman was guilty of 'plain bloody murder'.

'A leader of the pack has to have willing followers,' thundered Gunderlach, and each of the trio had been complicit in Wigginton's evil plan, a scheme, he mused, that sounded like a script from a late-night movie but which became a real-life horror story for Edward Baldock. 'Who amongst us here expects to find that kind of brutality from three such ordinary-looking persons and, of course, that is what makes it all the more abhorrent.' The defendants were not 'silly adolescents' but mature women who sat down together and planned a murder. 'They cared naught about what we value in our society: the right of a person to live.'

As the jury retired, the judge, Mr Justice MacKenzie, noted that the jurors 'would be unlikely to strike another case like this if they served on juries forever'.

On 15 February, the verdict was announced in a courtroom jammed with the families of the defendants and the victim, with the media and the public, including members of Brisbane's lesbian community. Ptaschinski was convicted of Baldock's murder and sentenced to life in prison. 'You knew what was likely to happen and you took no pity on Mr Baldock as a fellow human being,' said Justice MacKenzie. Jervis was found guilty of manslaughter and received an 18-year sentence, which was later reduced to twelve years. Waugh was acquitted. As their sentences were delivered, Ptaschinski stood with a grim expression, her tattooed arms folded; Jervis wept; Waugh allowed herself a relieved smile.

'They should all rot in jail,' said Eddie Baldock's son, Shane. 'My father was killed mercilessly. He was the most gentle man. He never saw any bad in people. I think his worst fault was that he trusted too many people.'

Tracey Wigginton kept her silence for nearly seven years, until in May 1996, in an interview with journalist Ella Riggert of Brisbane's *Courier-Mail* newspaper, she gave her side of the story for the first, and to date only, time. Riggert wrote how she had been nervous at the prospect of coming face to face with Wigginton in her cell in Brisbane's Boggo Road women's prison, but found her 'articulate, friendly and obviously intelligent'. Wigginton started by telling Riggert that she was not the 'Lesbian Vampire Killer' of the tabloids. Lesbian, yes. Killer of Eddie Baldock, yes. Vampire, no. She lambasted Ptaschinski, Jervis and Waugh's claims that she was a Satanist and a vampire and said she had never drunk Eddie Baldock's blood, nor any other kind of blood, human or animal, because the sight of it 'makes me sick, even a tiny cut on my finger'.

The implication was that the women at their trial, especially Ptaschinski, had tried to paint her as a malevolent mastermind with magical powers who had them helpless in her thrall. Wigginton said the only time she had discussed vampires with the other women was when they were watching *The Hunger*, a vampire film starring David Bowie and Catherine Deneuve, a week before Baldock's death.

So why, asked Riggert, did she so brutally murder the defenceless man?

Baldock's death, Wigginton explained, was the end result of the sexual and physical abuse she had suffered at her grandparents' hands when she was a child. The trauma had caused her to embark on a series of relationships with women, almost always destructive and abnormally possessive relationships, that ended badly. The night she murdered Baldock she had been, she told Riggert, pushed to her emotional brink by the infidelities of a lover. She had bought the woman a motorbike to win her affection, but to no avail. The two had had an angry break-up the day before. So distraught was Wigginton that she had turned into an 'animal' and lashed out. 'I remember thinking ... some bastard has to die. At that moment, me as a person ceased to exist. Nothing mattered. I didn't matter, they didn't matter – nobody mattered.'

Wigginton told Riggert, 'I had snapped. I knew I couldn't kill a woman or someone who I knew – but I didn't know what I was looking for.' In the car that night, she had been in the passenger seat, Ptaschinski was driving. Jervis and Waugh were in the back seat. When they saw Baldock, 'He was the one – I don't know why. He just was. I told Lisa, "Stop the car." Kim got in the front seat and he got in the back. I didn't even speak to him. He just got in. He was five sheets to the wind, rather than three. He was so drunk he fell asleep in the back of the car. Psychiatrists have told me Mr Baldock was a lookalike of my grandfather, but I don't see it. I said to Lisa, "Drive." She asked me where. I told her to go to West End near the big shed. They all knew something was up. I didn't have to say a thing.'

Wigginton and Ptaschinski had escorted the stumbling Baldock to the river bank, where he undressed. She thinks that was when her keycard fell into his shoe. When Ptaschinski was unable to stab Baldock, Wigginton told Riggert, 'I said, "Go!" Lisa ran so hard she smacked into a fence chain, which imprinted on her legs. It bruised her for days. Then I started to stab him. You think nothing. Nothing goes through your mind. There is no emotion – just blind fury. But once I had started I couldn't stop. I couldn't see Mr Baldock. I kept seeing my grandmother, my grandfather, my mother, my father and all the people in my life who had hurt me. It is all just pure adrenalin. It was such blind fury I was able to pick a dead man up with two knives. If someone had tried to stop me I don't think I would have gone through with it. But I know I had that option to stop, right up until I lifted the knife, and I didn't. Afterwards I sat down against the roller door with my arms resting on my knees. I thought he was still breathing. I remember thinking, "Hurry up and die", but I later found out he wasn't breathing. He had died after the second blow. I was like a husk or the shell of a volcano. There was no anger or love. There was nothing. I was spent.'

Later, in the car, she said, 'You could have heard a pin drop. The heater was on and all you could smell was blood. In court someone said they could smell blood on my breath. I don't know how that was possible. I had just killed a man who had lost 75 per cent of his blood – and a lot of it was all over me. So how could you smell blood on my breath?'

Wigginton seemed to believe that life in prison was her just desert. She says she regrets her crime – 'No one has the right to take someone else's life' – and she thinks in quiet moments of how she killed Baldock. At those times, she told Riggert, 'I cry.'

Given her notoriety, it was inevitable that Wigginton would be singled out in jail. Other prisoners in Boggo Road and at Brisbane Women's Correctional Centre at Wacol where she was incarcerated called her Drac, and made the sign of the cross as she approached. The kitchen staff thought it amusing to lace her food with garlic, the traditional vampire repellent.

Yet, as all who have known her attest, Wigginton is a formidable woman, not easily cowed, and within months she established herself at the top at both Wacol and Boggo Road. Knowledge of her celebrity and propensity for violence had preceded her and she became Queen Bee, imposing her presence on other prisoners quite early and reportedly getting into (and winning) fights which earned her even more respect. She has had several affairs. In 1996, after a spate of brawls, Wigginton was declared one of Queensland's most violent female prisoners and placed under strict security.

In time Wigginton curbed her violent ways and became a model prisoner. 'She is highly intelligent and did university studies by correspondence for several years and obtained a Bachelor of Arts from Deakin University, majoring in anthropology and philosophy. The degree included two high distinctions and ten distinctions,' reports one who has observed her in prison. 'Wigginton paid her education expenses from money she earned while working in the gaol.'

In September 2003, public outrage erupted when it was discovered that Wigginton had been transferred to the minimum security Numinbah Correctional Centre on the Gold Coast. She remained there for three years. Then, in June 2006, she punched another female prisoner and was charged with assault. The count was thrown out when the prisoner withdrew her complaint. After further inquiry, prison authorities stepped in and accused her of intimidating her victim into refusing to testify about the assault, and

Wigginton was transferred back to maximum security at Wacol. For good measure, she was also accused of hitting a prison officer.

Wigginton was devastated by the transfer and fought the decision in the Brisbane Supreme Court, but her application was denied and she remains in maximum security at Wacol, where she enjoys regular visits from former prisoners and women's rights activists.

Wigginton has been eligible to apply for parole for some time, but refuses to do so because she says it would generate too big a media circus. Prison officers say she has adapted to – and may even relish – life in prison.

CHAPTER 3

THE GRANNY KILLER

John Wayne Glover: Serial killer
1989–90

For years after his conviction for murdering six elderly women on Sydney's Lower North Shore in 1989 and 1990, at Sydney's Long Bay Gaol John Glover would every month or so welcome to his cell the man who helped to arrest him, Detective Sergeant Dennis 'Miles' O'Toole. It became part of Glover's little routine that, at the end of each visit, he would quip, 'Goodbye, Dennis, call in any time you see the light on. If I'm not here I'll leave a message.'

Glover looked forward to his chats with O'Toole who, of course, had an ulterior motive. He was convinced Glover had murdered a number of other elderly women, and lived in hope that the man known as the Granny Killer might confess. The serial murderer turned on the charm that had made him a pillar of the Mosman community and a successful pie salesman, even while he was slaughtering defenceless women in their seventies, eighties and nineties. He would greet O'Toole with the same blokey bonhomie he would once have expended on visitors to his palatial family home at the aptly-named Beauty Point or to the Four 'n Twenty Pies hospitality tent at the SCG when the Sydney Swans AFL team played. With twinkling eyes he'd indulge in mind games with O'Toole, tease him that he was about to confess to the other murders, then clam up. He'd chat away about his life behind bars, maybe tell the detective a few ribald jokes he'd made up or heard in the yard.

As did most who met him, O'Toole found it hard to reconcile the jolly, avuncular prisoner with the savage Granny Killer whose *modus operandi* was to bludgeon his victim to death with a hammer, sexually assault her body, tie her pantyhose around her neck, spreadeagle her legs, and steal from her handbag. But one day Glover's mask slipped to reveal the monster beneath. On this occasion, he had been chatting calmly and dispassionately to O'Toole about his crimes, when in passing O'Toole mentioned Glover's daughters Kellie and Marney. 'All of a sudden ... he lost control of himself and slammed his open palm down hard on the interview table,' recalled O'Toole. 'I could see all at once the naked rage beneath Glover's benign exterior, and I understood then that those women never stood a chance. I don't mind saying I was terrified at that moment and bloody relieved when warders ran from everywhere.'

John Glover had always been adept at keeping his dark side a secret. As a boy growing up among the mills and factories of working-class Wolverhampton, England, in the hard, depressed 1930s, he learned to bottle up the hurt and humiliation dealt him by his mother Freda. 'She had a will of iron and a sharp tongue when something upset her,' Glover would remember. Freda brutally tongue-lashed John, his younger brother Barry, and her husband, their father Walter, a quiet, serious-minded locksmith who played piano in the pub to make a few extra quid and, no doubt, to escape his shrewish wife. At last, unable to bear Freda's harangues a moment longer, Walter left, leaving 9-year-old John and 6-year-old Barry at their mother's mercy.

Freda Glover did what she felt was necessary to survive. She became a black marketeer and a prostitute, openly inviting her clients home. She married three times more, but between and during husbands there was a steady stream of men traipsing in and out of her bedroom. 'My mother was fast and loose and had many lovers,' said Glover who, until the day he died, could bring to mind the sounds of her lovemaking. As a boy, he was allowed to remain in the house when Freda entertained, but as he grew into a teenager she paid him small sums of money to go out and stay out.

Once Glover found a pornographic photo of his mother which, he said, 'disturbed me greatly'. That may have been a vast understatement for, later, when police found the bodies of his victims their legs would be arranged just like Freda's in that long-ago snapshot.

Yet while Glover despised his mother and was repulsed to the point of nausea by her promiscuity, perhaps because she owned the roof over his head and gave him pocket money, perhaps *because* she was his mother, he remained outwardly respectful towards her. When she abused him, he stood there stoically, taking it, never protesting, but seething inside. He wished her dead.

Glover was further traumatised at the age of thirteen when his best mate fell from a tree onto his head and died.

Glover's schooling effectively ended when his father left home, for he was shuttled from his mother to his father to friends to relatives, but at fourteen Freda took him back 'with open arms', said Glover, 'because I was old enough to earn a quid.'

That he never attended university rankled all his days, for Glover had delusions of grandeur and came to believe that if only his mother's promiscuity and obstreperousness hadn't cost him the chance to matriculate he could have been an academic, a captain of industry, a famous artist or musician. 'I was very intelligent and quick on the uptake,' he recalled with typical braggadocio, 'with a flair for music and languages.'

In his late teens and early twenties, although unable to hold any job for long because of his hair-trigger temper, crude tongue and thievery, Glover presented to contemporaries as a wannabe David Niven or Cary Grant. He affected airs and graces, was a smooth talker who always knew the latest risqué joke and could deliver the punchline well. He dressed as nattily as he could afford and was handsome, muscular and athletic. His thick brown hair was greased and fashioned into a racy pompadour. Women enjoyed his company. Though a long-term serious relationship eluded him, he claims to have had lots of sex. 'I was a mad rooter,' he bragged, 'and never had an unsuccessful sexual experience.'

Though Glover's jobs were always menial, he spent money freely. His friends assumed his wealth was inherited until he was caught robbing a house and it was all over the local paper – the source of his money now obvious to all. He laughed off the conviction: 'Stealing was something everybody did ... if somebody had something I wanted, I'd take it.' Glover was emboldened rather than chastened by his arrest and conviction. He went on to pull off a series of burglaries, fencing his booty – usually clothes, tools, a van, a handbag – and spending the money on women, clothes and beer.

He joined the army as a drill instructor and radar operator, and when his stint was up paid the rent by working fitfully as a bus conductor and van driver and by stealing. Freda continued to harass him, putting a crimp in his style in front of any friend he brought home with her constant putdowns and refusal to be impressed by anything he did. To get out of earshot of her abuse, as much as anything else, he paid the obligatory £10 fare and migrated to Australia.

Arriving in Melbourne in 1957, Glover worked as a tram conductor, factory worker, clerk. A fan of 'the Duke', the rugged actor John Wayne, he changed his name from John Walter Glover to John Wayne Glover and bought a macho bushman's hat which he sported on the streets. He would wonder aloud whether acquaintances thought he resembled Wayne, or perhaps Paul Newman. One night, 'three parts pissed', he got a tattoo on his arm. 'I chose an eagle carrying a shield over a mountain. It cost me 15 shillings and sixpence and I've regretted it ever since. The significance of the eagle and the shield? Fuck all!'

Glover's heavy drinking, one-night stands and thievery continued. He began getting into fights, usually sparked by one of his trademark smutty remarks to a woman, delivered with a sly smirk, at which her boyfriend would take offence. 'Gee, you've got nice tits!' was a favourite conversation starter.

Glover progressed from robbing houses and garages to mugging women in the street. Creep up behind them, knock them down and steal their handbags. He was caught peeping through a window at two women as they undressed.

Then, inexplicably to all her friends, wealthy, attractive and vivacious Gay Rolls fell in love with him. Glover was like no one she'd ever gone out with before. She enjoyed his jokes and his flash-as-a-rat-with-a-gold-tooth charm. She felt she could detect in him untapped potential to succeed in business, and that she could bring out his best. On his part, he was besotted by her class and intelligence, and her money would have had undoubted appeal. 'One day Gay said to me,' Glover would recall, '"I know what you've been like with women in the past, now what are we going to do about it?" I told her next time I was in Coles I would pick up a cheap ring and give it to her as a symbol of my faithfulness. But Gay beat me to it. She went out to a jeweller and bought an expensive engagement ring. All of a sudden we were engaged.'

They wed in 1968 and lived with Gay's mother, Essie, in Sydney's wealthy and picturesque suburb of Beauty Point, near Mosman. Soon Glover and Essie Rolls, who scarcely before the confetti had been swept from the church grounds revealed herself to be every bit as ornery as Freda, were sworn enemies. To one acquaintance, Essie was 'a nasty version of Dame Edna Everage'. Glover worked hard (although, typically, he continued to steal from his employer and was caught shoplifting) and seemed to be trying to be a responsible husband, but Essie browbeat and belittled him in front of Gay and, after they were born in 1971 and 1973, his daughters Kellie and Marney. As he'd done with Freda's harangues, he took Essie's without a peep, but boiled within and wished her dead too.

Came now the catalysts for the horrors to come. In 1988 Freda, who had migrated to Australia some years earlier, died, then Essie. And to his shame and alarm Glover contracted breast cancer and underwent a partial mastectomy. He became impotent. The ailment, which scuppered his self-image as a manly stud, and the deaths of the elderly women who had made his life hell, unleashed his devils.

After bashing 84-year-old Margaret Todhunter, who survived, in a Mosman street on 11 January 1989, Glover, now a portly, white-haired fifty-eight, began a murderous onslaught against elderly women.

On 1 March 1989, he cruised the streets of Mosman in his white Ford Falcon company station wagon, a heavy, wooden-handled Stanley Hercules claw-hammer under the front seat. At 3.50 pm in Military Road he saw 82-year-old Gwendoline Mitchelhill walking slowly home, laden with shopping bags. He stuffed the hammer into his pants, parked his car and shadowed her. When she reached the entrance foyer of her block of flats, he sneaked up and smashed his hammer down on her head, repeatedly. She died soon after he fled the scene with her wallet, which contained $100.

On 9 May, Glover murdered Lady Winfreda Ashton, 82. He stalked her to the foyer of her block of units and battered her before choking her to death with her pantyhose. He tied the underwear in a bow around her neck. 'Yes, for a little woman she put up a good fight,' he later mused.

After viciously assaulting women at nursing homes on 5 August and 18 October while there on the pretext of taking pie orders, Glover killed again on 2 November. Margaret Pahud, 85, lived in a retirement village in Lane Cove. As he drove slowly around the suburb trawling for a victim, Glover saw Pahud walking home from the local shops carrying her shopping bags. He stopped his car, took his hammer and followed her. He waited until she turned into the leafy walkway that led to her block, then smashed his hammer down onto the back of her head three times.

Next day, 3 November, he attacked and killed Olive Cleveland, 81, at the Wesley Gardens Retirement Village in Belrose. He sat chatting in the garden with her, then ambushed her when no one was around. This time he'd left his hammer in the car and killed her by repeatedly smashing her head onto a concrete path.

Twenty days later, Glover was comparing whisky prices in the bottle shop of the Buena Vista Hotel opposite the Mosman police station when he saw Muriel Falconer, 93, wheeling a shopping bag along the footpath. It was late afternoon. He followed her to her home. Staying close on her heels, he waited until she had opened her front door, then shoved her inside and rained hammer blows on her. Glover returned home, threw his bloodstained clothes into the laundry chute – amazingly, his wife never noticed blood on his shirts or trousers – cleaned his hammer with hydrochloric acid and settled down to watch the 7 pm news on ABC-TV.

More than once, as newsreaders reported on the atrocities of the Granny Killer, Glover would remark to Gay that it was a disgrace that such a terrible person could be on the loose in their suburb and he hoped he'd be caught quick bloody smart.

At Mosman RSL, Glover was an elected official and a major contributor to the club's poker machine revenue. He went to the club every day after work and pounded away on the pokies before going home in time to watch the evening news. He was known as a cheery soul, a decent chap, and he was always first up to dance with his wife and daughters and other patrons when the music cranked up on gala nights. At the height of Granny Killer hysteria, he was offering to drive elderly female members to their homes after a night at the club. He would accompany them to the front door, take their keys and insist on going inside first to ensure that the Granny Killer wasn't lurking inside. Having checked the premises, he would say, 'Coast's clear. In you go. Good night. Take care.' When John Glover himself was exposed as the killer, many of these patrons required treatment for shock.

In January 1990, Glover molested an elderly woman at Greenwich Hospital, but fled when she pressed an alarm buzzer. The distressed patient told police that it was Mr Glover, the pie salesman, who had attacked her. Two officers went to his home and asked him to go to the police station next day to be interviewed over the matter. Glover panicked. Terrified that he would be linked to the killings, he tried to end it all. He penned a suicide note, then washed down handfuls of benzodiazepine and normethadone tablets with whisky. But he survived, and police found the suicide note, in which he had scrawled 'no more grannies' and 'Gay, don't try to understand. Essie started it all'.

The task force searching for the Granny Killer made Glover a suspect, and a *hot* suspect when they checked his records at Four 'n Twenty Pies and found that his travels had him in the vicinity of a number of attacks at the exact times they were committed. Too, when police asked locals who lived and worked around the death sites what they had noticed that day, a number mentioned seeing a paunchy, white-haired man. The task force checked Glover's record and learned of his many crimes in Melbourne and England. They contacted family members, who told them of his hatred for his mother and for Essie Rolls, Gay's mother. Obviously, she was the 'Essie' in his suicide note. Did 'no more grannies' refer to his victims?

Suddenly the pieces were fitting together. Police 'stole' his company station wagon, by now a blue Ford Falcon, from Mosman while he was shopping, and planted a Quiktrak tracking device underneath the chassis. They called him to say they'd found the car and he came to fetch it, driving off oblivious to the fact that police were following his every movement on screen. With no firm evidence against him, the task force hoped he would do something to incriminate himself. They hoped he would not attack again, but if he did they planned to be close enough to move in before he could kill.

Glover was under heavy surveillance when he left home on 19 March 1990. At 10.26 am he pulled up outside the home of Joan Sinclair, a 60-year-old grandmother with whom he was having an affair, in Beauty Point, and went inside. The task force detectives surreptitiously parked up and down the street, and waited. As the day wore on they grew worried. Was Glover killing this woman? Should they invade the house? What if they charged through the door and Glover and Sinclair were merely having coffee together or making love? Glover would then know that police suspected him and possibly never transgress again and so evade ever being brought to justice. The detectives chose to sit and wait, and prayed that no harm had come to Glover's companion.

But, some hours later as dusk began to fall, when no lights came on and the dogs at the back of the house began to bark, the detectives could wait no longer. Shortly after 6 pm, Dennis O'Toole, Murray Byrnes, Paul Mayger and Paul Jacob stormed the premises. When they switched on their flashlights their worst fears were realised. Before them was an appalling tableau. The semi-naked body of Joan Sinclair lay on the bloodstained carpet, congealed blood pooled around her head. Her pantyhose were arrayed around her neck. Her legs were splayed. The bloody hammer with which Glover had caved in her skull lay nearby. When they examined her they knew she had been dead for around six hours.

O'Toole would recall: 'Something hit me then that had never hit me before. It was as though I was almost ashamed to be human. The senselessness of her death was like a literal weight on my shoulders. I felt enormous sadness and everything seemed to drain out of me. But then, standing there in the pitch black, I told myself to snap out of it. In our situation those feelings were a luxury I could not afford. All that mattered to me, to all of us, was catching John Glover – and, oh yes, getting out of that house alive.'

The detectives crouch-crept through the halls and passageways of the house, guns drawn, expecting Glover to leap out at them at any moment. Suddenly Jacob's voice rang out from the bathroom. 'We've got him! He's here!'

The men piled in through the bathroom's batwing doors. They saw a bath, at one end Glover's shock of white hair and at the other his feet sticking over the rim. He was naked, semi-conscious and the now-tepid water was polluted with vomit and blood. O'Toole grabbed Glover by the hair and with the help of the others hefted his bulk out onto the tiled floor. After killing Sinclair, Glover had drunk most of a bottle of Vat 69 whisky, taken a quantity of pills including the antidepressant sinequan, and made a half-hearted attempt to slash his wrists. Once more, he would live.

After his stomach was pumped at Royal North Shore Hospital, Glover admitted to killing Gwendoline Mitchelhill, Lady Winfreda Ashton, Margaret Pahud, Olive Cleveland, Muriel Falconer and Joan Sinclair, though he could offer no reason. 'I don't know why I killed them,' he repeated. He also confessed to a number of assaults and indecent assaults on the streets and in the nursing homes of the Lower North Shore. Why he beat and molested these women he did not know either. In questioning he allowed that he hated his mother and mother-in-law but as far as he knew that was not why he murdered other elderly women. He tearfully worried how his wife and daughters would cope with his being unmasked as the Granny Killer. He fretted that he would never see the ocean again.

In the days following his capture, Glover lurched between despair and a seemingly relieved jollity. One minute he would be weeping and moaning, the next entertaining police and hospital staff with jokes. He mock-seriously chided O'Toole for causing the lump on his head which he suffered when the detective dragged him out of the bath.

Crown prosecutor Wendy Robinson's reaction to Glover echoed that of many who came into contact with him. 'He looked so sedate and grandfatherly,' she recalled. 'It took me a while to come to grips with the fact that this man was one of the worst killers in Australian history. He had murdered six women. However, when I became fully acquainted with the case, the first thing I said to police was, "Where are the others?" It seemed overwhelmingly unlikely to me that he had not murdered more women than he was charged with killing.'

Before his trial, Glover was interviewed at length by eminent forensic psychiatrist Dr Rod Milton, who led Glover through his crimes. Of the murder of Gwendoline Mitchelhill, Glover reflected: 'She was walking down the street. This is where it becomes frustrating for me because as John Glover, sales manager of Four 'n Twenty Pies, there seems to be another personality or whatever comes out of me, sees this person and wants to harm her. This personality, alter-ego, whatever, like Mr Good Guy and Mr Bad Guy, picks up a hammer from under the seat of the car, kept there for work purposes, and follows her to her flat entrance. It comes to me that I recall it in detail because I was there, but not as the perpetrator of the act but as another part of me committing this act.'

When he stood trial at Sydney's Central Criminal Court on 18 November 1991, Glover pleaded not guilty to killing the six women on the grounds of diminished responsibility. Yes, he'd killed the women, but he was not completely responsible for his actions. In a statement to the court he again invoked 'Mr Good Guy and Mr Bad Guy'. Mostly, he remained composed, talking easily about the murders. Only three times did he show any great emotion. When it was posited by Dr Milton that he might have harboured incestuous thoughts about his mother, Glover's face reddened and his hands clenched in rage, and he spluttered noisily and tears coursed down his chubby, florid cheeks when he recalled the happy life he had led in Mosman with the family he would never know again: 'Everything was absolutely fine. We lived together amicably. The girls grew up. I was fortunate in having two bright girls and fortunate again in having them go to private school ... everything *I* should have had ... everything *I* should have had, they were getting ...' And he sobbed again when he apologised to his victims' loved ones.

Dr Milton told the court that Glover's behaviour fitted the pattern of a certain type of serial killer because he distilled anger and released it as an intense rage directed against women. Murderers of this type often resented an important woman in their life: 'He acts out on a lookalike of the mother or wife. He ... looks for women and takes his time sizing them up. He hunts the victim and moves at his own pace to rape or kill.' Killers such as Glover, Milton believed, may kill in a frenzied attack and with blunt force, and take a weapon to the murder scene. Glover committed sexual abuse on his victims because after the attack he was still expending energy and the murder was not complete until the sexual assault. Glover, argued Milton, had a narcissistic personality and lacked concern for his victims. Having no recognisable mental or emotional illness, a defence of insanity or diminished responsibility was invalid. In Glover's case, said the psychiatrist, 'the only thing abnormal is the nature of the killings themselves'.

Milton believed that one of Glover's problems was his relationship with his mother:

> One element was of a sexual arousal by his mother. I am sure that when he referred to her as being 'fast and loose' and described her more or less in various derogatory ways, I think that as an adolescent there was probably some sexual arousal there for him. I think that he also felt guilt at that sexual arousal and felt anger towards his mother arising from that guilt she inflicted on him. He was angry with her, he was stirred up by her, but at the same time was angry

> with her for stirring him up … as a result of early life experiences, in particular his relationship with his mother, John Glover remained emotionally at an adolescent level of development. He sought dependence on forceful and older women while at the same time resenting that dependence and associated incestuous feelings.

It was at these words that Glover had gone into meltdown.

Summing up, defence counsel Andrew Leary, however, contended that Glover's responsibility was necessarily diminished, for surely a sane person would not irrationally continue to commit murder after murder in the very face of a concentrated police presence and the attendant intense publicity about the killings. Also, said Leary, Glover had no real motive because he knew only one of his six victims.

Prosecutor Wendy Robinson referred to Dr Milton's findings and declared that the defendant *was* fully responsible for his actions because in keeping his hammer and gloves handily under the seat of his car, 'he had organised himself in a premeditated fashion so that he was able to strike again when the opportunity arose'.

As the jury was considering its verdict, Glover remarked, 'Milton has got me hung, drawn and quartered. All they have to do now is flay my hide and nail it on the wall.'

Which, in essence, is exactly what happened.

On 28 November 1991, after two hours and forty-five minutes of deliberation, the jury returned to the court and the foreperson declared that they had found Glover guilty.

Glover stood to receive his sentence. After recapping the defendant's life of crime and emphasising his responsibility for the murders and assaults, Justice James Wood called him:

> a man of extreme cunning, and of extreme dangerousness who is prepared to attack whenever and wherever it suits him, and to stay his hand when it does not. The threat he poses to the community denies him any mitigation otherwise available. In order to protect the society, and also to provide the appropriate punishment for

> the appalling murders of which the prisoner is guilty, I have no alternative other to impose the maximum available sentence which means that the prisoner will be required to spend the rest of his natural life in jail. John Wayne Glover, in relation to each count of murder for which you have been found guilty, I sentence you to penal servitude for life.

His papers would be stamped 'Never to be released'.

Before he was hustled out of the court, Glover, the only serial killer in criminal history known to prey on elderly women, tried to meet Detective Sergeant Miles O'Toole's eye to commend him on a job well and fairly done, but the detective was having none of that and looked in another direction.

Like Wendy Robinson, O'Toole was certain that Glover had killed many more times than six. He felt he could have been responsible for the unsolved murders of Josephine McDonald, 73, in 1984, and Wanda Amundsen, 83, in 1988, on the New South Wales Central Coast, both killed in periods when Glover's sales beat took him to the region. Of Elsie Boyes, Christina Yankos and Irene Kiddle, all 63, who were slain in Melbourne when Glover lived there. Of Sydney artist and socialite Florence Broadhurst, 78, who knew Glover, who was bludgeoned to death in Paddington in 1977. And of the vicious assaults of five other elderly women on the Central Coast in the early 1980s.

Glover spent the next two months in Long Bay Gaol's classification centre being assessed by psychiatrists and prison staff. During this period, he received two visits. One was from journalists Steve Barrett and Simon Bouda for the book *Garden of Evil: The Granny Killer's Reign of Terror* (co-written with this author). The other was from his wife Gay, to tell him that she was divorcing him and taking their daughters away. The three moved to New Zealand where they changed their names and began a new life. It is understood that they have since returned to Australia, and that they never saw Glover again.

After being classified 'non-dangerous', Glover, who'd grown a luxuriant set of mutton-chop whiskers, was transferred to Lithgow Gaol, west of Sydney. Apart from prison staff, social workers and medical staff, the only visitor he received was his nemesis, O'Toole, for their bouts of mind games. Glover did receive phone calls from and correspond with one woman – her name has been withheld and her identity remains a mystery – whom, it is understood, he had first met when he was selling pies.

Glover called his cell 'the garden gate', cockney rhyming slang for '12 × 8', its dimensions. The corner with the toilet, he would pompously declare, was 'my en suite'. He kept his domain pristine and decorated its walls with brightly-coloured towels. It was there that he spent his long, lonely days and nights reading, playing chess, listening to the radio, watching television – the ABC exclusively, he let everybody know – and hopefully suffering nightmares about the terrible things he'd wrought.

'John Glover is a very strange and complex man,' said Miles O'Toole in 1992. 'But – and there's no other way to say it – we get on very well together. He speaks easily to me. He has a very winning personality and I can see how he would be a very successful sales representative. It's easy to be swayed by his charm, but I keep remembering the despicable crimes the bastard committed.'

In 2003, Glover developed prostate cancer and rapidly lost weight. By 2005 the once hulking, big-gutted bully boy weighed just 58 kilograms. Depression engulfing him, he refused to leave his cell. He told a warder, 'I've had enough. I want to kill myself.' In late August Glover collapsed in his cell and was put on suicide watch due to his condition and his depressed state.

At 1.25 pm on 9 September 2005, a fellow inmate found Glover, now seventy-two years old, dead in his cell. He had twisted his bed-sheet into a noose, wrapped it around his neck, tied the other end to the shower fitting and strangled himself. Most people thought he had suicided, but a few who knew him believe that, as with his other attempts he would never have had the courage, and that his death was by misadventure. His ploy, they say, was to pretend to hang himself so that when he was rescued during the regular 1 pm inspection by a guard he would be relocated to Long Bay where he would be closer to the woman he'd been corresponding with – but he'd miscalculated when he twisted the noose, the 1 pm inspection had not taken place that day, and so he had died before help could arrive. At the inquest, Detective Senior Constable Ian Mitchell pointed out that Glover had recently seemed 'future oriented' and had in fact planned a visit the following Sunday with a woman. On the morning of his death, Glover had phoned the woman and later told staff he was getting married the following January. Still, the coroner disagreed and found that Glover had meant to kill himself. The cause of his demise was officially suicide.

When in the days after his death no one – not his wife, nor his daughters, nor his surviving sister – came forward to claim Glover's body and arrange for burial in a cemetery, it seemed that he would be buried in a pauper's grave. But in mid-September, the mystery woman took responsibility for the body and paid for a funeral. The burial site was kept a secret.

CHAPTER 4

THE LAW OF THE RAZOR

Tilly Devine and Kate Leigh: Gang leaders
1920s–1930s

East Sydney in the 1920s and 1930s, when it was the kingdom of vice queens Tilly Devine and Kate Leigh, was one of the most dangerous places on earth. Paddington, Darlinghurst, Kings Cross, Surry Hills and Woolloomooloo were sprawling slums of ramshackle rat- and roach-infested terraces and shacks where lived criminals, violent alcoholics and drug addicts and those too poor to escape to more salubrious suburbs. It's incredible to think that Sydney's inner east, today among Australia's most sought-after and priciest places to live, where a couple of million dollars might buy a small bungalow, was home to Tilly and Kate's razor gangs who rampaged through the labyrinthine alleys and dunny lanes.

Tilly and Kate's kingdom, reported *People* magazine, comprised 'sly-groggeries and gin mills, full of prostitutes, pimps, thugs, blackmailers, thieves, bludgers and strong-arm toughs, [located in] the noisome slum which begins across the road from Central Railway Station and whose squalid, dirty, narrow streets rise and fall across Surry Hills ... the Hills are crammed with ancient hovels and terraces and life is characterised by the personalities of people, the rottenness of crime, the roughness of jungle justice ...'

It was a lucrative milieu for brothel-keeper Tilly and sly grog and cocaine dealer Kate. When they ruled 'Razorhurst', as the inner east was then known, they ranked among Sydney's wealthiest citizens. Their heyday fortunes, estimated at around £250,000 each, would be the equivalent of many millions of dollars today.

Never before, in any city in the world, had the kingpins of crime both been women. Tilly and Kate outdid their male counterparts simply because they were smarter, more ruthless and more violent. Each notched more than a hundred convictions and served more than a dozen prison terms, but on release they returned to their gangs, their brothels and sly-grog shops unchastened and even more determined to make crime pay. They could both have turned their backs on it all and lapsed into cushy retirement when they'd made their money, but the truth is that they *enjoyed* breaking the law.

The long criminal careers of Tilly Devine and Kate Leigh were spawned by laws enacted by the government of New South Wales in the early twentieth century designed to beat crime but having the opposite effect. Illegal sly-grog shops raked in money by slaking the thirst of anyone wanting a drink after the pubs were made to close their doors at 6 pm. (Kate, in prison when the Liquor Act became law in 1916, set up the first of her grog shops immediately on her release in 1919.)

Cocaine, long sold over the counter by chemists as a nerve-soother, was banned. So naturally criminals sold crudely adulterated coke at high prices to those eager for a fix. Street prostitution was criminalised, so illegal brothels flourished, presided over by proprietors who paid their 'girls' with addictive drugs to keep them loyal, and robbed them and their clients.

Standover gangs fastened themselves to the criminal entrepreneurs like fleas on a mangy pooch. They demanded, and usually were paid, protection money.

Handguns were outlawed in 1927, so crooks armed themselves with cut-throat razors with which they killed, maimed and intimidated. Victims bearing an L-shaped scar, extending down the left cheek and across the mouth, were ubiquitous. There were more than five hundred recorded razor attacks from 1927 to 1930. However, because of the gangster's code of never informing, these statistics represent but a small percentage of the attacks that actually took place.

At the height of her criminal career in the early 1930s, Tilly Devine ran as many as thirty brothels, mostly around Palmer Street, East Sydney. With her platinum blonde sausage-roll curls, heavily mascaraed eyes, lurid rouge and the full-length furs she wore even in summer, she stood out in any crowd. After a day's work in her brothels or scheming with her gang in pubs, more often than not the Tradesman's Arms in Palmer Street where fights broke out regularly to the strains of 'The Wild Colonial Boy', played on an accordion by an amputee World War I veteran, she would repair with her abusive and brutish husband, Big Jim, to their expensive home at seaside Maroubra – which featured candelabra, state-of-the-art wireless, polished silver, grand piano and a clutch of pampered Pomeranian dogs.

Tilly was a (mostly) benevolent despot. She and her henchmen protected her 'girls' from pimps and standover men. She paid them well and took care of their food, shelter and doctors' bills. But if they betrayed her by not paying her 50 per cent of their takings, or did a runner to a rival madam, she took horrifying revenge. Once she ordered her heavies to hold down a sex worker who had betrayed her while she shredded the girl's face with heavy blows from her be-ringed fists.

Most of her convictions were prostitution related, but with a hair-trigger temper and predilection for violence, her rap sheet also contained many convictions for assault. Police, innocent members of the public who stared at her too long, a butcher, a fishmonger, a too-forward admirer whose attentions were repaid by Tilly jabbing a pair of scissors into his cheek, anyone who objected to her noisy streams of profanity, or flirted with Big Jim ... no one was safe.

On one occasion, sentenced to six months in Long Bay Gaol, Tilly stood in the dock and, reported *The Truth*,

> flew into a frenzied rage. Her face turned a rich purple, her eyes became piggish, and in a berserk shriek that could be heard all over the building she poured out a stream of vile abuse: 'You don't f------ give a f------ woman a f------ chance. You're all f------ against me!'

Matilda Mary Twiss was born in Camberwell, a south-west London slum, in 1900. As a teenager she'd walk out on whatever factory job she was doing to escape across the river to the more respectable parts of town to linger in art galleries and music halls and gaze longingly at sumptuous shop windows. It was on these jaunts that she vowed to one day be a wealthy and important woman – whatever it took.

To realise her dream she became a prostitute on the Strand in London's West End not far from Buckingham Palace. One day, at the height of World War I, she was chatted up by an Australian digger named James Devine, an overbearing larrikin who claimed to his ingenuous companion that back home he was the rich squire of a kangaroo farm. They married at the Church of the Sacred Heart of Jesus in Camberwell in 1917. Leaving their baby son Frederick at home with her parents, who refused their daughter permission to take him to Australia, she followed Jim to Sydney as a war bride in 1920. Photos of her then show a pretty, open-faced girl in poor clothes. A contemporary later wrote that Tilly had 'a complexion of milk and roses and hair the colour of a hayrick in summer'. In the mean streets of the Harbour City she was a popular addition to the ranks of prostitutes, the beneficiary of her toil being Big Jim. In the late 1920s, as she aged and her features and disposition hardened, she became a madam, opening one brothel, then another, and another ...

Kate Leigh took advantage of the 1916 Liquor Act's requirement that pubs close their doors at 6 pm to corner the market in sly-grog shops, establishments where the thirsty could get a drink after the 'six o'clock swill' that resulted from the Act. Her grog shops, usually a back room in a Surry Hills terrace house where drinkers could illegally guzzle down beer, wine and spirits of varying quality, numbered more than twenty in the 1930s. Kate also sold cocaine and fenced goods shoplifted by her gang. She had a lucrative sideline accepting bribes from police in return for apprising them of the activities of other gangsters, notably Tilly Desine.

Born one of thirteen children in 1881 in Dubbo, central-west New South Wales, Kate decamped for Sydney at the age of ten, and soon was serving time in institutions and prisons for vagrancy, prostitution, assault, receiving stolen goods and perjury. Like Tilly, Kate was attractive when young, but a lifetime of crime bloated her features. By her thirties she was obese, with an oft-broken nose and rotting teeth, greasy hair and a loud gravel voice. In photos of the time she wears a wide, floppy-brimmed hat festooned in feathers. Expensive rings adorned every finger and, again like Tilly, she wore thick fur coats all year round.

Later in her life Kate exhibited kindness and a rough good humour, but in her criminal prime she was a nasty piece of work: 'a bad woman, a foul-mouthed old bitch', said her frequent nemesis, policeman Ray Blissett. She had a murderous temper, as local hoodlum Snowy Prendergast discovered when he invaded her home at 104 Riley Street, Surry Hills in 1930, intent on doing harm to Kate's lover Wally Tomlinson. She bailed up Prendergast on her stairs and told him to leave. When he did not, she shot him dead. She always carried a pistol in her handbag, but wasn't fussy what weapon she used. 'She wouldn't think twice about hitting a bloke over the head with a tomahawk,' said Blissett.

Another celebrated detective of the day, Greg Brown, had many a run-in with Leigh. He told this writer how thieves would make a beeline to her to fence their stolen goods. 'She was a rough, tough old bird.' Brown remembers, as if yesterday, the time she held off at gunpoint a gang of crooks who were beating a young police officer: 'She said she'd shoot them if they didn't let the copper go, and she would have, too.'

Kate Leigh's and Tilly Devine's criminal activities rarely collided, but the pair had a fierce personal rivalry and despised each other. Each longed to be known as Sydney's unchallenged crime czar with all the wealth, power, fear and headlines that status guaranteed. Former policewoman Maggie Baker told this writer, 'In a lane near Palmer Street, Darlinghurst, I came face to face with Tilly. She was blocking the footpath, preventing me from proceeding. She said, "You're the new copper, aren't you? Well, you're not comin' down this bloody street ..." She grabbed me and started shaking me. Next thing, a woman wearing a big black hat got off a tram. It was Kate Leigh. She came up to where Tilly was shaking me like a rag doll and, without a word, she king-hit Tilly Devine and then sat on her in the street. But Tilly could handle herself. She was a dirty fighter and very strong. I saw her and Kate have a blue in Oxford Street one day. Tilly had Kate's hat off and was pummelling her on the ground. Kate got much the worst of it.'

And just as their bosses clashed, whenever Leigh or Devine gang members met the razors flashed. Kate ordered the beating and slashing of Tilly's men and her prostitutes. Tilly's hoodlums ransacked Kate's grog shops, smashing barrels and breaking bottles, and attacked her cocaine sellers. In Kate's pay were such charmers as Wally Tomlinson, Gregory 'The Gunman' Gaffney, Bill 'The Octopus' Flanagan, Bruce Higgs and Barney Dalton. Tilly's gang included her husband, Frankie 'The Little Gunman' Green, Guido Calletti, Sid McDonald and the beautiful doomed prostitute Nellie Cameron.

The Leigh–Devine gang wars were ignited on 17 July 1929, when Devine man Frankie Green was shot and wounded in Woolloomooloo by Leigh hireling Gregory Gaffney after the pair had fallen out over Nellie Cameron. Tilly and Big Jim decided Green should lie low at their Maroubra home until his wounds healed. But Gaffney discovered where Green was hiding and, with Wally Tomlinson and Barney Dalton, set out to finish the job, knowing that as soon as he could Green would come gunning for him.

At midnight, Tilly and Jim Devine, the bandaged Green and another henchman named Sid McDonald were listening to the wireless when a voice rang out from the street. 'Come outside! I want Green's blood!' It was Gaffney. Jim Devine switched off the interior lights and peeked through the front blinds to see Gaffney, with a pistol, clambering over his front fence. Devine opened fire through the open window with a Lee Enfield .303 rifle. Gaffney screamed and collapsed as his blood pooled around him. Tomlinson and Dalton, a talented Eastern Suburbs rugby league player, fired their pistols at the house. To neighbours it must have sounded like the Battle of the Somme. Devine, a crack shot, hit Tomlinson in the arm. Tomlinson and Dalton fled the scene, leaving Gaffney, whose chest had been blown open, to die on the road.

Big Jim was arrested, and the two gangs were out in force at the 2 August inquest into Gaffney's death. Reported the *Sydney Morning Herald*:

> Evil-looking men with battered faces rubbed shoulders with bejewelled women in fur coats at the Coroner's Court yesterday when Mr May inquired into the gang duel which occurred on July 17. Seldom have so many criminals convicted of serious offences, some of them with a notorious police history, assembled in the public section of the Court. Factions between them were noticeable. Belligerent glances were freely exchanged.

At the inquest Devine was ordered to stand trial for murder, but he was found not guilty when the jury accepted his explanation that he was merely defending his hearth and loved ones.

Reprisals were inevitable. Nowadays Kellett Street in the heart of Kings Cross is an innocuous cluster of coffee shops and restaurants. But eighty years ago it was a grimy and forbidding row of doss houses, sly-grog shops, coke dens and brothels – no place for a stroll, and most certainly not on the icy evening of 8 August 1929. The rival gangs of Leigh and Devine had been gathering in Kellett Street since mid-morning. At first the forty or so mobsters were content to trade insults, but as the day wore on and cocaine and alcohol took effect, the nastiness escalated. A brick was thrown. A car window was smashed. Cut-throat razors were drawn. A shot rang out. Suddenly a pitched battle erupted as the gangs went at each other with pistols, razors, fists, clubs and bottles. Police were powerless to restore order, and it was only the heavy casualties on each side that brought hostilities to an end. Amazingly, there were no fatalities, but no combatant escaped without bullet wounds, slashes and bruises.

Kate now offered Tomlinson and Dalton many thousands of dollars to kill Jim Devine and Frankie Green. Green, a psychotic hoodlum whose life would end when he was stabbed in the heart by his lover in April 1956, got wind that there was a price on his head and pre-empted matters. At 4.30 pm on 5 September 1929, Green strode into Sharland's Strand Hotel on the corner of William and Crown Streets, East Sydney. He knew Tomlinson and Dalton were drinking there with razor-men Ed Brady and Charles Connors. Brazenly confronting the four men, Green said he'd be happy to accommodate them if they wanted trouble out on the street at closing time. Leering at the group, he sauntered outside.

At 6 pm, the Leigh gangsters warily exited the pub. As promised, Green and Jim Devine were lurking in the shadows. Green advanced on his quarry, pulled out a long-barrelled revolver, snapped 'Cop this, you bastards!' and fired at Dalton and Tomlinson. Dalton fell dead, shot through the heart. 'You cop this too!' snarled Green and fired at Tomlinson, who fell with a bullet in his arm. As he lay on the footpath Green approached. Tomlinson looked up at the hitman standing over him, clutching his gun. 'Have another go,' he gasped. Green obliged and blasted Tomlinson in the chest. His lung punctured, Tomlinson coughed blood, closed his eyes and lay still – but somehow he survived to fight another day. Green and Devine fled down a nearby laneway, Green hurling his pistol over a fence as they hared back into the depths of Razorhurst.

Open warfare between the Leigh and Devine gangs and other mobs raged until the mid 1930s. Sydney in that period was like a battlefield littered with the corpses of the dead – who included Gregory Gaffney, Barney Dalton, Snowy Prendergast and a score more – and the wounded. Leigh and Devine, Frank Green, Guido Calletti, Wally Tomlinson and Jim Devine all bore lifelong razor and gunshot scars.

Eventually, new consorting laws that levied heavy fines and gaol terms on 'anyone who habitually consorts with reputed thieves or prostitutes or vagrant persons' broke up the razor gangs.

One day in 1936, NSW police commissioner William McKay laid down the law to Tilly and Kate. He told them he appreciated that both were simply supplying the recreational demands of otherwise law-abiding punters, and that in future the police would leave them in peace so long as they ran their brothels and grog shops 'quietly, cleanly and without violence'. Ageing and with their gangs decimated, Tilly and Kate had no option but to clean up their acts.

The two of them continued to profit from crime, and served the odd stretch behind bars when the police, usually as elections loomed, needed to be seen to be taking a hard law and order line. But by the 1950s they had become relatively harmless 'colourful identities'.

Kate would don her floppy hat and sit – sometimes shelling peas for dinner – in the gallery at Central Criminal Court, offering a raucous commentary on proceedings. She gave money and shelter to the homeless and held Christmas street parties for the poor of Surry Hills. Never mind that the toys for the urchins had been swiped from Mark Foys and David Jones. Tilly donated thousands of pounds to children's hospitals, the Jesuits and the Salvation Army. When newspapers and magazines wanted a photo of the two old supremos hugging, they cheerfully agreed.

Tilly and her second husband, a good-natured villain and barman at the Tradesman's Arms named Eric Parsons, travelled to London in 1953 for the coronation of Queen Elizabeth II. Tilly, who'd had her hair set into a towering helmet in Paris two days before, and Eric were in the Mall as the royal carriages clattered past to Buckingham Palace. Eric died of cancer just four years later.

Kate married the old lag Ernest 'Shiner' Ryan, an accomplice from as long ago as 1916, in 1949. At the wedding she bawled, 'I'll see he doesn't get to the bloody pub! If this marriage doesn't work out, I've got a good, sharp razor!' The marriage ended a few months later. Shiner survived.

Now that riches and territory and criminal kudos were no longer at stake, the pair could even afford to compliment each other. Said Tilly of Kate, 'Aww, she ain't a bad old bitch at heart.' And Kate of Tilly: 'She and me, we were enemies for years. Tilly would put the dirt in about me to friends, and then I'd tear into Tilly and we'd chase each other from one street to another. But that's all done now. When poor old Til came down from Long Bay last time, we had a real nice couple of hours together. Til's a very good woman, mind you, no matter what the police say about her. In that, she takes after me.'

By the mid 1950s, the women's wealth was largely gone, spent on parties, homes, trips, cars, clothes, jewellery, charity and hangers-on. After a long overdue investigation, the Taxation Department realised that neither had filed a tax return since the 1920s, and exacted retrospective punishment. What was left of their fortunes and virtually every possession they had left – including furs, rings and cars – was confiscated.

Kate was reduced to selling illegal rotgut alcohol to down-and-outers from dingy rented rooms, the days when movie stars, sportsmen and politicians were her patrons a distant memory. Then in 1955 the government allowed pubs to stay open until 10 pm and Kate, like the good old bad old days, was history. She lived alone in a sad and tiny first-floor room over a shop in Devonshire Street, Surry Hills, until her death after a stroke, aged 82, on 31 January 1964.

Her funeral caused gridlock in Surry Hills. Tilly, herself shockingly wasted and ill with cancer, was there to honour her old enemy at a packed St Peter's Church. She was joined by senior police, politicians, newspapermen and minor radio celebrities. Recalled policewoman Maggie Baker, 'When Kate died, I felt, well, there's a bit of good old Australian history that's gone. I couldn't fit into the church. I've never seen so many cars, so many people from all walks of life.' In the eulogies, Kate's criminal career of 70-odd years was not mentioned.

Tilly didn't fare as well. When she died on 24 November 1970, few came to bid her farewell at Botany Cemetery. *Daily Telegraph* journalist Ron Saw wrote a scathing eulogy in his column: 'She was a vicious, grasping, high priestess of savagery, venery, obscenity and whoredom ... one of the most frightening creatures spewed up by the razor gangs [who was] charged with everything from consorting to malicious wounding, from indecent language to attempted murder. She was a wretched woman.'

CHAPTER 5

THE HODDLE STREET MASSACRE

Julian Knight: Mass murderer
1987

On Sunday 9 August 1987, the accumulated stress, shame and disappointments of his wretched existence finally overwhelmed Julian Knight. His fragile psyche shattered, and his brain snapped. At 9.50 pm, he kneeled military-style on a nature strip in Hoddle Street in Melbourne's Clifton Hill, and opened fire with a Ruger .22 semi-automatic rifle, a 12-gauge shotgun and a .38 M14 semi-automatic rifle. Later he would say, 'I saw the police and the public as targets. The object was to take out as many as I could and I didn't see them as human beings.'

In twenty-three minutes of horror and mayhem, Knight shot seven people dead and wounded nineteen. One woman was nursing her baby in a car when she was hit, others died trying to help the wounded. Some of Knight's victims stood transfixed, rooted to the spot as the 19-year-old approached and gunned them down. One witness who had seen bodies strewn all over the street likened the scene to a war zone.

If Knight came across that comment in the aftermath of his random shooting spree, and it's probable he did, for he read the newspaper reports voraciously, a smile of satisfaction might have scuttled across his weasel face. For a war zone was precisely what Knight, who had been discharged from the army in disgrace just eighteen days earlier, after stabbing an officer, was hell-bent on creating. 'I wanted to see what it was like to kill someone in combat,' he told police, 'and I wanted to know what it was like to die in combat.' (Many consider it unfortunate that he never got to find out.) Knight bragged to arresting officers that he had planned to kill himself before he could be captured but did not because he mislaid the bullet he had saved for this purpose.

In fact, and typically, the loser who dreamed of being a war hero scurried rat-like for his life when he ran out of ammunition, and was easily overpowered by police. Later, when he was arrested and encased in a straitjacket, he screamed and wailed. Hardly heroic.

The massacre that Julian Knight perpetrated in Hoddle Street was the terrible culmination of a life marked by failure, rejection and humiliation and his obsessions with the military, firearms and himself.

As a baby, Knight was adopted by Ralph and Pamela Knight. Ralph was a career soldier who would be promoted to major and who, at the time his son went berserk, was commanding the education centre at Laverack Barracks in Townsville, Queensland.

In 1980, the 12-year-old Julian was devastated when his adoptive parents split up and his beloved father, the military man he idolised and whose approval and admiration he so desperately sought, left the boy with his mother and embarked on a new life and, in time, a new marriage. Psychologists would say Knight felt sorely rejected by both Ralph Knight and his birth mother, and their perceived abandonment contributed to his low self-esteem.

Julian Knight grew into a socially inept and friendless teenager with a snarly temper and ready fists who took refuge in guns and dreams of war and battlefield heroism, of standing alone and mowing down wave after wave of his enemies. He studied the rise and demise of Hitler's Third Reich and frequently imagined himself in a last-ditch gun battle in the ruins of Berlin.

The year his family disintegrated, Knight was given his first weapon, an air rifle, and no bird in his neighbourhood was safe. By fourteen he had learned to fire an M16 rifle and by sixteen, as a member of the Melbourne High School cadet unit, was adept at ambush tactics. That same year, 1984, he made a ludicrous and inevitably unsuccessful bid to join the South African army, but succeeded in joining the Australian Army Reserves in 1986. Though an intelligence test rated his IQ among the top 3 per cent in Victoria, he scored a succession of Cs in his final year at Melbourne High and had a short and abject stint at Latrobe University. Still, he couldn't care less that he flunked at university, because his failure left him free to realise his ambition of being like Ralph Knight and becoming a soldier.

After passing two rounds of interviews, in January 1987 Knight was accepted into the elite Duntroon Military College in Canberra as an officer cadet. In the light of what was to come, the Duntroon screening system came under heavy fire. 'Our ideal is to find responsible people with an amount of controlled aggression who can work well in a team,' responded one army psychologist. 'We certainly don't want Rambos, but sometimes the wrong person slips through the net.'

Julian Knight was just such a person. At Duntroon, he became highly skilled at handling and firing machine guns and submachine guns, 9 mm pistols, automatic rifles, grenade launchers, hand-grenades and anti-armour weapons. But it wasn't long before it became obvious that his master-plan of becoming a decorated soldier would never eventuate. His sullen and disagreeable demeanour made him a pariah at the college, and his gung-ho carelessness in the field convinced peers and officers alike that he lacked discipline and leadership qualities.

There's little doubt Knight was telling the truth when he claimed to be a victim of bastardisation at Duntroon, nor that the physical and mental abuse he received could only have contributed to his feelings of alienation and rejection. One who knew him at the time told journalist Tess Lawrence, '[Knight] wasn't good enough ... You wouldn't go out and die for this man. You just wouldn't trust his judgment.' This soldier called Knight a 'wimp [and a] coward – that's why he was picked on. He was scared shitless ... He was always saying he wished [a war] would start in Australia. Well, he started his own war ... Not one of us was surprised when we found out it was Knight. He was a real sicko ...'

Knight, by now tall and slim with thinning hair, a blotchy complexion, receding chin, prominent nose and the wispy moustache of a B-movie villain, struggled out of college too. He was often drunk. He got into fist fights, usually because, being self-centred and immature, his first reaction when contradicted, rebuked or criticised was to lash out. In a pathetic bid to impress, he affected a swaggering gait and a querulous tone of voice. To anyone who listened, he big-noted himself as a crack soldier who had accomplished many brave deeds. Few were fooled, however, and his very presence got on people's nerves. Women shied from him and the few relationships he had didn't last long.

On 24 April 1986, Knight applied for a shooter's licence at Collingwood police station. To qualify, he had to answer twenty questions, a typical one being: 'When do you load, then point, a rifle? A) When you're leaving on the great duck chase and your wife and kids get in the car?; B) When a duck flies overhead?; C) When your wife and kids get out of the car?' Knight, like just about everyone else who took the quiz, scored 100 per cent and, after a routine background check confirmed there were no criminal convictions or nervous breakdowns in his history, he was granted his licence. Over the next few months he registered a number of .22 rifles, a shotgun and a semi-automatic rifle. The registrar of firearms, Inspector Lex Newgreen, would tell reporters that 'Knight held those weapons lawfully. It is not unusual to have a spread of firearms like that'.

At Duntroon, Knight continued to be a lightning rod for trouble. Just six months into his 18-month course, a senior cadet prodded him in the chest with a fixed bayonet. Knight pushed the officer away and stormed from the scene without being officially dismissed. A few days later, another officer ordered Knight to strike him, with the idea of being able to level a charge of assault against the despised cadet. Other cadets stepped between the two before a blow could be struck. Knight was hauled before the company sergeant major, who accused him of disobedience (for leaving the scene of the earlier altercation without waiting to be officially dismissed by his superior), revoked his weekend leave pass and confined him to barracks.

Knight ignored the order and that weekend showed up at a Canberra nightclub with a girlfriend. Unfortunately for him, the sergeant major also chose to go there. The officer upbraided Knight in front of his girlfriend and ordered him to return immediately to barracks. At this point, injury was added to insult when Knight was punched by another soldier. Reeling from the blow, humiliated and enraged, he staggered out of the club but soon returned. He calmly approached the sergeant major, now sitting with friends, and slashed him twice across the face with a knife.

Knight was charged with malicious wounding and ordered to resign from the army. It's understood the police charges over this incident still stand.

In July 1987, his Duntroon days over, Knight was back in Melbourne, living with his adoptive mother Pamela, his 14-year-old brother Mathew and 12-year-old sister Sarah in their home in Clifton Hill. Along with his other belongings, he stashed his small arsenal under his bed. He attempted to contact his girlfriend, saying he wanted to see her, but she would have nothing to do with him.

Sunday 9 August was Pamela Knight's birthday. Julian and his siblings wished her happiness – and then things went to hell.

Knight learned that a group of acquaintances had held a party the night before to which he hadn't been invited, which made him seethe. Then his modified Torana V8 broke down. He tried again to cajole his estranged girlfriend into taking him back, without success. In the early evening, in his upstairs bedroom, he donned his dark blue polo shirt, jeans and runners, pulled on a zip-up jacket to ward off the cold, and went to the Royal Hotel around the corner in nearby Hoddle Street. Over the past weeks, Knight had developed a crush on a 29-year-old barmaid at the Royal and he hoped she'd be working that night. She'd rejected his advances but he was sure if given the chance he could convince her of the error of her ways.

When Knight walked into the pub, he saw the barmaid, but she was chatting and dancing with a bunch of tough and boozy Irish guys. Knight bought a packet of John Player cigarettes and a schooner of beer and sat alone, glowering at the barmaid. For an hour or so he continued to sit and drink and glare. He later claimed to have scoffed fifteen pots (15-ounce beers) but patrons who saw him that night put the number at five or six. After an hour and a half, the barmaid left the Royal with some of the Irishmen. Knight remained, radiating hostility, for another fifteen minutes. He said later it was then that he decided to pay the world back.

At 8.15, Knight left the Royal and walked home. He went straight to his bedroom. He took two rifles and a shotgun from under the bed and strapped on his ammunition belt. He sat alone for a while, then around ten past nine left the house and returned to Hoddle Street, where he kneeled on the nature strip, raised one of his rifles and took aim ...

Knight shot dead a woman nursing her baby in her stationary car. He picked off a motorcyclist who tumbled off his bike and lay sprawled in the middle of the road. He blasted a man and a woman who died huddled together in the gutter. Another woman was fatally hit when she left shelter to try to drag a wounded person to safety. A man was killed at the wheel of his car. As authorities converged on the scene, Knight peppered ambulances and police cars, shops and buildings. He fired at a police helicopter and punctured one of its fuel tanks. Though *he* harboured delusions of heroism, it was the people in his cross-hairs who showed unimaginable bravery. Citizens, police and ambulance staff risked their lives to help the wounded and dying.

Hoddle Street became a Goya-esque nightmare of twisted bodies, screams and moans and pooling blood, of sirens and spotlights. A number of cars, many with windscreens shattered and bodywork riddled with bullets, careened off the road. People ran and hid as best they could. Knight shot as many of them as he could, firing more than 125 rounds. Then, mercifully, he ran out of ammunition.

The father of one victim, 24-year-old Vesna Markovska, wept when interviewed by a reporter from *The Age*:

> 'Why was my daughter shot for nothing? [he demanded.] 'She was all the time wanting to help everybody. My family never make trouble in Australia, never. We vote, we are friendly to everybody. Australia is the best country in the world, but the gun laws are no good. If somebody wants to buy a shotgun they should go to the doctor and have their brain checked. Too many criminals, too many idiots buy guns and make trouble. I gave my daughter everything I could, we worked for our kids, but now she is gone. I have lost my daughter for nothing.'

Knight pleaded guilty in the Supreme Court on 28 October 1988 to the murders of Vesna Markovska, Robert Mitchell, Georgina Papaloannou, John Muscat, Dusan Flajnik, Keith Stanton and Tracey Skinner, and to the attempted murders of forty-six other people. His counsel, Robert Richter QC, told the court that Knight had succumbed to an accumulation of stresses that 'sent him into depression and despair'. Members of the families of his slain victims and several people bearing the scars of bullet wounds sat in the gallery. Many were in tears.

On 10 November, Knight, straggly hair now trimmed into a crewcut, stood stock-still and expressionless before Mr Justice Hampel as sentence was delivered. The judge said that he accepted psychiatric evidence that Knight suffered from a serious personality disorder although he was neither medically nor legally insane:

> Your inability to cope with an accumulation of pressures and stresses, your fragile and disordered personality, and rejections including being forced to leave Duntroon Military College after stabbing a sergeant with a pocket knife only weeks earlier, coupled with an obsession with military life and combat, produced the background to the shooting. War history, battle scenes and combat became part of your fantasy world. Your fantasy life was built around heroic killing in battle situations, ending up in victory or your own death in the so-called 'last man' stance.

The Hoddle Street massacre, said the judge, was one of the worst in Australia's history. 'The surviving victims and the community at large are understandably horrified and justifiably outraged by what you have done,' Hampel told Knight. 'There is a sense of bewilderment as to why a highly intelligent man of nineteen with no criminal history could have done what you did.'

He sentenced Knight to life imprisonment on each murder count and ten years' jail on each attempted murder charge, the sentences to be served concurrently. Twenty-seven years would have to pass before he would become eligible for parole. At that, Knight deferentially bowed his head to the judge, like an obedient soldier, as if to say he had it coming and would serve his time like a man. A court officer gripped him roughly by the elbow and led him away, to be transported in an armoured police vehicle to Pentridge Prison's maximum security H division.

Knight has not served uneventful time. Soon after his arrest he began writing a report in which he profiled mass murderers – such as James Huberty, who shot dead twenty people at a McDonald's restaurant in Los Angeles in 1984, and Charles Whitman, who climbed to the top of a tower at the University of Texas in 1966 and fired on students below, killing sixteen – who had used guns to kill strangers. Like himself, noted Knight, other mass murderers found it difficult to feel sympathy for people they've never known. A major life event was almost always the catalyst for the killings. In his case, he mused, it was being discharged from the army. Mass murderers, again like himself, felt 'isolated and frustrated, with a great sense of failure' and typically had had 'an unhappy home life'.

When ABC-TV aired the documentary *Hoddle Street* about the mass killing, the producers received a letter from the perpetrator himself, congratulating them and rating the film 'an accurate and reasonably comprehensive examination of the whole event'.

Not long after he was sentenced, in Pentridge at the end of 1988, Knight gave an extraordinary interview to journalist, broadcaster and filmmaker Tess Lawrence, which was published in the *Good Weekend* magazine in *The Age* and the *Sydney Morning Herald*. Lawrence reported Knight as shockingly unrepentant, indeed gloating over his crime, and had found herself on the pointy end of a grilling. Knight, she wrote, had demanded to know where the article would be placed. How much did Lawrence know about *the* night? How much did she *really* know about *the* night? Had she seen the pictures of the victims? Did she have any photos or press clippings of the massacre and if so could she *please* send them to him. The reason, he said, was that he wanted to make sure Lawrence didn't 'get anything wrong. The media are fucking incompetent. You're like the police. Fuckwits'.

Knight preened and postured and came on like Hannibal Lecter:

> 'You see [he carefully explained to the journalist], I'm not just a straight-out killer. Have you read about Son of Sam, have you read about the McDonald's massacre? I'd like you to read up on them before you get back to me, so you have more of an understanding, so we can more thoroughly discuss this type of killing process. I'm not like these guys [his fellow inmates]. No way. Don't even put them in the same class.'

When the article was published, Knight's 27-year non-parole period looked to be on decidedly shaky ground.

And that ground grew shakier still when, on 2 May 2001, authorities searched his cell in Barwon Prison's Acacia unit, supposedly the most secure unit in the Victorian prison system, with an A1 security rating, and were astonished to find, tucked away, a large trove of banned items. According to prison records, the stash included two blades in paperclip boxes; one blade in a typewriter disk container; one Stanley knife blade; one sharpened butter knife; numerous articles to do with the Ku Klux Klan, White Power and the Racists Party; articles about weapons; war magazines and books; a prison medical centre medication bottle; a black leather belt; two TV/video remote controls; one extension lead; one can opener; a quantity of bale hooks; a sharpened metal spike; permanent markers; a large quantity of computer disks – many containing information about prison security and staffing; one metal shiv approximately 25 centimetres long; two metal shivs approximately 23 centimetres long; a large quantity of pornographic material; a quantity of sandpaper; a quantity of unauthorised stationery (masking tape, date stamp, Post-It labels, etc.); solvent-type liquid paper; a very large quantity of prison security-related items including sections of Core (Public Correctional Enterprise) operating procedures, a quantity of Barwon visits muster lists, Barwon staff pictures, a Port Phillip Prison daily prisoner status report; a Victorian Department of Corrective Services head office phone list; TAB betting information; Department of Justice memoranda; the Barwon staff roster; a prisoner named Johnson's phone pin ID and phone names and numbers; and telephone hints for prisoners, including information on how to divert phone calls. On another occasion he was in trouble for secreting in his cell a picture of Adolf Hitler and cards with such slogans as 'Stop the Asian invasion', 'We hate all queers', 'White Power' and 'Dial-a-Racist'.

Knight has been a difficult and obstreperous prisoner. He has committed offences against departmental regulations, and numerous acts of violence. On a number of occasions he has spent time, sometimes as long as months, in solitary confinement. It is believed that he stabbed another inmate, a fellow murderer, and that he planned to escape after taking a prison officer hostage.

As part of his punishment for these offences, Knight lost privileges – which spurred him to repeatedly take the Victorian Corrective Services Department to court to redress what he said was a terrible miscarriage of justice. Between September 1992 and October 2004, he landed the department in the Victorian Supreme Court on sixteen occasions. His series of legal challenges cost the government more than $250 000, while a further $128 000 was spent on external legal advice to deal with Knight's legal appeals and Freedom of Information requests. His law suits included demanding Austudy payments while he was in jail, and claiming abuse of human rights when the Nazi and racist material was confiscated. He also asked the court to grant him access to prison staff rosters and to prevent prison staff opening his mail.

One after the other, each legal sortie was dismissed. In 2004, state Attorney-General Rob Hulls began proceedings in the Victorian Supreme Court to have Knight declared a vexatious litigant. Justice Philip Cummins granted the request, and barred him from bringing another case for ten years. He can still apply for material under the Freedom of Information Act, and he continues to do so, occasionally with success.

In 2007 Knight, now aged thirty-nine, was at it again, petitioning the Supreme Court of Victoria to have his security status downgraded and to order that a management plan be instituted to facilitate his re-entry into society. 'I wish to be rehabilitated and the defendant [Corrections Victoria] has a statutory obligation to facilitate that,' he declared.

It emerged in proceedings that prison officials had intercepted a letter Knight had recently written to the family of one of his victims. Knight said the confiscation was unjust because the letter was one of apology for what he had done, and an attempt to explain why. Writing letters of apology to those whose lives he had destroyed that icy night back in 1987 was, argued Knight, 'part of my rehabilitation and a small measure towards me making amends' and it was 'the prerogative of the victim in question to determine whether he or she wishes to receive the mail ... not for Corrections Victoria to vet it'.

Save your apologies, save your explanations, chorused his victims, who believed Knight was trying to ingratiate himself with prison authorities to win early release. 'I don't want [an apology],' survivor Andrew Hack told a reporter. 'I have five scars on my body that will be there for life. I have two girls and a wife and I'm just trying to get on with my life. I don't want an apology and I don't think anyone would.'

These days, in Barwon's Acacia unit Julian Knight spends twenty-two hours a day alone in his tiny, bare cell with concrete floor and stainless steel toilet and sink. The remaining two hours he can be found in the prison's tiny, high-security exercise cage in the company of other dangerous prisoners. He will be eligible for parole in 2014 and will undoubtedly apply. It's thought unlikely that his application will be granted.

CHAPTER 6

OUTBACK RAMPAGE

Kevin Crump and Allan Baker: Kidnappers, rapists, murderers

1973

Just before 11 am on Tuesday 13 November 1973, as Constable Brian Neale of the Special Traffic Patrol was cruising the New England Highway at Hexham, near Maitland on the New South Wales central coast, the radio in his supercharged Torana crackled into life. It told him to be on the lookout for two men driving a stolen blue Holden Premier sedan, registration BJD 666. A couple of minutes later, as he turned into John Renshaw Drive, Kurri Kurri, Neale saw the very car approaching at high speed. Seconds after it flashed past, he spun into a U-turn, flipped on the siren, radioed for support and for other police vehicles to cut off escape routes, and gave chase.

Neale could see the silhouettes of the fleeing men in the car ahead, which had ramped up to 145 kilometres an hour as it entered Minmi Road bound for Maitland, but the constable was nudging 160 and closing the gap. Now at East Maitland, he was joined in his pursuit by senior constables Millward and Jones in their Valiant Charger, Millward at the wheel.

Drawing level with the stolen car, Neale motioned to its driver, a scabrous punk whose name was Kevin Crump, to pull over. Crump's response was to swerve sharply and deliberately side-swipe the police car, which careened off the road in a storm of dust and gravel.

Respite for the fugitives was temporary, for Millward and Jones had caught up and were now only metres behind, siren screaming, lights flashing. Unexpectedly, the man in the passenger seat, Crump's fellow lowlife Allan Baker, turned in his seat and fired a .308 calibre rifle through the rear window at the pursuing officers. Millward swung his wheel hard. The bullet missed. Baker battered a hole in the rear window of the Holden with the muzzle of his rifle, stuck the weapon through and fired again and again. Two bullets slammed into the police vehicle's rear mudguard. As Senior Constable Millward struggled to keep the car on the road, his partner returned fire with his service pistol.

In the car ahead, Baker yelled to Crump, 'When I get ready to shoot, slow down so I can get better aim!' Crump obeyed, and Baker fired. The windscreen of the pursuit car disintegrated and Millward felt pain in his head. 'I knew I'd been shot,' he said later. 'I saw blood dripping and instinctively threw my hands to my head. I managed to stop the car. Blood was pouring onto my shirt.'

As the stricken Millward brought the Valiant to a stop, another police vehicle carrying detectives Ken Sneddon and Wayne Hore powered onto the scene and took up position behind the stolen car. As the wild pursuit continued, pedestrians and other motorists, uncertain whether this was for real or they'd been caught up in an action movie, took the sensible option and got out of harm's way.

Again and again Crump slowed down, almost to a halt, so Baker could fire more accurately at the police car behind. There followed the dull *crack! crack! crack!* of the rifle firing, and bullets whistled through the air. Several punctured Sneddon and Hore's vehicle, but many more missed. 'Baker was taking deliberate aim at us,' Hore reported afterwards. 'It was close.'

The stolen car sped up once more and raced for the Woodville Bridge over the Paterson River, on the way to Morpeth. Nearing the bridge, Baker and Crump realised that a police roadblock manned by officers bristling with weapons had been set up at the far end. They drove off the road and into a paddock lush with lucerne, where the car almost immediately became bogged. The fugitives, both armed with a rifle, leaped out and ran towards the river. Every 10 metres or so they turned, crouched and fired at the following officers, who were forced to duck and weave for cover.

Having bought themselves a few precious seconds each time the police had to scramble to their feet to resume the chase, Crump and Baker plunged into the cold waters of the river.

Meanwhile around ninety police, armed with shotguns and high-powered rifles, had converged on the site from surrounding commands and were scouring the banks of the river, nearby scrub and dense thickets of willow trees for the fugitives, who seemingly had vanished. Locals gathered, one of them offering the officers access to the armoury he kept on his farm. Police boats plied the river and a private plane piloted by its owner, businessman Bernie Saroff, in radio contact with police, swooped low across the water.

For two hours the two men avoided capture, hiding in a dense growth of rushes in water up to their necks, submerging to breathe through hollow reeds when searchers came close. But their cause was hopeless – there was simply nowhere for them to run, the water was icy, and police reinforcements were arriving en masse.

When Baker was finally spotted, he hastily threw his rifle into the water, where it sank, and gave up quietly, emerging from the river bedraggled and forlorn, 'like a mouse', recalled one officer. Crump was hauled out soon afterwards. Police thought it was the cold water that was making him shiver and tremble and his teeth chatter so hard that he could not say his name. Later they realised it was abject fear at what the police would now inevitably learn about him and his partner in crime that had rendered the man unable to speak.

Handcuffs were snapped on their wrists and Baker and Crump were hustled away to Maitland police station, both still in their sodden clothes.

They were not offered blankets. Members of their heavy guard recalled that Baker stared into their eyes with a defiant, arrogant expression. Crump, however, looked disconsolate and frequently shuddered.

Senior officers felt sweet relief that the manhunt was over without loss of life – Millward had suffered only a surface head wound and would soon recover. But something was worrying the life out of them: Would these blokes have fought so desperately, even to the extent of trying to murder police, to avoid capture if all they had done was steal a car? Highly unlikely, they suspected, and their suspicion was well founded.

It was speedily established that Crump, 24, and Baker, 25, had long criminal records. By now, too, searchers had recovered from the river Baker's discarded .222 rifle with its telescopic sight and Crump's .308. In the stolen car they found, among many items, a .22 calibre Winchester pump-action rifle, a box of .222 ammunition, a sheepskin-lined leather coat, some male toiletries, and a badge from the Collarenebri RSL club in north-west New South Wales. Bells rang at this discovery, and a phone call to northern New South Wales, where two huge murder investigations were under way, elicited stunning news.

On 3 November, 43-year-old itinerant cotton-picker Ian Lamb had been shot dead in his station wagon at Wee Waa, near Narrabri. His sheepskin-lined leather coat with a Collarenebri RSL badge pinned to the front, a quantity of toiletries, and $60 in cash were stolen from his vehicle. And on 7 November, a .22 Winchester pump-action rifle, a .222 with telescopic sights and a box of ammunition had been taken from the farm of 36-year-old mother-of-three Virginia Morse, almost certainly by whoever it was who had abducted her, driven her across the Queensland border, tied her to the ground, tortured and raped her and shot her dead.

The guard on Crump and Baker, already massive, was strengthened.

Allan Baker's first recorded run-in with the law was at the age of fifteen when the boy, who had scarcely spent a day in school, was sent to a child offenders' institution for stealing. He was fascinated by firearms. At the age of sixteen he shot and wounded his best friend in the head, although he maintained it was an accident. Taking his youth and explanation into consideration, a magistrate placed him on probation and ordered him not to go near guns. But Baker paid no heed, and in his late teens committed a series of armed robberies. Guns were not all that beguiled him: twice when he was arrested he was found to be wearing women's underwear, and a stash of panties and bras was found by police at his rented room. Baker, small of stature with a mop of curly dark hair and a straggly beard and moustache, met Crump in Maitland Gaol in 1972 and they became lovers.

Kevin Crump, also short and slight, affected surfie-like blond locks and the same scrappy facial hair as Baker. Also like Baker, with whom he was besotted, he had notched numerous childhood convictions, mainly for theft, and spent a number of terms in institutions. Crump was of low intelligence, and could barely read and write. It's recorded that on one occasion, after he'd shoplifted a pair of socks from a Woolworths store in Sydney he committed the dim-bulb act of returning to the store an hour later, wearing the pilfered socks, to try to steal a pair of swimming trunks. He was nabbed on both counts. His limited intellect was also in evidence at parties, where he would invite friends to hit him in the face as hard as they could, betting them $10 that they wouldn't be able to knock him down. He almost always lost his bet. In one of his early stints in prison he'd raped another prisoner.

Mid 1973, and the pair were out of jail. Baker was in north-west New South Wales seeking labouring jobs. He reckoned there'd be work about, because in October the previous year he had briefly found employment at Banarway, the property of Brian and Virginia Morse, 25 kilometres north of Collarenebri, where he was paid and fed and given shelter. Brian Morse later said that he had no problems with Baker's work, and found it up to standard. One day Baker had just moved on.

Baker contacted his old prison pal Crump, then mooching around Newcastle on the central coast of New South Wales, and invited him to join him. Still deeply in Baker's thrall, Crump did not need to be asked twice. He stole a blue Holden Premier belonging to one Phillip McBride of nearby Kearsley and headed north to rendezvous with Baker. The pair drifted through the bush, surviving on the cash they gleaned from minor robberies and a few days' menial work here and there.

On 3 November, broke and hungover and wearing overalls and balaclavas, they pulled up alongside Ian Lamb's station wagon, parked by the roadside in an isolated area. Lamb was inside asleep. They thought they'd rob him, but something in Baker snapped. 'Hey!' cried Baker through the open car window. Lamb gave a start and opened his eyes, and Baker shot him through the throat with his .308 calibre rifle. 'He just woke up and got shot,' Crump would recall. They stole the coat, toiletries and cash, siphoned the petrol from the station wagon's petrol tank and sped off across the border into Queensland, leaving their victim to die.

On his arrest, Baker was asked why he shot Lamb. He replied sullenly, 'I don't know.' By the time of his trial he had changed his tune, now saying it was an accident. 'I didn't mean to shoot him,' he blathered. 'The gun was a scare weapon. All I meant to do was tie the man up and rob him. When I went over to the car and knocked on the door I said, "Hey, you!" and the guy in the car sat up suddenly and made a noise and I jumped backwards and the gun went off. I didn't know I had shot the man until Crump told me. I didn't know my finger had pulled the trigger. I had no reason to shoot the man and he did not know us.'

On 7 September, around 8 am, Crump and Baker hid their car near the home of Brian and Virginia Morse and their three children, then aged thirteen, nine and five. The men sat atop a haystack for three hours in the rising heat and watched the homestead through binoculars. They saw Brian Morse working on a wheat header and his wife going about her chores. The children left for school. At 11.30 Brian drove off, heading for Moree to have a part for his header machined. Virginia Morse, now on her own, iced her brother's wedding cake, then sat sewing in the cool shade on the front porch.

The killers advanced stealthily on the farmhouse, intent on robbery but fully prepared to murder Virginia Morse if she recognised her former employee. Which she did. Crump and Baker crept up behind her and Baker warned her not to turn around or he would shoot her. Virginia, said by all who knew her to be a kind and loving soul, turned and cried, 'Oh Allan, you scared me.' Baker now pointed his rifle at the startled woman. 'Allan,' she said, 'don't be silly.'

They stole the guns from the house, bundled the bound and gagged Virginia Morse into the blue Holden Premier and drove 170 kilometres into Queensland, for twenty-two hours inflicting unspeakable horrors on their victim. They beat her, burned her with cigarettes, and raped her repeatedly. Baker later recalled: 'Mrs Morse said, "What's going to happen to me? The kids will be home by now. I love my children. Please let me get home to them. What time is it? Brian will be starting to worry about me." I kept telling her to shut up.'

Meanwhile, Brian Morse had returned around 9.30 pm to find his wife and his rifles and ammunition missing. Deeply concerned, he telephoned friends to see if she was with them; she was not. Hours later, at a complete loss, he phoned the police, who began a search. Next morning Brian and his father found Virginia's car, drained of fuel and hidden under sheets of tin in a patch of bracken at an abandoned police station 2 kilometres from the property. Inside they found a notepad with the unmistakable impression of the word 'HELP' on it, as if the kidnapper had surprised Virginia writing the message and ripped off the top page. A team of police and volunteers converged on the area but no trace of the missing woman was found.

By the Weir River, 80 kilometres north of the border town of Goondiwindi, Crump and Baker, who had been drinking beer during the drive, dragged Virginia Morse from the car and staked her out on the ground with tow ropes and straps. They continued their atrocities. In her agony, Virginia asked why the men were doing these things to her – Baker told her he didn't know. Then they gagged and blindfolded her again, tied her to a tree and, despite her pleas for her life, Crump executed her with her husband's gun, the .222 rifle. 'She wasn't crying because I think she was beyond that,' Baker would tell police. 'She had been crying all the time before. She was blindfolded and I aimed at her and her hands came up to her face and they were shaking and she fell over. If Kevin hadn't shot her I would have because she could identify us … and we done these terrible things to her. It was like a firing squad.'

Crump would claim at his trial that Baker had threatened to shoot him if he didn't kill Virginia Morse. 'He wanted me in as deep as him. Your Honour and gentlemen of the jury, it was a choice of either me or Mrs Morse ... Allan told me to aim at the right side of her face. If I shot her there it would probably kill her outright. Allan told me I had to prove myself. Allan had his gun aimed at her too.'

Death was instantaneous. They burned their victim's clothes, then committed further depraved indignities on her body before they hurled it into the river and covered it with stones and branches.

Hardly had Crump and Baker washed the blood from their hands when they knocked at the door of a Goondiwindi farmhouse seeking work. There was none, but they helped the farmer fix a vehicle. They went on to the Boggabilla Hotel, where they got roaring drunk and were ejected for unruly behaviour.

By now a massive police search was in full swing for Virginia Morse, and a manhunt under way to find the killers of Ian Lamb, whose body was discovered on the day Virginia was kidnapped.

By 13 November, the killers had moved south, to the central coast of New South Wales. At Kearsley, on the coalfields 50 kilometres from Newcastle, they parked the blue Holden behind a stand of trees across the road from the home of the Pemberton family. Robert Pemberton had been Crump's boss during a short stint at Seppelts Vineyard near Cessnock and Crump was under the impression that he was a wealthy man and would have money and valuables in his home. They waited for the Pembertons to leave for work and around 9.30 am parked in the driveway and broke into the house.

While they were inside, stashing cash, cameras, watches, rugs and radios into bags, a taxi drove down the street. In a remarkable coincidence, the taxi driver, Kevin Marks, was a friend of Phillip McBride. He recognised the blue Holden Premier as the car stolen from McBride earlier that month. Crump and Baker saw Marks noting down the licence number and speaking on his two-way radio. They ran from the house juggling their loot, leaped into the vehicle and sped away toward Kurri Kurri. They pulled into the Stanford Merthyr service station, where proprietor Kelvin

Sweeney, another friend of McBride's, also recognised the car. He too notified police.

On receiving the calls from taxi headquarters and Kelvin Sweeney, police broadcast an alert. Soon afterward, Constable Neale saw the blue Holden Premier powering towards him along John Renshaw Drive, turned and gave chase. The vicious duo's crime rampage was about to end in the cold waters of the Paterson River.

After their arrest, Crump and Baker were confronted with the circumstantial evidence against them – the stolen rifles, the coat, the toiletries – and confessed to their involvement in the deaths of Virginia Morse and Ian Lamb. They told investigators where they would find Virginia's body. NSW police charged both men with murdering Ian Lamb, with kidnapping and conspiring to murder Virginia Morse (because they killed her in Queensland, the murder itself came under that state's jurisdiction), with maliciously shooting at police with the intention of preventing lawful apprehension, and with breaking into and stealing from the Pemberton home at Kearsley.

Some six months later, on 10 June 1974, Crump and Baker's trial began at Sydney's Central Criminal Court, under Mr Justice Taylor. The public benches were jammed with spectators. Both men, who sniggered and smirked at each other on numerous occasions throughout the proceedings, heedless that every callous chuckle was breaking the hearts even more, if that were possible, of their victims' loved ones, pleaded not guilty to the charges, claiming, in a nutshell, that while they were definitely 'involved' in the murder of Ian Lamb, of conspiring to murder Virginia Morse, and in the wounding of the police in the 13 November car chase, they were the helpless victims of a variety of circumstances that had landed them in their present plight.

The jury took just 105 minutes to find Crump and Baker guilty of all charges. When, on 20 June 1974, Justice Taylor sentenced them to life imprisonment, Baker was typically emotionless while, equally typically, Crump stared at the floor and trembled and swayed. Taylor refused to fix a non-parole period. 'This is a clear case where you two should spend the rest of your lives in jail and there you should die; this is a case where life imprisonment should *mean* life imprisonment.'

The judge said he was satisfied that the men were always going to kill Virginia Morse:

> but first you had to use her to satisfy your lust. You secured her while she was helpless and raped her. She pleaded to be released for the sake of her children and her husband but when, to use your own phrase, she was beyond tears, you decided to execute her. You raped her again before you, Crump, shot her through the eye. Both of you, however, had not exhausted your depravation of this woman and not even her dead body escaped being inflicted with obscenities, evidence of which I have excluded. You then dragged this woman, this wife, this mother, into the river. I do not find a worse case …

During the trial the brave and dignified Brian Morse had sat in the gallery, often with his head in his hands. Now, unable to bear any more, he stood and left the courtroom.

Justice Taylor went on to say that he hoped that if ever the defendants came before a parole board seeking clemency and mercy they would be shown the same amount that they showed Virginia Morse when she begged for her life:

> For sheer cruelty there was a complete absence of a spark of human decency in what you did. What you have done to the children and husband of this poor woman has outraged all the accepted standards of men. The description of men, however, ill befits you and the description of obscene animals would be more apt.

In the wake of the judge's words, one H.C. Grant-Frost of Singleton, New South Wales, wrote a letter to the editor of the *Sydney Morning Herald*:

> May I dissent from one part only of Mr Justice Taylor's judgment … May I suggest to Mr Justice Taylor and people generally that whatever else animals are, they cannot be obscene. Of all life on

earth only humans are capable of the obscenity and depravity condemned by the judge.

Given the extent of their evil, Baker and Crump, who have been incarcerated separately in different maximum security prisons, were inevitably going to serve hard time. On 16 October 1974, soon after he was locked up in Goulburn Gaol, Baker was attacked by another prisoner wielding a lump of wood. He needed six stitches in his face. In years to come he and Crump were abused and bashed by fellow inmates and, it's rumoured, warders who were appalled by their crime. Baker was once stabbed in the head by a gang of inmates and more than once has found faeces smeared in his bunk. In 1993, Crump was charged with raping another prisoner, but the man committed suicide before the charges could be heard.

Baker has served the majority of his time in Grafton but today is back in Goulburn Gaol. Crump has spent most of his sentence at Maitland Gaol and Sydney's Long Bay. For eighteen months he was locked away in the notorious (and now-defunct) Katingal section, where he never once saw sunlight. In recent years he has been housed at Junee Correctional Centre in the Riverina.

Neither man has much interaction with other prisoners or staff, and both have devoted themselves to finding a legal loophole that might get them out of gaol. They have been supported in their efforts by a number of people in the community, including clergy and some Labor and independent politicians, who believe that prison should be about rehabilitation rather than retribution. Baker, who has long insisted that he is a changed man and has found religion, and Crump have made repeated attempts to overturn Justice Taylor's decree that they should never be released.

In 1993 Crump applied to have his sentence redetermined into a definite term that would offer him hope of release one day, but this was denied him by Justice Brian Sully in the NSW Supreme Court. Four years later, he tried again; this time, Justice Peter McInerney set his sentence at a minimum of thirty years. Responding to the ensuing public outcry, the NSW Government introduced legislation saying 'special reasons' must exist for a judge to even consider a parole hearing. In July 2000, Baker applied to have his life sentence redetermined so that he could eventually apply for parole. When the appeal was refused, Baker took his fight for freedom to the High Court of Australia. In October 2004, the High Court's full bench handed down its judgment: a 6-1 rejection of Baker's plea, which seemed to effectively end his and Crump's hopes, and those of other criminals such as the killers of Anita Cobby and Janine Balding, also sentenced to life behind bars with no chance of parole, of ever being released.

The decision was applauded by the vast majority of those who recalled what Crump and Baker had done. NSW Premier Bob Carr was one who concurred with the ruling, calling Crump and Baker's crimes 'evil incarnate, pure wickedness. [The concept of rehabilitation] applies to them but there are categories of crimes that every justice system in the world recognises as so horrific, [that a life sentence] does mean life'. A deputation from the Country Women's Association said that the prospect of Baker and Crump one day being freed was causing sleepless nights in rural areas, places whose innocent rustic aura had been destroyed by the men's evil deeds. Certainly, after these two had wrought their damage, farmhouse doors, once traditionally left unlatched, were deadlocked, and people who once thought nothing of sleeping outside on the veranda in warm weather, moved inside.

Brian Morse, who remembers Virginia as 'a vibrant but ordinary wife, mother and friend who loved life and family' and to whom he was 'fortunate to be married for thirteen very happy years', attended one hearing, brought on by Crump to affect a redetermination of his sentence, in April 1997. Afterwards, Morse told *Sun-Herald* reporter Martin Warneminde:

> I could hardly look at him. I felt like leaping at him and throttling him with my bare hands. The animal did not even show the slightest suggestion of remorse. Every time you looked at him he seemed to be smiling. He must never be free to walk the streets again. I hope they rot in a total living hell.

CHAPTER 7

THE KILLING OF DR VICTOR CHANG

Chiew Seng Liew and Phillip Choon Tee Lim: Murderers, robbers

1991

When Victor Chang was shot dead on 4 July 1991, motives for the murder of the brilliant and revered surgeon flew fast and thick across the nation. The shooting, said some, was payback after Chang had said no to conducting a heart transplant operation on a Triad boss. No, claimed others, the 54-year-old Chang was assassinated by Chinese government agents because he was an outspoken supporter of the pro-democracy movement in the land of his birth. Others maintained that the doctor was refusing to pay blackmail to persons unknown. That he was a victim of murderous Chinese illegal organ traders after he baulked at suppling them with the organs of deceased Australians. That his brutal and bloody demise was connected somehow to the 1985 slaying by Triad agents of

Sydney businessman Stanley Wong, the life of whose wife, Yung Wong, had been saved by Dr Chang and his team.

As is often the case when evil is committed, the truth was much more banal.

The life of one of the world's pre-eminent surgeons was snuffed out in a bungled $3 million extortion attempt perpetrated by three hamfisted amateurs who had picked out his photo at random in a Chinese magazine feature on wealthy Asian-Australians. Two of them had never heard of Dr Chang, had no clue that he, with his team at Sydney's St Vincent's Hospital, had performed 187 heart transplants, including fourteen heart-lung operations, in just seven years, with a patient survival rate of a phenomenal 85 per cent. Dr Chang, who was born in Shanghai, China, and who came to Australia in 1953 and was inspired to become a doctor after seeing his beloved mother die of breast cancer in 1951, was a Commander of the Order of Australia, the first Chinese Australian to achieve the honour. Among his patients were former NSW Premier Neville Wran, media magnate Kerry Packer and 14-year-old Fiona Coote.

When police began investigating the murder of Victor Chang, they were convinced that the clues left strewn around the crime scene revealing the seeming ineptitude of the killers were deliberate red herrings, designed to throw them off the trail. Surely no criminals could be so hapless. The men had attacked their victim in broad daylight during morning traffic peak hour in front of as many as thirty witnesses. They wore no masks. The first shot, fired at point-blank range, passed through Dr Chang's cheek and had it not been followed by a second shot to his temple would have caused no lasting damage save for a scar. The person who turned out to be the shooter, Chiew Seng Liew, dropped his wallet, containing full ID, on the grass beside the body.

The blunder was in character for Liew, a 48-year-old Malaysian national whose criminal career had been considerably less than auspicious. The eldest of four children, Liew at the age of five was taken in by his aunt when his father died and his mother abandoned him and his siblings. He quit school at eight and never picked up another book. In 1965, the year he fathered a son to his live-in lover, he committed an armed robbery in

Kuala Lumpur, was quickly caught, and sentenced to nine years in Pudi Prison. On release he married a woman named Chong Soon Yep, and had three children with her in rapid succession. His son from his previous relationship joined the family.

Liew, who was gauged by prison psychologists to be of low-average intelligence, emotionally unstable and with a propensity for violence, worked on and off on construction sites, but believed, erroneously, that his real talent was for crime. In May 1968, he and three henchmen mugged a man in Kuala Lumpur. Liew pulled a handgun and relieved his victim of his $150 watch. He evaded capture until the following year when police swooped. This time he was sentenced to twelve years in Pudi Prison, and dealt eight strokes of the rattan for good measure. While in prison, evidence came to light that he had committed another robbery, bursting into a jewellery store with a pistol and dashing out carrying watches with a total value of $50 000. The six-year sentence he received was to be served concurrently with that for the mugging.

On 29 January 1991, Liew, tall and chubby-faced with a towering bush of woolly brown hair, entered Australia on a tourist visa and stayed, an illegal immigrant, broke and unemployed in Melbourne. Exacerbating his poverty were the relentless demands for money from his wife and four children at home in Malaysia. One day soon after his arrival, Liew was passing the time over a meal at the Jade Tree Chinese restaurant in South Yarra with his friend and fellow Malaysian, Australian citizen Phillip Choon Tee Lim, 34, who was a cook at the restaurant. Liew mused to Lim that there had to be a way for them both to make some easy money. If only, agreed Lim who, despite being $20 000 in debt and hamstrung by liabilities that grew bigger daily thanks to his rampant gambling addiction – he had, when chatting to Liew, just lost a week's wages at the TAB – dreamed of opening a massage parlour or a gambling club. What to do? Well, suggested Liew, let's rob a rich guy.

Shortly afterwards Lim travelled to Malaysia and, seated on a barstool at the Hot Legs Pub in Kuala Lumpur, put his get-rich-quick plan to his fellow Jade Tree cook and former brother-in-law, Tiang Ha 'Stanley' Ng, 37. Ng was more than interested. The pair returned to Australia.

Back in Melbourne, Liew, Lim and Ng got down to business, trawling for likely candidates for a hit. To make the selection process easier, Liew produced a Chinese magazine feting wealthy Australian-based Asian businessmen. 'Any of these men will do,' enthused Liew, but after some thought they zeroed in on Dr Victor Chang who, he had to explain to the others, was a celebrated Sydney heart surgeon who had operated on famous people and was fabulously wealthy.

Robbing Dr Chang, they decided, was a risk worth taking, and the trio drove to Sydney. On 18 June, they set up home in a rented flat in Summer Hill in Sydney's inner west and began shadowing the surgeon in Ng's blue 1984 Toyota Corona. They lurked outside his luxurious three-storey hacienda overlooking Sandy Beach in affluent Clontarf on the northern side of Sydney Harbour, and surreptitiously observed the doctor coming and going in the car parks, corridors and reception areas of St Vincent's Hospital in Darlinghurst. They followed him, always a couple of car lengths behind, as he drove his $235 000 midnight blue Mercedes-Benz 500SL sports coupe, licence plate 2000, from Clontarf, over the Spit Bridge, along Military Road through Mosman and Cremorne and Neutral Bay and across the Harbour Bridge to East Sydney and St Vincent's Hospital.

Light-headed from the prospect of the money they would soon have and increasingly confident that they could carry out the robbery, Liew, Lim and Ng bought balaclavas, rope, a knife, adhesive tape and rubber gloves. They stole the MPY 812 licence plates from a parked car in Punchbowl in south-west Sydney, removed the personalised NG 818 plates from Ng's Corona and substituted the stolen ones. They acquired four guns, including a .32 calibre pistol, for around $100, three silencers and a number of boxes of bullets.

On 28 June, the three steeled themselves to make the move. They drove to the Chang house, their mission to stage a home invasion, tie up the family and demand $3 or $4 million. When Lim and Ng asked Liew what they should give the Chang family to eat should they become hungry before the ransom was delivered, Liew snapped, 'Don't worry about it.

Smash them. They don't matter.' The robbers agreed that if Dr Chang resisted their demands to hand over the money they sought, they would threaten to hang his family one by one. But when they arrived in the street they saw a red car unfamiliar to them parked in the driveway, assumed the family had visitors, and abandoned the scheme.

The following day, 29 June, the men put another plan into operation. They would follow Dr Chang from his home into the city, stage a minor collision by driving into the rear of the doctor's car, and when he got out to inspect the damage and exchange insurance details they would rob him at gunpoint on the roadside. Again their scheme was stymied at the last minute, for as they drove closer to Dr Chang's car they saw that, unusually, the doctor had a passenger whom Ng recognised as his son.

Frightened and shaken by their lack of success – stealing from Dr Chang was not turning out to be the cinch they thought it would be – the trio argued. It was decided that instead of robbing the surgeon they would knock over the J. Farren-Price jewellery shop in Sydney's St James Arcade. Sensing that his cohorts were totally disorganised and their scheme for robbery and ransom was doomed, Ng announced he'd had enough. He was out. He would return to Melbourne. Liew and Lim accused him of having 'no guts', then thought up yet another scheme for robbing Dr Chang.

They would fake the accident and confront the surgeon beside his car, but instead of demanding $3 million with menaces, they would try to evoke his sympathy by telling him of their straitened circumstances and heavy debts and cajole him into giving them just $30 000. They would admit that they had planned to murder him and his family in a bid to rob him of $3 million, but had seen the error of their ways, and would now settle for much less and no one need get hurt. Though Liew would have the .32 pistol concealed under his jacket just in case things turned nasty, there would be no need for violence, for surely this great humanitarian would take pity on them and happily hand over a lousy $30 000 to his poverty-stricken fellow Asians. Congratulating themselves on this master-plan, they set the date for 4 July.

Around 7.30 on that fine and chilly morning, Dr Chang, alone this time, turned out of his driveway en route to St Vincent's. His Mercedes-

Benz was in the centre lane, stop-starting its way along Military Road in Mosman in heavy traffic when the robbers' blue Corona loomed from behind and collided with the rear left side of the doctor's car.

Both vehicles pulled into Lang Street, the first available exit 200 metres further along Military Road. Dr Chang, Lim and Liew got out of the cars and stood on the footpath inspecting the damage to the doctor's Mercedes. It was 7.45 am. The doctor, far from being in the generous mood that the pair hoped to find him in, was furious. 'How could you do this? How could you do this?' he shouted at them.

Had they known Dr Chang, they'd have realised he was never going to be an easy mark. For all his smiles and the bonhomie of his public image, Victor Chang could be feisty, argumentative and sharp tongued. He suffered neither fools nor those he believed were taking unfair advantage of him or thwarting his work. This pair ticked all three boxes. Self-confidence of this calibre was never going to be cowed by clumsy strong-arm tactics.

Liew addressed Dr Chang by name, which must have alarmed him, and went into his prepared spiel. He explained that they needed his help. Could he please give them some money because they were poor men, deep in debt with numerous dependants? What Dr Chang said next is unknown, but after around ten minutes of heated discussion, he turned to walk away. Liew panicked, grabbed Dr Chang by the arm and tried to drag him into the Corona. When his victim pulled away, Liew slammed his head into the windscreen of the vehicle, sending the doctor's glasses flying, and opened his jacket to reveal the handgun tucked in his belt.

Liew said later that Dr Chang had cried out, 'Don't hit me or I will call my wife', and he had retorted, 'Don't do any tricks or I will harm you.'

Dr Chang, by now probably fearing for his life, pulled out his wallet, opened it and showed them that he was carrying only a small amount of cash in notes. He offered them the money and suggested that he write his assailants a cheque, neither of which were of any use to Liew. Suddenly Chang saw a chance to escape. A Mosman resident named David Goff came into view and the doctor cried to him, 'Call the police! They have guns!'

Liew really panicked then, putting his revolver to Dr Chang's cheek and firing. The bullet passed through the doctor's cheek. Dr Chang dropped to his knees on the grass verge, cradling his bleeding face in his hands. Liew fired again, this time into the doctor's temple. The bullet entered his brain and lodged there. Dr Victor Chang fell dead into the gutter behind the rear wheel of his car.

Liew aimed his handgun at Goff but fortunately for the local man thought better of firing it. Liew and Lim leapt into their car and sped away.

There was never a need for Liew to fire the second, fatal shot. It was an act as senseless as it was callous. Why did he do it? Acting Justice Slattery, at Liew's sentencing the following year, believed that he fired out of 'frustration or revenge'.

Liew, knowing that witnesses would have noted their car's registration number and told police, who'd have put out an all-points alert by now, drove to a side street in nearby Crows Nest. There he and Lim removed the pilfered plates and replaced them with Ng's, and dropped the stolen plates and the murder weapon in a bin in a car park. Lim stayed to skulk about in Crows Nest while Liew caught a bus south across the Harbour Bridge to Chinatown in Sydney's Haymarket. This is where he reached in his pocket for his wallet and found it missing. His horror at the discovery can only be imagined. Borrowing money from a friend, he caught an interstate bus to Melbourne and sought refuge in the outer suburb of Sunbury with his friend Jimmy Tan, a 39-year-old restaurateur.

Police, including members of the homicide and scientific squads, arrived at Lang Street, covered Dr Chang's body with a white blanket, and established a crime scene. Dr William Hock of the nearby Mosman Medical Centre, who was the first medico to arrive at the scene, reported, 'There was this guy lying in the gutter. He was very dead. He had no pupil movement and he'd stopped bleeding. There was nothing I could do.' Witnesses – pedestrians, drivers, and those who had witnessed the crime from passing buses and taxis – came from everywhere offering information.

Police scoured Lang Street and neighbouring thoroughfares and driveways for evidence, took fingerprints and photographed the area. They door-knocked local residents and quizzed them on what they had seen and heard. They found Liew's black leather wallet lying on the grass just 1.5 metres from the doctor's body. Inside was $30 and small amounts of Singaporean, Malaysian and Brunei cash, his identification papers with photographs, a Malaysian driver's licence, a number of addresses in Melbourne, the Qantas ticket on which he had flown to Australia on 29 January, and a Tattslotto ticket for draw number 1032. That was a start, although, as Detective Dennis 'Miles' O'Toole noted at the time, 'We thought the wallet was a set-up. [The murderers] could have stolen it or picked it up on the street and then thrown it in as a furphy.' O'Toole was over-estimating the intelligence and cunning of Chiew Seng Liew.

Australia was saddened and shocked by the needless and terrible loss of one of its finest citizens. People brought armfuls of flowers to the place where Dr Chang died. He was eulogised in parliament and the media by politicians, celebrities, broadcasters and ordinary people whose lives had been touched, perhaps saved, by his genius. The medical fraternity was distraught.

Valerie Lawson, in the *Sydney Morning Herald*, wrote of the scenes of despair at St Vincent's:

> Nurses wept. Doctors cancelled their operations. On the day of the murder, St Vincent's reminded the then-chief executive, Dr Ron Spencer, of the time John F. Kennedy was assassinated. 'The same stillness and silence hung over the place.' Having used new techniques to perform a successful heart transplant operation on Fiona Coote in 1984, Chang's reputation had risen to that of a saviour. His death shocked the country and on July 10 more than 3000 mourned him at St Mary's Cathedral. Some wore badges announcing their membership of the Australian Heart Transplant Club. The card on one bouquet read, 'Dear Victor, you did everything to save our lives but we could do nothing to prevent your life being taken. God rest your soul.' Those who could not squeeze into the cathedral stood under umbrellas in Hyde Park, listening to a broadcast of the service.

Meanwhile, Task Force Oak, an elite 35-strong squad led by Detective Inspector Jim 'Tip' Counsel, Detective Senior Sergeant Ron Smith, Detective Sergeant 'Miles' O'Toole and Detective Inspector Mike Hagan, who had led the hunt for Sydney's Granny Killer, John Wayne Glover, in 1989–90, was established to arrest Dr Chang's killers.

The investigators placed under surveillance the people whose addresses they found in the dropped wallet. They saw Liew enter one man's house and later photographed him meeting with Lim on 7 July, at 2.45 pm, in Melbourne's Swanston Street. Lim, after he'd bade farewell to Liew in Crows Nest, had driven Ng's car back to Melbourne. There is a photograph taken, police say, at the very moment when Liew tells Lim he thinks he might have left his wallet at the murder scene. The look on Lim's face is one of shock and anger. After this revelation, on 11 July a terrified Lim, certain that his arrest was only a matter of time, absconded to Malaysia.

Liew's associates were interviewed. Jimmy Tan told police that Liew, who was now hiding out at Ng's North Melbourne flat, had admitted to him that he shot Dr Chang. 'I have killed a doctor,' Liew had said. 'We extort him $3 million. The doctor didn't want to pay and he took out his wallet. There were a few $10. I didn't want that. I wanted millions of dollars. I then banged the doctor's head on the windscreen of the car ... Then I fired ... He loved his money more than he loved his life.' Liew, now clearly needing to vent, told another acquaintance, Ka Chan, that his victim 'wasn't afraid of death. I don't know why. He had so much money, he wasn't afraid of death. Pointed him with a gun and the doctor say, "Don't afraid. I don't afraid." Then the doctor struggle and there were people passing by, the time is right, I don't know why, moved twice and fired two shots and he fell down.'

At 1 pm on 13 July, nine days after the slaying, Liew, sporting a new short, spiky, dyed-black hairdo, was arrested at Melbourne's Tullamarine Airport as he attempted to board Singapore Airlines flight SQ228 to Singapore, where he planned to make a connection to Kuala Lumpur. Liew went quietly, answering only a subdued 'Yeah' when asked by the arresting officers if he was Chiew Seng Liew. He was interrogated by detectives Ron Smith and Paul Tuxford with the aid of a Chinese interpreter at Melbourne CIB headquarters. Liew admitted that the wallet was his, that he was in Sydney on 4 July and that indeed it was he who'd been noted travelling in the blue Corona seen at the murder scene and which had by then been located in Melbourne. But, contrary to the information they'd gleaned from Jimmy Tan, Liew swore that he had had nothing to do with the extortion attempt and certainly had not shot Dr Chang. He had no idea who had done these terrible things, and he had no idea how his wallet came to be beside the body.

At the end of the interview Detective Sergeant Smith came to the point: 'From indications or a number of persons we have spoken to, the persons responsible for the murder of Dr Chang were two Asian men, one of whose description is not unlike yours. Is there anything you wish to say in relation to that?'

Liew: 'I did not do that thing.'

Smith: 'Mr Liew, from the inquiries that we've made and from the fact the wallet was located in very close proximity to the scene of the murder of Dr Chang and from our interview today – [in] which I believe you have not given me satisfactory explanations as to the movement of your wallet – I believe that you were party to the murder of Dr Chang and it is my intention to charge you with that murder. Is there anything you wish to say in relation to that?'

Liew: 'So you are going to charge me with that offence. I never did that.'

Liew was later taken – by car rather than by air, for officers, at that stage not knowing whether the Triads were involved, feared an attempt on his life – to Sydney and charged with the murder of Dr Chang. Liew listened impassively, his expression vacant, as in Central Local Court he was charged with murder, detaining Dr Chang with intent to hold him for advantage and demanding money with menaces. His solicitor, Leigh Johnson, did not seek bail.

Meanwhile, acting on Liew's statement, police in Melbourne arrested Stanley Ng, the conspirator who'd dropped out of the action, charging him with plotting to detain the surgeon and demand money with menaces from him in the weeks before the shooting, and Liew's friend Jimmy Tan, who was charged as an accessory to murder. In exchange for immunity from prosecution, both immediately agreed to become Crown witnesses and testify at Liew's trial that he had confessed to them that he had killed Dr Chang, and that Lim was the second man who had bailed up the doctor on 4 July. Ng and Tan also informed the officers that Lim had fled to Malaysia. Interpol was alerted and Lim was nabbed at a Kuala Lumpur bus terminal on 12 November after police there had kept a watch on his girlfriend, a bar girl. Lim was extradited to Sydney and charged with murder.

On 19 October 1992, in Sydney's Supreme Court on the first day of his joint trial with Lim, Chiew Seng Liew brought proceedings, for himself at least, to a speedy end when he pleaded guilty to the murder of Dr Chang.

Lim claimed that while he was in on the plot, and was party to talking Dr Chang into giving them $30 000, he was taken by surprise when Liew shot the surgeon. Nevertheless, on 31 October he, under the doctrine of common purpose, was found guilty of murdering Dr Chang and detaining unlawfully for advantage. As the jury forewoman announced the verdict, a woman in the public gallery leapt to her feet and cried, 'Hang him! Dr Chang was my doctor!'

At sentencing, three days before Christmas Day 1992, Acting Justice Slattery damned the defendants' scheme as 'absurd, impractical and almost certainly doomed to failure'. The crime, which Slattery called 'the brainchild' of Liew, deserved the 'severest' of sentences:

> Liew and Lim had misjudged the strong resolve and attitude of their victim in any attempt to detain or kidnap him. When the deceased failed to cooperate with them in their amateurish plan, they were unable to meet the challenge and resort was had to a gun ... The shooting of the deceased was precipitated by the refusal of the deceased to enter a car. Chiew Seng Liew shot the deceased not only once but twice. Whereas it might be said that the first shot was fired in the heat of the moment or in panic, the second shot in circumstances where the deceased was wounded and partly immobilised and falling to the ground was more likely fired either to effect his escape or in frustration, for revenge.

Slattery sentenced Liew to twenty-six years in prison with a non-parole period of twenty years. He will be eligible for release in 2011. Lim was given twenty-four years. He could be back on the streets in 2009.

There was anger in the community that Liew and Lim got off so lightly in view of the enormity of their crime and the amount of planning that the plotters, wrong-headed and haphazard as it was, devoted to it over a prolonged period. Too, many believed, Liew and Lim were guilty of more than simply killing Dr Victor Chang. As Detective Sergeant 'Miles' O'Toole said sadly outside the court, 'There were literally hundreds of people waiting on having their heart transplant performed by Dr Chang. We don't know how many of those people have died as a result of this.'

The Victor Chang Cardiac Research Institute was established in the deceased surgeon's honour in February 1994. Funded by the Federal Government and public donations, the Institute is a world leader in research into the prevention, diagnosis and treatment of heart muscle diseases.

Solicitor Leigh Johnson has visited her old client Liew, now sixty-three, at Lithgow Correctional Centre west of Sydney. She says he cries a lot.

CHAPTER 8

THE CROSS-DRESSING KILLER

Eugenia Falleni: Murderer
1917

Sydney in 1920, just as it likes to do today, revelled in its reputation as Australia's most cosmopolitan, sophisticated and unshockable metropolis. Yet the jaded denizens of the Harbour City were reduced to stunned but salacious incomprehension when the bizarre life of Harry Crawford was unveiled at his trial for murdering his wife, Annie. For Harry was not the gruff, grizzled bloke he pretended to be. He, in fact, was a she, whose real name was Eugenia Falleni.

The genesis of Falleni's gender-bending ruse was, simply, that she was lesbian. Today gay people can be seen in public together, set up house together, get married, adopt a child, kiss and hold hands in public; no big deal. It's normal. Society can cope. But in Falleni's day such behaviour was universally considered to be depraved, monstrous and evil. Those discovered in a compromising position with a member of the same sex were routinely bashed and gaoled. Falleni's solution was to pose as a man. That way she could be with women without attracting attention.

Unfortunately, she also had murderous instincts.

In Falleni's 1920 mugshot, her salt and pepper hair is oiled and parted on the left (the practice of most men back then). Her skin is deeply lined, making her seem decades older than her forty-five years. Her ears are heavy, eyes mean and piercing, masculine mouth set in a grimace, nose strong, chin set firm and square and looking as if it could withstand a hefty punch. She wears a suit with a white shirt and patterned tie. Her hulking shoulders are encased in a shabby double-breasted brown serge suit jacket. Her hands, one of them gripping a grey felt hat, look powerful enough to have battered Annie Crawford and heaved her dead weight onto a bonfire, which is what she was accused of.

Falleni was again dressed this way, as a man, at her July 1920 committal hearing, when the murder charges against her were aired and Crown and defence attorneys made their cases. But four months later, after her masquerade was blown and she was standing trial for her life, she wore women's clothes. On the day she was sentenced to death she was dressed in a demure white blouse under a black jacket, with a white skirt, black velvet hat and button-up boots.

The trial was a national sensation as revelation followed revelation. Each morning a crowd, comprising mostly curious women and teenage males anticipating further titillation, queued outside the court. When the doors opened at ten they rushed for the best seats in the house, those that offered a good squiz at the person the press was calling the 'man-woman'. (Roll up, roll up and ogle the freak! Just like Sideshow Alley at the Royal Easter Show.)

Eugenia Falleni was born in Florence, Italy, in 1875. Why her parents chose to relocate themselves and their young daughter in New Zealand is not known. At the age of sixteen, Falleni left home to go to sea. From her early teens, to conceal her sexual orientation, she had passed herself off as a boy, and on vessels throughout the South Pacific she posed as a male named Eugene. This, however, did not stop her falling pregnant in 1899. It is not impossible that she was raped after her identity was discovered in some seaside dive.

Her daughter Josephine was born in Newcastle, New South Wales. When the child was a toddler, Falleni placed her in the care of an Italian couple she had met in Sydney's harbourside suburb of Double Bay. Falleni fabricated the tale that she had taken Josephine under her wing after the child's mother had died and her father had absconded, but that she was no longer able to care for the little girl. She would, however, keep in contact with Josephine.

This left Falleni free to once more pull on a pair of trousers and pose as a man. Now, however, she called herself Harry Crawford and made ends meet by taking on a series of low-paid, hard-scrabble jobs around Sydney. Her act was convincing. As Falleni toiled away in pubs, laundries, abattoirs and a rubber manufacturing company, none of her employers – nor, it seems, her workmates – detected anything remotely feminine about her demeanour, speech or bearing. Certainly Annie Birkett didn't.

In 1912, while Falleni was working as a yardman and driver for Dr G.R.C. Clarke in the upper North Shore suburb of Wahroonga, she met Birkett, who was doing domestic duties for Dr Clarke. Birkett was an attractive 30-year-old widow with a 9-year-old son, also named Harry, who had saved a tidy sum of money. As Harry Crawford, Falleni courted Birkett, treating her and young Harry to visits to the circus and to buggy rides. She told Birkett that she was the son of a master mariner and convinced her to buy a lolly-shop in Balmain where they could work together. Falleni also told Annie that she loved her. They became man and wife, Annie and Harry Crawford, on 19 February 1913, at the Methodist parsonage in Balmain South.

Incredibly, Annie had no idea that her 'husband' was a woman. Casting about for explanations, one can only grasp at flimsy straws. Perhaps Annie never saw Harry naked, never saw Harry shave or urinate. Perhaps they only made love in the dark and Annie was unaware that Harry's erection was in fact a dildo. The machinations to which Falleni would have had to resort to pull off such a subterfuge beggar belief. Still, she did succeed in doing so, and for three years, it seems, Annie was none the wiser. Indeed, apart from claims to the contrary from a couple of prosecution witnesses during the murder trial seeking to portray Falleni as a brute, it seems the Crawford marriage was largely harmonious as the newlyweds set up home, first in Balmain and a year or so later in Drummoyne, in Sydney's inner west.

From time to time, Falleni's daughter Josephine would come to stay and an element of tension would enter the household for Josephine, naturally, knew her mother's secret. Later, she would declare in a written statement, '[Annie] always thought that Mother was a man. I said to my mother, "She will find you out one of these days." My mother said, "Oh, I'll watch it. I would rather do away with myself than let the police find out anything about me."'

In its prosecution of Falleni, the Crown told the jury that in its view she decided to murder Annie Crawford when, God knows under what circumstances, in early 1917 she at last discovered her 'husband's' ruse and threatened to, so to speak, expose him.

The Crown asserted that on Friday 30 September 1917, a public holiday commemorating Eight-Hour Day, and while young Harry Birkett was conveniently away from home, Falleni insisted Annie join him for a picnic lunch at Lane Cove River Park. They set up their blanket and refreshments in a lonely clearing. At some point, Falleni attacked Annie, battering her unconscious, then tossed her onto a bonfire and fled.

In the days and weeks that followed, Falleni did not report Annie missing. Rather, she told daughter Josephine, stepson Harry and various friends that Annie had walked out after an argument: 'I gave her a crack and now I don't know where she is. She may never return.'

Then, the Crown contended, around 2 October, Falleni took her stepson, who doubted the story he'd been told, to The Gap, the notorious suicide spot at Watsons Bay, intending to hurl him off the cliff. Sensing danger, the lad had refused to go close to the edge. Thwarted, Falleni took Harry home. In the next weeks, Falleni sold the confectionery shop and all the furniture from the rented Drummoyne home in which she and Annie lived and moved to inner Sydney with young Harry.

On 3 October, a lad strolling in the bush in Lane Cove River Park stumbled onto the charred remains of a woman in the scrub about 200 metres from Mowbray Road. Police were summoned and Superintendent Tait, Constable John Walsh and government medical officer Dr A. Palmer attended the scene. They found the corpse sprawled face upward, badly burned from the head to the knees. The face was beyond recognition. There were six cracks in the skull, which police assumed had been caused by the heat of the fire. The woman's clothes were destroyed save for her black stockings and black lace-up shoes, one of which had been half-soled and patched some time before. Though unable to determine the dead woman's age, the investigators were able to determine that she was 5 ft 1 in (152 cm) tall. Strewn around her body in the pyre were a broken bottle, the wire frame of a wide-brimmed hat, a hatpin, a brooch and a greenstone pendant, hinges from a satchel, a metal tumbler, an enamel mug, and a corked bottle containing kerosene.

Unable to identify the corpse and with no reports of anyone going missing, police were at a loss, and the death of the mystery woman was consigned to the unsolved crimes file. At about this time Eugenia Falleni, still pretending to be Harry Crawford, moved to another inner city location after divesting herself of Annie's son, who went to live with an aunt.

In a weird coda, on 29 September 1919 Falleni wed a second time. She and Elizabeth 'Lizzie' King Allison, who was in her fifties, were married at Canterbury Registry Office and moved in together. It's possible that Falleni's surreptitious donning of the dildo in the dark worked again with this new bride. But it's more likely that Lizzie Allison, as many women in their fifties and sixties did in those days, considered herself past fleshly pleasures and that the union was unconsummated. Whatever, the marriage seemed to be working well right up until Falleni's carefully constructed make-believe world careened out of orbit.

Worried sick by his mother's failure to contact him in three years, in early July of 1920 Harry Birkett went to the police and told them he believed that Harry Crawford had murdered his mother and that the burned remains of the woman found in October 1917 in Lane Cove River Park might have been hers. On 5 July, Detective Sergeant Stuart Robson went to the Empire Hotel in central Sydney and asked for Harry Crawford, who worked there as a bar useful. Questioned by Robson, Falleni, keeping up the appearance of a tough-looking man, assured the officer gruffly, 'I am a Scotchman, born in Edinburgh ... and I did not kill my ex-wife.'

Not at all convinced by this, Robson escorted Harry to police headquarters, where 'he' was charged with Annie Birkett's murder. The accused made a statement, but then asked to be incarcerated in a women's ward should a gaol sentence be imposed. Nonplussed, Robson asked why, and that was when Eugenia Falleni revealed her real name and that she was a woman. The bombshell was confirmed by the police medical examination that was hurriedly ordered.

Falleni was taken to the scene of the crime, where she again denied guilt and insisted that she had no knowledge of the area. However, when the officers asked whether it was true that she, as Harry Crawford, had in fact been an employee of the nearby Chicago Flour Mills early in 1917, Falleni sighed and admitted that it was.

The murder trial of the 'man-woman', as the tabloids had tastefully taken to calling Falleni, was a national sensation. The Crown played blatantly on the furore to win a conviction. Formidable Senior Crown Prosecutor Coyle (aka 'The Bloody Bulldog') declared in his opening remarks, 'I find it difficult to refrain from referring to the accused as he, but when I do you will understand that I mean the accused, who posed as a man, and definitely stated that she was a man, and married two women as a man ... All her actions since then have been characterised by cunning and deceit.'

At Falleni's preliminary hearing in July 1920, the prosecution argued that she had perpetrated 'sex fraud' and had killed to cover her deceit. The defence, in turn, countered that Falleni was innocent of murder and no fraudster, well, not purposely, anyway, because she was at the mercy of an 'innate congenital condition' over which she had no control.

Found at the hearing to have a case to answer, Falleni was charged and remanded in custody. Her trial for murder began on 5 October 1920 in Sydney's Criminal Court. When the defendant took her place in the dock she had discarded her male garb and was dressed as a woman. The members of the public gallery craned and tittered throughout.

After Falleni pleaded not guilty to feloniously and maliciously murdering Annie Crawford – though she never did explain in so many words why she chose to live as a man – the prosecution witnesses were wheeled out. Harry Birkett, now aged seventeen, declared that his mother and father-in-law were always quarrelling, that Falleni drank excessively while his mother did not, and that Falleni had called his mother 'horrible names'. Young Harry said that after his mother disappeared, Falleni seemed preoccupied and mumbled incomprehensibly. One day, he recalled, Falleni, who was illiterate, had produced a copy of the *Evening News*, showed him a photograph of the shoes found on the mysterious burned corpse which had recently been found in Lane Cove River Park, and asked Harry whether the word 'murder' was used anywhere in the article. When told no, Falleni seemed vastly relieved, but made a point of warning the boy, 'If the police ever come and ask for me, don't tell them I'm here.'

A dentist named McManus inspected a lower set of false teeth taken from the burned body and testified that while they did resemble a set he'd made for Annie Crawford in February of that year, he could not be certain they were the same ones. However, another dentist, named Burnham, confirmed that the corpse's upper dental plate was the one he had made and fitted for Annie in 1910.

Clara Bone, who employed Harry Birkett in her Drummoyne grocery shop, told the court she often saw Harry Crawford and his wife Annie and that she understood they were an unhappy couple. Her husband Ernest weighed in with the information that on 2 October 1917 he had encountered the accused who, when Ernest wondered why he hadn't seen Annie around lately, told him, 'The bitch has cleared out ... She goes away with other men [and] I can bloody-well prove it! I have letters.' The defendant, went on Bone, had been very agitated and smelled strongly of whisky. 'I was glad to get out of his company,' he shuddered.

Henrietta Schieblich testified that Falleni, in his Harry Crawford guise, came with the boy in October 1917 to stay briefly with her at her home in Cathedral Street, Sydney. 'Crawford' had told her sadly that Annie had 'left me, after a jolly good row, and I gave her a jolly good crack to go on with'. Schieblich said that throughout his stay, the defendant had acted strangely, once running down the stairs crying, 'Madam, Madam, your house is haunted!'

Detective Sergeant Robson, who had detained Falleni at the Empire Hotel, was called to the stand. To gasps from the gallery, he recounted how he had found a dildo (politely described as 'a wooden object wrapped in dirty rags, covered with gauze and capped with rubber') among Falleni's possessions. 'I opened the bag. I got the article from it and asked the accused, "Did your first wife know you were using anything like this?" The accused said, "No, not until ... the latter stages of our married life."'

One Elia Carroll testified that on 30 September 1917 she saw the accused, dressed in a dark suit, sitting disconsolately on a rock by the Lane Cove River, about five minutes' walk from where the body was later found. She said she had a good look at the person's face and noted that his eyes were grey and he had a drooping mouth. 'Thirty minutes later, when I passed the same spot, the person in the suit was still there. This time, when he saw me he became alarmed and jumped over a rock.' During cross-examination by defence counsel McDonnell there was an unintentionally comic exchange. McDonnell said that Elia Carroll must have been mistaken in identifying the defendant, because Falleni's eyes were not grey, but blue, and he ordered Carroll to approach the dock and look into Falleni's eyes. Carroll did so, then announced unequivocally, 'Her eyes are grey.' Retorted McDonnell: 'Well, I think they are blue. And what would you say about the accused's mouth? Is it a drooping mouth?' Carroll came back, 'Yes, it is a drooping mouth.' 'But,' continued the hapless McDonnell, whose attempt at discrediting the witness's testimony was by now in ruins, 'Do not the mouths of most women droop at the age of forty or forty-five years?' Carroll, a woman in her forties, retorted emphatically, '*Not* necessarily!'

McDonnell then tried to convince the jury that Annie Birkett had indeed walked out on her husband and was lying low because she feared she would be ridiculed for her naivety in not realising her husband was female. The burned body, maintained McDonnell, was not hers but that of a 'half-witted woman carrying a briefcase' seen in the park on 20 September. But that ploy came to grief when the Crown proved that the woman in question was alive and well.

The defence lawyer's reasonable, to modern sensibilities at least, insistence that Falleni's dressing as a man and marrying a woman were not due to 'sex-fraud' but to 'innate sexual inversion' also fell on deaf ears.

The Crown called James Hicks and James Woodbury, labourers from the Cumberland Paper Mills, located close to where the woman's body was found. Each said they had seen Falleni in the bush on 30 September 1917. They had noticed the accused's peculiar walk and the swing of his right arm.

Author Ruth Ford, in 'The Man-Woman Murderer: Sex Fraud, Sexual Inversion and the Unmentionable "Article" in 1920s Australia', a chapter in the book *Gender & History*, maintains that the Crown, strategically, as the trial drew to a close, invoked the dildo, never mentioning it by that name but as 'the article', to horrify and sway the jury into returning a conviction:

> The prosecution implicitly invited the jury and the court audience to speculate on sexual acts too abhorrent and offensive to be mentioned. This was most apparent in the dramatic importance of the dildo in the prosecution's case. Referred to euphemistically as 'the article', the dildo was constructed as evidence of Falleni's guilt and used by the prosecution to emphasise Falleni's deception, sexual perversion and guilt ... The find of 'something artificial' was followed by laying charges of murder, as if the discovery of 'the article' – too vile and scandalous to be named – proved Falleni's guilt.

Throughout the trial, the tabloid press was in a frenzy. And in much of its coverage, the lost life of poor Annie Birkett, beaten to unconsciousness and most probably burned alive, took a back seat to sensationalism. *Smith's Weekly* declared Falleni a 'fiend' and that her 'repellent sex-perversion' had made her 'alien from public sympathy'. Elsewhere she was branded as a 'monster', a 'pervert', 'despicable' and 'evil-incarnate'.

Yet one of *Smith's Weekly*'s commentators, skulking behind the *nom de plume* 'The Man in the Mask', differed in his analysis. He felt that Falleni was more sinned against than sinning. In an article unearthed by Ruth Ford, the 'masked man' aired some novel insights into Falleni's condition, musing that her body had been possessed by demons:

> Within that body there had lurked the ghoulish wrath of some unclean ancestor. As the body grew, so that usurper had grown, an unnatural monster that bullied the timid soul-thing into surrendering its rightful sovereignty ... The ghoul had seized that frail soul, tortured it and warped those fragile wings so that its flights became grotesque acrobatics ... its beautiful dreams and its exquisite desires torn and distorted by that evil intruder. The body was a house divided ... an ugliness where nature hid its naked beauty in rags of bestiality. The dwelling that had been designed for the sacred ceremonies of motherhood had become a ribald clubhouse for mock rites of masculinity. The cowering soul-thing was forced to witness these rites, even to participate in them ...

In his summation to the jury, Chief Justice Sir William Cullen left no doubt as to his personal opinion of Falleni, saying to the jurors, 'You are not, because a person is of bad character, deceitful, untruthful, to come to the conclusion that the person is guilty.'

On 6 October, at 6.15 pm, the jury retired to consider its verdict and returned two hours later. Falleni was guilty. When asked by the judge if she knew of any reason why he should not impose the death sentence, Falleni answered in a sad, low monotone:

> Your Honour and gentlemen of the jury, I have been three months in Long Bay Gaol, and am near a nervous breakdown. I would like to make a statement but my constitution will not allow me. I do not know anything at all about this charge. I am perfectly innocent, and I do not know what the woman done. We never had any serious rows, only just a few words, but nothing to speak of. Therefore I

> am absolutely innocent of this charge against me. It is only through false evidence that I have been convicted.

Sir William Cullen sentenced her to death.

Falleni probably did murder Annie Crawford, but there's little doubt that her trial was shamefully prejudiced. The Crown was represented by the vastly experienced and whip-smart Coyle, while Falleni's defence was in the hands of McDonnell. The prosecution called twenty-eight witnesses. The defence called one. Nor did McDonnell question the Crown's use of police line-ups to identify Falleni as having been in the vicinity of the death scene, *after* photos of her had been published in the press.

Not only that, looking back on the transcripts of proceedings it seems that Falleni was being judged as much for her flouting of the prevailing sexual mores as for her crime. The Crown insisted that her abnormal sexuality was the motive for murder because she wanted to prevent Annie Birkett, after she had discovered that her husband was a woman, from broadcasting the fact. And, the prosecutors argued, a sexual deviate who had lived a life of such outrageous deception would surely be eminently capable of murder. The subtext was that here was a woman who was a sexual invert, a freak of nature, who had adopted a masculine identity, who had married and had unnatural sexual relationships with women with, no less, a dildo. She had to be punished for that. And, for good measure, she had slain Annie Crawford. So the noose was her just reward.

Falleni endured two soul-destroying months waiting for the hangman's knock on the door of her cell until, without notice, her sentence was commuted to life imprisonment. In February 1931, aged fifty-six, she was granted early release and walked free from Long Bay, wearing women's garb and calling herself 'Jean Ford'. She found work as a landlady and lived an unremarkable life until she was struck by a car in Oxford Street, Paddington, on 9 June 1938. She was rushed to Sydney Hospital and died there the following day.

CHAPTER 9

EXPELLING THE DEMONS

Ralph Vollmer and the Exorcists

1993

Ralph Vollmer came prepared. As his wife Joan's body was lowered into its grave at Horsham Cemetery, the slight, deeply lined farmer stood in the vanguard of a host of mourners, curious spectators and fifty television, radio and press reporters. He was carrying an overnight bag which contained one red and two pink dresses, stockings and underwear. 'Because,' declared Vollmer, 'Joan will need something to wear when she rises again.'

For the past week, Vollmer had been exultant at the prospect of Joan's resurrection, exhorting the media and the general public to join him for the great event. 'I am not sad, only humble and excited that God has chosen me to be part of this miracle,' he fervently told all and sundry. 'I want you all to come and see this fantastic event. My very word! Joan will be alive and she will talk to you. She will tell God's story to people around the world and get sinners to repent.'

But by the time the first spadefuls of earth were thumping onto the top of the simple pine coffin, Vollmer, like everyone else, knew that there would be no miracle today. Looking hopelessly insignificant, he stood there in the red dirt, clenching his left fist, then extending his fingers as if imploring Joan to rise from her grave. As the realisation set in that she was not going to return to him – not in this life, anyway – his face crumpled in grief. 'Maybe she didn't want to come back because it's so beautiful up there,' he managed to gasp through loud sobs as he was supported by his sons Geoffrey and Gary, from his first marriage. But he had no regrets. 'If we hadn't delivered her, she wouldn't be in heaven now ... Out of this, God's name is going to be glorified because people have been hearing His word and the gospel in the last few days as I have been talking about Jesus. People will realise there is more to life than chasing the mighty dollar. I will continue to preach the mighty, mighty word of Jesus. And I will see Joan again in heaven, and when I do it will be a great, great day!'

The deliverance that Vollmer was referring to was an exorcism conducted at his farm in the tiny (population 21) western Victorian wheatbelt town of Antwerp, 55 kilometres north of Horsham, during the last week of January 1993, an undertaking in which 49-year-old Joan was literally beaten to death.

The tipping point in the lead-up to the tragedy occurred on 26 January. Ralph Vollmer, 54, known in the community as 'gentle, simple, caring and a religious sort of bloke', returned to his 42-hectare pig farm from nearby Dimboola in his white Toyota with its 'Smile, God Loves You' sticker on the back window. He could not find his wife. He looked in each room of their small cottage, out the back, around the pig pens. No Joan. Becoming alarmed, he searched the property at a run, calling her name. Then he saw her. She was standing, he would later say, in the middle of a paddock, barefooted, making strange animal-like sounds and swearing obscenely while 'doing a kind of war dance'.

The episode was yet another instance of Joan's recent strange and troubling behaviour, thought Ralph, after he and a friend had manhandled and sweet-talked her by turns indoors. Of late, God knew, Joan had been depressed, restless, wilful and sharp-tempered, especially when he tried to discuss with her the glory of God as he understood it. She had refused to bathe, seemed excessively anxious, and sometimes said irrational, nonsensical things and babbled about colours, numbers and letters. Occasionally she would break into song, sounding, he said, 'like a nightingale'; other times she would rant in the gruff tones of a man.

Joan Vollmer had had a troubled life. Growing up in Victoria's Gippsland region, she had been sexually abused and later diagnosed with schizophrenia. Withdrawn and emotionally erratic as a teenager and young woman, she had few friends. She married in her twenties and gave birth to a daughter, but her alcoholic husband later committed suicide, and as a teenager her daughter became estranged from her. Joan was living in the town of Moe when she read an ad placed by widower Ralph Vollmer in a newspaper lonely-hearts column. They met and hit it off, and she wed the mild-mannered, ever-smiling German migrant in 1986. In 1991 she was treated for three weeks in a Ballarat hospital for hypomania, a form of psychosis. Perhaps, thought Vollmer now, her hypomania was rearing its head again. Then again, perhaps it was something else, something worse ...

Vollmer, like Joan, was a member of the Horsham Salvation Army congregation, but he also had friends among a breakaway sect of charismatic or 'true spirit' Christians who spoke in tongues to confound the devil and believed that Satan and his evil spirits were among us. Vollmer telephoned sect member John Reichenbach, 38, farmer, father of four and former member of the Lutheran Church, who ran a Bible study group which he had attended in Gerang Gerung, a small township nearby. He told Reichenbach of Joan's strange behaviour and his friend agreed to come to the farm and observe her. After spending some time with Joan, Reichenbach sat with Ralph and the two men prayed. Then, according to Vollmer, Reichenbach told him, 'There is no physical problem with your wife but she had Satanic influences during her childhood which took her out of God's care and kept pouring demons into her. She is now possessed by them and they have to be removed.'

Vollmer told Joan what he and his friends had in store for her, a 'deliverance session'. She did not want to be the subject of an exorcism, and was angry and perplexed, but her husband would not be deterred.

On Saturday 23 January, Vollmer, Reichenbach and his 30-year-old wife Leanne gathered in the Vollmer farmhouse and together prayed for Joan, sang hymns to her, read Bible passages and played tapes of Bible readings non-stop. Their mission: to cast out the demons that had taken up residence within her. '[Joan],' Ralph later said, 'ran all over the place, throwing things about. We all tried to calm her down.' They held her fast when she struggled to escape, and that night they put a mattress on the floor and held her down on it. She mimed giving birth, and tried to take off her clothes. One of them turned the mattress east-west to thwart the 'evil spirits of the north'. She hardly slept and was given only minimal amounts of food and drink.

After three days of this, Vollmer and the Reichenbachs were joined by David Klingner, 28, a harvesting contractor who was also a member of John Reichenbach's fellowship group. Klingner had suspected that Joan was possessed ever since he'd seen her 'with a really blank expression [and] eyes rolling around in their sockets' at a New Year's Eve prayer meeting. Klingner would say that when he arrived at the farmhouse, Joan Vollmer showed many signs of being possessed – wild mood swings, muscle twitching, her stomach distended by the demons roiling inside her, and able to read the exorcists' minds when they were not praying.

'She was aggressive and showing many manifestations of evil spirits,' Ralph Vollmer would tell reporter Norm Lipson of *Who Weekly* magazine. There were, Vollmer said, from eight to ten demons possessing his wife. Among them was the Spirit of Abuse, which made Joan say disparaging things. The Spirit of Filth caused her to 'use words I couldn't repeat, words I'd never heard of, *yucky* words!' The Spirit of Jezebel coerced Joan into attempting to shed her garments and seduce the very people who were trying to save her soul. When the demon named Legion took hold of her she had the strength of two thousand which, he explained, made it rather difficult for him and his colleagues to hold her down. At other times she was gripped by the spirits of a dog and a pig, which made her bark and snort, and by malignant spirits named Princess Joan and Princess Baby Joan. These two, Reichenbach insisted to Ralph, had attached themselves to his wife's womb when she was three and had lurked there ever since, waiting to make their move.

After six days the exorcists, frustrated by their lack of success – for Joan was continuing to resist them in spite of everything they were doing for her – decided that more serious methods were required. Her eternal life depended on it.

In the early afternoon of 30 January, a blazing hot Saturday, a towering, snowy-haired fellow named Matthew Nuske arrived. Nuske, only twenty-two years old, an assistant greenkeeper at Melbourne's Ringwood Municipal Golf Club, was believed by the Reichenbachs and Klingner to have been granted special powers by God and to be a whizz at banishing evil spirits.

Nuske set to work. Taking a roll of cling-wrap, he held it above his head and ran around the house seven times. The protective plastic, he assured the others, would shield them all from Satan. That done, he ordered Vollmer, Klingner and the Reichenbachs to gather up Joan's personal possessions and destroy them. Among other things, the group enthusiastically smashed her prized collection of porcelain vases and figurines to shards and splinters. Not content with that, Nuske demanded that the gardens and a greenhouse be ripped up, because evil spirits had been known to hide in foliage.

Then Nuske cleared the kitchen of all furniture but a single chair. He seated Joan, now weak and dazed, bound her hands and feet to the chair's arms and legs with stockings and, as the others gathered round, commenced his ritual. First he called on the spirits inside the woman to make themselves known to him, then, for more than two hours, he ordered them to vacate Joan Vollmer's body 'in the name of Jesus Christ!'

Ralph Vollmer would report that a titanic battle between the gangling exorcist and his wife's demons ensued in those few hours, in which the spirits coiled within the poor woman responded to Nuske's high-decibel shouting and Leanne Reichenbach's and David Klingner's slapping and vigorous massaging of her womb, stomach and breasts, by 'hissing, cowering and manifesting themselves'. To ensure that Joan was aware of the Lord's presence while all this going on, Klingner kept her eyes prised open wide with his thumbs. Soon, claimed Ralph Vollmer, the only spirits remaining inside Joan were Princess Joan and Princess Baby Joan, and they were refusing to budge.

It was last-resort time, the group decided, time to get doubly serious. 'I was holding Joan's arm and had one leg between her two legs,' recalled Ralph Vollmer. 'Leanne had one of Joan's legs between her legs and Matthew had one arm and David was standing behind her holding her head up and her jaw open with one hand and his other hand was on her eyes to hold [them] open. [Leanne] was just pushing against Joan's stomach [as] the rest of us were holding her ... there were many times when we couldn't hold her ... we got very physical with her, yes.' At last, the exorcists believed they had succeeded in driving the demons from Joan Vollmer's stomach and into her mouth. Ralph Vollmer said the spirits had anchored themselves to his wife's tongue and held there fast. All it would have taken was for Joan to open her mouth and Princess Joan and Princess Baby Joan would have skittered out and away. But no, Joan, or the devil himself, clamped her mouth shut. 'Some force,' allowed Ralph, 'had to be used to open the mouth.'

All the while, Joan Vollmer struggled and screamed and foamed at the mouth, which the exorcists interpreted as the spirits expressing their fury at being thwarted.

'Then, at around 5 pm, we heard a final groan,' said Vollmer. 'When the demons finally let go of her tongue there was just a final groan and she died instantly ... I was standing in front of her and the light in her eyes was gone.'

Neither hymns 'proclaiming God's victory', nor prayer, nor mouth-to-mouth nor cardiopulmonary resuscitation could revive Joan Vollmer. Nuske departed at 6 pm. Ralph Vollmer did not blame him for Joan's death. They knew he had done what was right. In fact, the group felt at peace: sad they had lost Joan, but glad to have done the Lord's will. It was the malevolent spirits, Ralph Vollmer believed, that killed his wife. Too, his grief was assuaged by his confidence that, like Jesus and Lazarus, Joan would be resurrected, today, tomorrow or, if not then, surely at her funeral.

Leanne Reichenbach prostrated herself on Joan Vollmer's body so that, she later explained, God's power could flow from her into the dead woman.

In the 40-degree heat the corpse, covered in red and purple contusions, was laid in a bed under an eiderdown and by Sunday evening was decomposing rapidly. A terrible smell emanated from the body, and it had swollen grotesquely. The head was turning black and was twice its normal size, and blowflies and maggots were making themselves at home.

On Monday 1 February, Vollmer, sure now that Joan's resurrection would take place at her funeral, called the authorities. Local doctor Lindsay Swalwell supervised the removal of the body from the farmhouse.

As word of Joan Vollmer's fate spread to a disbelieving nation, local church leaders made it clear that they had not sanctioned the exorcism. Such approval was granted only in 'the most extraordinary cases' after painstaking evaluation and psychiatric assessment of the person thought to be possessed. These people at Antwerp had acted off their own bat.

Members of Joan Vollmer's family were also disturbed by the manner of her demise. They suggested that rather than spirits causing Joan's recent odd behaviour, she was suffering a nervous breakdown initiated by the way Ralph relentlessly bombarded her with religion, and compounded by his tightness with money. 'The only place he ever took her was to church,' quipped Joan's sister Dorothy Smith.

Vollmer, the Reichenbachs and Klingner were questioned by police. In Vollmer's taped statement to police, he defended his and his fellow exorcists' actions. 'We thought the demons had put her in a coma,' he explained. 'We slapped her face a few times but we realised she was dead ... She was quite stiff and quite cold ... There was an odour and one side of her face was black. At this time I began to realise that it wasn't Joan. We were dealing with an evil spirit, not with the flesh and body of my wife.' Their attempts to rid Joan of her spirits 'would have hurt my wife dearly. But we weren't dealing with my wife any more ...'

The exorcism had been 'a spiritual battle between the kingdom of God and the kingdom of Satan'. He told police that Joan had been baptised by the devil at the age of three (a claim derided by Joan's sisters). Officers asked Vollmer why he felt that Joan needed to be exorcised. 'She was becoming more abusive,' he offered, 'she acted like a prostitute ... snorted like a pig and acted like a dog.'

God, he went on, his expression beatific, 'was going to do a complete resurrection job on Joan'. In that, too, he was wrong.

In October and November 1994, in Horsham Courthouse, Vollmer, clutching a Bible, David Klingner, Leanne Reichenbach and Matthew Nuske faced charges of manslaughter, recklessly causing serious injury and false imprisonment. Each pleaded not guilty.

Prosecutor Peter Jones QC told the five-woman, seven-man jury that Joan Vollmer had died of a heart attack as a result of the compression of her thyroid cartilage, or adam's apple. The pressure, he went on, had been placed on the deceased's neck by the participants in the exorcism. He said the defendants had caused involuntary manslaughter involving aspects of criminal negligence and/or unlawful dangerous acts. The exorcism 'was a very, very violent situation that got out of control ... They had no consideration for Christianity, they went right past that. They were on a frolic of their own and an unlawful frolic'. Jones said that 'common sense [had given] way to zealotry' and that Ralph Vollmer 'should have realised that [his wife] was ill and that no amount of exorcism or exorcising or whatever was going to cure it'. He castigated the defenders for not calling a doctor when they realised that Joan's condition was deteriorating and said Ralph's claim that the exorcism was performed on evil spirits and not on his 'real' wife was 'just a load of nonsense'.

Charles Francis QC, for the defence, countered that because the defendants were members of a charismatic Christian movement and believed that they could commune with the Holy Spirit, it was reasonable for them to hold an honest belief in the reality of demonic possession. They were doing what they truly felt God wanted them to do.

Witnesses included 77-year-old Rainbow woman Leah Clugston, a member of the Reichenbachs' Bible study group, who testified that Leanne Reichenbach had telephoned her late in January and told her of her suspicions that Joan Vollmer was possessed by evil spirits. Clugston, who claimed to receive frequent 'confirmations' from God, said she had asked the Lord if Joan's body had been invaded by demons and God had told her that indeed it had.

During the 'deliverance' the exorcists had repeatedly called Clugston and asked her to check with God whether there were still spirits in Joan Vollmer's body. Each time she had consulted the Lord and passed His Word on to them.

Clugston had gone to the Vollmers' house on Sunday 31 January and seen Joan's corpse. God had then told her to lay hands upon the body. Recalled Clugston, 'I said, "No, not me," and He said, "Yes, you. There is no salvation without obedience."'

So she had laid her hands on the corpse and cried, 'In the precious name of Jesus, rise and walk!' but Joan did not obey. Clugston had then prayed with the others for Joan's resurrection, but still her condition did not improve. Finally, she testified, God had instructed her to return home.

Prosecutor Jones was scornful of Clugston's claim to a 'hotline to heaven'. 'If you really had that power you'd never have to work again,' he said, to chortles from the gallery. 'You'd go to the racetrack and get the straight six. You'd get millions. It's just not real.'

In his final instructions to the jury, Judge Graeme Crossley stressed that the practice of exorcism was not on trial in this case, and the members had to decide whether the acts performed by those carrying out the exorcism were lawful.

On 1 December 1994, Crossley declared that in his view their treatment of the deceased had been 'rough, unwarranted and absolutely unjustified'. He dealt Ralph Vollmer a twelve-month suspended sentence for recklessly causing serious injury and the false imprisonment of Joan Vollmer. Court observers said it was likely that the light sentence had been handed down because Vollmer had had minimal physical contact with his wife during the exorcism. Leanne Reichenbach was found guilty of manslaughter and false imprisonment and, as tears flowed down her cheeks, ordered to serve four months of a two-year sentence. David Klingner was deemed to be guilty of the same charges and was jailed for three months. Matthew Nuske was guilty only of false imprisonment – the manslaughter charge against him had been dropped – and was dealt a three-month suspended sentence.

Leanne Reichenbach and David Klingner appealed against their sentences, but their appeals were turned down and they served their time. On their release they returned to the service of the Lord.

When last contacted by reporters, Ralph Vollmer was missing his wife desperately, but defiant that he and the exorcists had done no wrong. 'We didn't go against God,' he insisted. 'We were acting in His name.'

CHAPTER 10

PARTNERS IN CRIME

Catherine and David Birnie: Serial killers

1986

The girl ran for her life. For the past day and night since her abduction, she had been raped and tortured by a man and woman she knew only as Cath and Dave in a room of their rundown white brick bungalow in the Perth suburb of Willagee. Now her captors had taken time out to buy some cocaine, Dave saying he would inject the drug into his penis to keep him hard for what was to come. Left alone for a short time, the 16-year-old realised that her captors had omitted to lock the window. She memorised the number on the dial of the telephone on the bedside table, cleverly hid her handbag and her pack of cigarettes in the ceiling to prove she'd been there and that this nightmare had really happened, climbed out the window and tore off to a local shopping centre, running so fast she feared her lungs would burst. Before long she was spilling out the terrible details of her ordeal to detectives at Palmyra police station.

That night of Monday 10 November 1986, police returned to the house in Willagee, and interviewed the residents, whose names were Catherine and David Birnie – not only about what they had done to the teenager, but about what they might have done to a number of women who had vanished in recent weeks. The pair, for hour after hour, angrily denied knowledge of the missing women. All Birnie would admit to was having had 'consensual sex' with the girl who'd escaped.

Then Detective Sergeant Katich, exhausted and frustrated, said, almost as a throwaway line, 'David, it's getting dark. Let's go dig them up.' The stringy-haired, thin-faced Birnie considered for a moment and then, out of a clear blue sky, replied, 'Okay. There's four of them.' *Paydirt!* thought Katich.

Later, when both were charged with multiple murders, Catherine Birnie sighed that she had killed because 'I wanted to see how strong I was within my inner self. I didn't feel a thing. I was prepared to follow David to the end of the earth and do anything to see that his desires were satisfied.' Catherine's voyage of self-discovery cost the lives of at least four innocent women.

Incredibly, the killers' fatal attraction to each other seems to have taken root when they were babies for, reportedly, Catherine Harrison (as she was christened) and David Birnie were inseparable when they played in a council playpen near their family homes in Subiaco. Their parents knew each other through the fathers' jobs in the laundry of Royal Perth Hospital. Both the Harrisons and the Birnies were deeply dysfunctional folk. In 1952, when Catherine was ten months old, her mother died and she went to live in South Africa with her father who, a court was later told, sexually abused her. At four, she returned to Australia and the custody of her maternal grandparents. In spite of their care, Catherine grew up a sad, uncommunicative girl who was unable to form lasting friendships – until, when she was fourteen, her old playpen pal re-entered her life.

David had grown up the eldest of Margaret and John Birnie's six children. When he was ten, his parents were charged with neglect – their home was filthy and garbage-strewn and both drank heavily. Mrs Birnie was also racked with chronic pleurisy and pneumonia. On the orders of the West Australian Social Welfare Department, David and his siblings were fostered out. David was soon fending for himself, and looking for trouble. Catherine, who was desperately seeking someone to love her and whom she could love in return and who would give her wayward, disappointed life direction, *any* direction, accommodated him.

He was her Svengali and she was his Trilby, delighted and desperate to do his bidding. They drifted together, had sex, partied and survived on welfare payments and what they could steal. Birnie had grown into a small and surly man whose squinting eyes framed a large blade of a nose. He worked as a truckie and labourer and in 1966 was apprenticed as a jockey to trainer Eric Parnham until he was fired after being arrested for assaulting and robbing the elderly proprietor of a boarding house. Birnie's passions were pornography and drugs, which also became the obsessions of the brooding, foul-mouthed and promiscuous Harrison, by now a diminutive, tawny-haired woman with a slash for a mouth and whose normal expression was sour, as if she had just bitten into an especially acidic lemon.

Like Bonnie and Clyde, the young lovers hurtled headlong into crime, getting what amounted to a sexual buzz from breaking the law. They broke into houses and stole cars but, stupid and careless, were almost always caught. Magistrates for a while cut them slack for their youth, placing them on good behaviour bonds or imposing minor fines. Once out of the courtroom, however, they offended again and again. After one too many arrests, when they pleaded guilty to eleven charges of breaking, entering and stealing goods worth around $3000, the judge sentenced Birnie to three years' gaol in Karnet Prison. Catherine Harrison, eighteen and pregnant (whether to Birnie is not known), was paroled.

Harrison gave birth and waited for Birnie to get out of prison, which happened rather sooner than expected – he escaped. They continued to ply their crime wave around Perth, squalling baby in tow. In June 1970 they were arrested and charged on fifty-three counts of stealing, receiving, breaking and entering, and unlawful use of motor vehicles. In their possession were wigs and other items of disguise, gelignite, detonators and fuses. Birnie was gaoled for two and a half years, and Harrison given a six-month custodial sentence. The baby was taken from them and put in a home. A judge, remarking on Birnie's 'evil influence' on Harrison, advised her to leave him while she still could. Start afresh with a new man, he cautioned, someone less dangerous and manipulative, someone less surely doomed.

In fairness, Harrison tried. After she was released from prison and was working as a domestic in Fremantle, south of Perth, on her twenty-first birthday she married Donald McLaughlin, the son of her employers, who had fallen in love with her. She quickly became pregnant to McLaughlin and they had a son, also Donald, whom they called Donny. Tragically, when he was seven months old, Donny was run over by a car near their Victoria Park home and killed. Catherine saw it happen. In a sad attempt to erase her loss, she had five more children with her husband over the next twelve years. Yet, even as she had child after child, a big part of her heart still belonged to David Birnie.

Then in 1985, like the scary goblin in a recurring nightmare, Birnie was back in her life. Freed from prison, he was living with a hairdresser when he located Catherine and made contact with her. The spell he'd cast upon his old partner in crime had lost none of its malignant potency. With scarcely a thought, Catherine walked out on Donald McLaughlin and their children to live in a threesome with Birnie and his lover. The hairdresser soon left, unwilling to compete with the soulmates' intensely perverse feelings for each other (by now their usual sexual accoutrements were hard-core pornography and drugs – Birnie liked to inject his penis with a cocaine solution because he believed it helped him maintain his erection). Catherine became Birnie's de facto wife and by deed poll changed her family name to his. David got a job in the spare parts department of a car wrecking yard and supplemented that income by stealing.

After David and Catherine Birnie's arrest for murder in 1986, David's brother James, then twenty-one, told the Nine Network's *Willesee* program of the dark world his brother and Catherine had come to inhabit. James, who had been twice convicted of 'indecent dealings' with his 6-year-old niece and who allowed, somewhat unnecessarily, that his and his brother's upbringing had been 'very bad' and that the family had 'severe sexual problems', told how Catherine had relieved him of his virginity when he turned twenty-one after David gave her to him for a night of sex as a birthday gift. James said his brother was a sex addict who 'cracks up, just crawls into a hole and closes up, when he can't get any'. David slept with many other women, with his partner's knowledge and approval, every week. Often Catherine joined them. Once, while James was living with his brother, he had woken to find David in his bed. David had then raped him. He did not go to the police 'because Dave threatens to kill me all the time'.

By 1986, however, neither perverted sex nor petty crime was providing the danger or excitement Catherine and David Birnie craved, and they decided it was time to turn into reality a fantasy – that of being serial killers – that had long turned them on during sex.

The pair became deadly predators, trawling Perth's highways and back roads for female hitchhikers to rape and murder. Over thirty-five appalling days in October and November, they abducted four young women, chained them to the bed in their ramshackle house in Willagee, drugged them, raped them, and then stabbed, strangled or axed them to death. Said one detective, '[These are] the most macabre and sadistic crimes in the history of Australia.' (The Birnies' killing spree may well have been even more horrific. David in 1992 reportedly confided that he and Catherine had murdered three more women but, when pressed by police, refused to say more.)

The first known victim was Mary Neilson, 22, a psychology student at the University of Western Australia, who in early October had the tragic misfortune to turn up at the wrecking yard when David Birnie was manning the spare parts counter, seeking second-hand tyres for her Galant sedan. The scrawny bloke by the cash register said he could help with a good cheap set, and why didn't she drop around to his house in Willagee that night and pick them up. When Neilson knocked at the door, the Birnies pulled a knife on her, tied her up and gagged her, then chained her to a bed. While David raped her, Catherine watched. Neilson was then driven to the Gleneagles National Park pine plantation where she was raped again, strangled with a nylon strap and stabbed to death. Catherine illuminated the horrific scene with a torch. The killers buried her in a shallow grave.

Susannah Candy was just fifteen, the daughter of a prominent Perth ophthalmic surgeon. On 21 October, hitchhiking on the Stirling Highway at Claremont, the brilliant schoolgirl made the fatal mistake of accepting when the Birnies offered her a lift in their red Sigma. The pair drove Candy to Willagee, where they took turns defiling her, one holding a knife at the child's throat while the other raped her. Next day, in the depths of the Gleneagles National Park, Catherine Birnie strangled her and then she and David buried the body.

Noelene Patterson, 31, a vivacious and popular computer operator, was standing by the roadside on the Canning Highway, East Fremantle, after her car ran out of petrol, waiting for a kindly motorist to give her a lift to a garage. She would have been delighted when the Birnies pulled up alongside and offered assistance. Back at the Birnie's house, Patterson was raped. They kept her there for three days, because David Birnie developed a crush on the attractive former air hostess, who had recently worked on businessman Alan Bond's luxury private jet. Catherine had no problems with David having sex with another woman so long as it was cruel, loveless, detached sex. But an emotional attachment was not part of the bargain. She would not accept him being unfaithful. On the third day, the furious Catherine held a knife to her own chest and threatened to plunge it into her heart if David did not kill Noelene Patterson. Shocked by this rare show of assertiveness, he complied. When they buried her in the forest, Catherine spat on Patterson's grave.

On 6 November, the Birnies picked up 21-year-old Denise Brown and subjected her to the same pattern of incarceration and rape. Next day they drove her to their killing fields in the Gleneagles National Park. David Birnie raped Brown again, then stabbed her. When their victim bravely fought for her life, Catherine Birnie produced a larger knife and handed it to her lover to finish the job. They dug Brown's grave, laid her in it and stood alongside gasping for breath. Suddenly Brown sat straight up. David hit her twice in the head with an axe.

Three days later, as the disappearances of the four women, each a much-loved and admirable person from a stable home, were raising fears of a serial killer on the loose in Perth, the Birnies struck again when they gave a lift to a 16-year-old girl hitchhiking along the Stirling Highway at Nedlands. The atrocities were proceeding according to plan – the kidnapping, the bed chains, the rapes at knifepoint – and next day they'd kill the girl in the national park just as they had the other women. But when Catherine and David Birnie called a halt to fuel up on more cocaine, their captive's desperate dash to safety brought the murders, and the Birnies' reign of terror, to an end. As Justice Wallace in Perth's Supreme Court would later say, 'That young girl's cool head and initiative, coupled with providence, undoubtedly enabled her to escape the fate of her predecessors.'

On 10 November 1986, acting on information from the girl who escaped, police arrested the Birnies in the house where they had committed their dreadful acts. The interior reflected the squalor of their lives. In the living room, where they were read their rights, every surface was grimy and soiled. Ashtrays and bins overflowed, while drug paraphernalia including numerous syringes, beer bottles, cigarette butts, rotting food, newspapers open at pages with reports about the vanished women, and filthy clothes and bedding, were strewn all over the floor and on every other horizontal surface.

Later the Birnies took police to where they had buried their victims, and David Birnie was heard to sigh, 'What a pointless loss of young life.'

After they were charged, neighbours described the Birnies as a couple who 'kept to themselves', seemed 'reasonable people' and were 'kind to their two Alsatian dogs'. The fellows at the wrecking yard called David Birnie 'a well-liked, average, everyday person'.

On 6 November 1986, the Birnies pleaded guilty in Perth's Supreme Court to four counts of wilful murder, five counts of deprivation of liberty and two counts of aggravated sexual penetration of a 16-year-old. Sitting together in the dock, they showed no remorse at any stage, and snarled when their crimes were recounted. Catherine often placed her hand on David's knee or held his hand.

Giving testimony was a 19-year-old university student who had narrowly avoided being a victim. She told how on the morning of 7 or 8 November she had been walking along Pinjar Road, Wanneroo, when a red car eased to a halt alongside and the occupants, whom she identified as the Birnies, he driving, she in the front passenger seat, asked her whether she wanted a lift. The student could see someone slumped in the back seat and immediately assumed it was their sleeping son or daughter: 'I felt uneasy. I didn't recognise the car. There was a man driving and a woman in the front seat. The man kept looking down, not looking at me, and the woman was drinking a can of UDL rum and coke. I thought the fact that she was drinking at that time of day was strange. He didn't look at me the whole time. It was the woman who did all the talking. She asked me if I wanted a lift anywhere. I said, "No, I only live up the road."' The people in the car had then, without a further word, driven off in the direction of the Gleneagles National Park pine forest. 'It wasn't until I saw a really good photo of Catherine Birnie that I realised who they were. Somebody must have been looking after me that day. I don't know what would have happened to me if I had got into that car.' The figure in the back seat was Denise Brown, the woman whom the Birnies would murder with an axe.

David Birnie was sentenced on 10 February 1987. He and Catherine entered the court together. He was stolid and stony-faced, appearing small and insignificant in a tight blue prison shirt that accentuated his narrow shoulders and chicken chest, and blue flares. Over his right eye and on his lip was sticking plaster to cover injuries he'd received when, police insisted, he slipped entering the Supreme Court cells. She, wearing a yellow blouse and checked skirt, seemed deranged. As she mounted the steps to the dock she shrieked and swore and spat and tried, unsuccessfully, to twist out of the iron grip of her police escort. When order was restored and she'd been admonished by Justice Wallace, the judge sentenced David Birnie to life in prison under strict supervision, saying he should stay in gaol for the rest of his days and that no matter how heavy a sentence he imposed it would be an inadequate reflection of the community's horror at what he had done. As Birnie was led from the court he responded to the mob that was demanding that he be strung up by waving to them and blowing them a rancid kiss.

Catherine was not to receive her sentence until a psychiatric examination was carried out. One doctor who interviewed her declared that hers was 'the worst case of personality disorder' he'd ever encountered.

She appeared for sentencing on 3 March. David sat alongside as she, too, received life in gaol under strict security. When the sentence was brought down, she squeezed his hand. Justice Wallace told Catherine Birnie:

> While your pleas have spared the relatives of your victims the trauma of trial, I do not accept such pleas as demonstrative of remorse. This is because of my understanding of the active part you played and I believe the actions would have continued if you had not been discovered. Each was premeditated, calculated and carried forward to its conclusion without mercy. You willingly joined in the selection of your unfortunate victims, carried them off at knifepoint and held them in captivity for the sole purpose of the sexual gratification of your partner in crime and then murdered them, lest you be identified, and then finally mutilated them. You personally extinguished the life of two of your victims and certainly participated in the death of a third. The only appropriate punishment is the sentence I intend to impose: strict life security in prison.

He repeated what he had told David Birnie, that no sentence was long enough to reflect the community's horror at the crimes and that she should end her days in prison. This was one way of ensuring that the pair would never meet again.

Catherine had made no effort to contact her five children since she had walked out on them and Donald McLaughlin to join David. But a couple of weeks after she was sentenced, she wrote them a letter from Bandyup Women's Prison. Whether a cynical attempt to portray herself in a loving light, to allay blame, or a genuine attempt to establish some kind of contact with her kids, the letter seemed to reveal a facet of herself, a softness perhaps, that was not evident to anyone who had known her as the scowling and implacable partner of David Birnie, or who had observed her snapping and squirming at her trial – and which certainly was never experienced in any degree by her poor victims. She wrote:

> Dear kids,
>
> Hi, Mom here and I'm not sure if indeed you'll receive this, but I'll try. First, the reason I changed my last name to Birnie was so that you kids wouldn't be hurt by the newspapers and the television people. I'm not proud about what has been said about me, but I have to live with that and the memories. As to why this happened, I can only hope that the doctors can help me find out. Maybe they can do tests or something so then I can come to grips with all of this.
>
> I never stopped loving any of you kids, but I thought you'd be safer with your father. Maybe, I was wrong, about leaving you with him and if that's the case I'm truly sorry. Secondly, the reason I'm asking for a divorce [from Donald McLaughlin] is because I'll be in here for a long time and he can't get on with his life if he is still tied to me. My two lawyers and QC don't hold out much hope for me getting out before 10–15 years have passed. I would like it very much if your dad would allowed you to, if you would write to me please. Also, if he'd allow you's and if you's wanted to, would you please come and see me one day. I bet all of you have grown up so much and are a credit to your father. The address is at the top of this page and so just write to C.M. Birnie at that address and your Mum will receive it.
>
> I have a TV and a radio in my room so I can see all of the shows and I can keep up with all of the latest songs. I'm sending this letter to

the Busselton Police Station, as I don't know your address. Hope you dad doesn't get upset by this ... I'd better close now because it's almost tea time. I hope I do hear from you really soon and if you and dad agree, could I have a photo of all you kids – Your hopeful Mother

PS: I've been told that the Welfare are looking in on you kids so I'll send it to them to pass on to you. Please kids, try and go on and behave yourselves and don't get into any trouble, because of what I'm supposed to have done. I love you kids very much and I don't ever want to hear that any of you have got into trouble of any kind. Once again, my love to all of you kids and I hope one day you'll come to see your Old Mum. Maybe you'll write to me cause I'd really love to hear from all of you. I love you kids.

Her children were not the only recipients of her missives. She and David Birnie exchanged 2600 letters in their first few years of incarceration. Then she claimed to have found God, and wrote no more. He scribbled on for another year or so but eventually, receiving no replies, gave up.

Even in Perth's Casuarina maximum security prison, David Birnie found it impossible not to transgress. After he was found under the influence of an illegal drug, he had fourteen days added to his life sentence, and in 2004 another prisoner was awarded $70 000 in criminal injuries compensation after he successfully claimed to have been raped by Birnie and paedophile Adrian Barrett in 1999.

On 7 October 2005, David Birnie, then aged fifty-five, hanged himself in his cell. On hearing the news, the young woman who'd brought about his arrest by escaping through the window said that her only regret was that he had not been executed when he was convicted nineteen years before. She had put the horrors of Willagee behind her, as much as she was able, and in glorious irony had given birth to her second child on the night that Birnie died. 'We are now able to have closure,' she said in a statement, 'and are looking forward to a life without the constant reminder that a criminal such as David Birnie is alive and well in gaol at the taxpayers' expense.'

Catherine Birnie, fifty-two when Birnie died, applied to attend his funeral. Her request was denied.

She was also turned down in 2007 when she sought parole after twenty years in prison. 'Catherine Birnie should never be released. She committed crimes at the shocking end of the scale,' said WA Attorney-General Jim McGinty. 'I don't think that the community should ever expect to see Catherine Birnie walking the streets again as a free person.'

CHAPTER 11

THE NIGHT STALKER

Mr Cruel: Kidnapper and murderer

1988–91

In 2002, on the tenth anniversary of the abduction and murder of her daughter, Karmein Chan, Phyllis Lam addressed the killer in the pages of Melbourne's *Herald-Sun* newspaper. She told the man known to police and public alike as 'Mr Cruel', the man who lived then, and continues to live, in the nightmares of parents everywhere, that she forgave him. 'Every day by God is penned and that's why I am not angry with the murderer any more.' She ventured then that by giving himself up he might find a kind of peace, because there would not be a day he spent on earth that was not shadowed by guilt and remorse at the horrors he had wrought on innocent children in Melbourne in the late 1980s and early 1990s.

After abducting and assaulting up to ten children before releasing them and then, in April 1991, kidnapping and killing Karmein Chan, Mr Cruel went to ground, and despite the efforts of a crack task force and police who have never stopped looking for him, he has never been caught.

Police believe Melbourne's very own bogeyman may have begun his abductions as long ago as the late 1970s, but the first kidnapping they can definitely ascribe to him took place the day after Boxing Day of 1988.

The Christmas of the Wills family of Ringwood, was shattered on 27 December when their 10-year-old daughter Sharon, a quiet and well-behaved girl who sang with the Victorian Children's Choir and played a number of musical instruments with skill and grace, was stolen from her bed by an armed intruder. The kidnapper broke into the Wills' home at 5.30 am. He wore a ski mask and carried a handgun. He rousted Sharon's parents from their bed and bound them with copper wire, then took $35 from a wallet before going to the bedroom where Sharon was sleeping with her three sisters. He woke her by whispering her name and when she opened her eyes threatened her with his gun: 'Make a sound and you will die.' He blindfolded the terrified girl, gagged her by placing a round object in her mouth, and hustled her from the house and into the night.

Eighteen hours later, nearing midnight on 28 December, the man in the ski mask dropped Sharon off, exhausted and traumatised by the assaults she had suffered, on the Mountain Highway near Bayswater, just a few kilometres from her home. She was found wandering in the street by a passing motorist. After she was treated in hospital, Sharon, surrounded by her tearful and desperately relieved family, was able to tell police that she had a sense that the man's car was small and that he had taken her to a flat or small house. His voice seemed to be that of a man in his twenties.

The kidnapper had planned his crime meticulously. He had gone to great lengths to conceal his face, and had made sure that he left no personal traces on his victim or her clothes. 'We are dealing with a dangerous, cunning person who has set out to capture this girl right from the beginning,' detectives told reporters. They believed he was not known to the Wills family, and that he had possibly targeted Sharon after he read a newspaper article in June that year about a fire that had broken out in her bedroom. 'To get hold of the girl was his primary aim and the robbery was just something by the way,' said an officer. In posting a $100 000 reward for information leading to the kidnapper's conviction, investigators suggested that their quarry was 'a very cunning person, very dangerous and with an unknown potential'.

Police had a better idea of the man's potential for evil when he struck again on 4 July 1990.

Brian Lynas had every reason to be happy and proud. The English chartered accountant had come to the end of a successful three-year Melbourne stint with international accounting firm PriceWaterhouse. On 3 July, he and his family were days away from returning to London where he would take up his role as a partner with the company. To celebrate a job well done, Brian Lynas and his wife went to dinner, leaving their daughters Nicola, described later by her father as 'a normal 13-year-old who has always been a happy girl', and Fiona, 15, at home in their luxury, high-security home in Canterbury.

At 11.40 pm, a man wearing a balaclava and armed with a revolver and a kitchen knife breached the house's security, forced a rear window, and slunk through dark corridors to the bedroom where the sisters slept. He tied up Fiona and told her to tell her parents that it would take $25 000 to secure Nicola's freedom. Then, after ordering Nicola to pull her blue blazer over her green pyjamas, he hustled her outside and into her father's Holden Berlina, parked in the driveway. Fiona, beside herself with terror, heard the car drive away. When her parents returned home at 12.30 she told them what had happened and they called the police.

Investigating officers immediately noticed checkpoints between this kidnapping and that of Sharon Wills – the balaclava, the weapons, the description of the thin abductor, a man in his twenties or thirties, and his seeming prior knowledge of where the victim was sleeping. 'There are obvious similarities between the two crimes but we are not hanging our hat on the possibility that the same man was involved,' said Detective Inspector Ron Blackshaw of Melbourne's major crime squad. But most likely, in his heart, he knew that it was, and that a serial kidnapper was on the loose. An abductor who had taken not only Nicola Lynas and Sharon Wills, but perhaps as many as ten women and girls and a 14-year-old boy, all kidnapped, assaulted and then released over the past eleven years in metropolitan Melbourne. The state government increased the reward to $200 000, the highest on record, for information leading to an arrest and conviction.

Soon after Nicola's disappearance, the stolen Holden Berlina was found in a nearby street, and Brian Lynas held a press conference. Red-eyed and distressed, he pleaded for his daughter's return and said that he would pay the ransom 'at a moment's notice'. Fiona, he said, was being strong and was 'holding her parents together'.

When Nicola was still missing after thirty-six hours, twice as long as Sharon Wills had been held captive, and with no word from the kidnapper regarding collection of the ransom, Detective Inspector Blackshaw announced, 'Fears for Nicola's safety are growing. [This is] a long time for a girl of thirteen to be in the hands of an abductor. We now hold incredibly grave fears.'

Melbourne's *Herald* newspaper contacted Julie Wills, the mother of Sharon, who had been thrust back into her own horror by Nicola's vanishing, and she had a message for the Lynas family: 'We really feel for these people. We didn't want it to happen to another girl.' When Sharon was snatched from them 'it was worse than a death ... just a totally numb feeling of disbelief ... nothing helps you through until the police knock on the door with the news'. Like them, all the Lynases could do 'was a lot of praying. I am really feeling for the girl. I hope she doesn't go through what Sharon went through. She looks to me just like another sweet, innocent kid like Sharon was'.

Fifty-two hours after he took her, held her hostage and assaulted her, on Nicola's fourteenth birthday the kidnapper set her free. At 2 am on 7 July, he pushed the traumatised girl, wrapped in a blanket and wearing a blindfold, from his car onto the kerbside in Kew, again only a few kilometres from her home. Ordering her to sit with her head between her knees, he ripped off the blindfold before making off into the freezing night.

Nicola told officers from Task Force Spectrum that she had been tied up and blindfolded for the entire time so she could not identify the man or the place where he had taken her. Her reunion was tearful and joyous, and the Wills family sent flowers. Before the Lynases returned to England, there would be psychological counselling for them all. Police warned people to take extra precautions to ensure their children were safe because they believed this 'dangerous man' would offend again.

On 11 July, prominent forensic psychologist Tim Watson-Munro published an open letter to the kidnapper who had become known as 'Mr Cruel' because of his callous manner, calculating attacks and painstaking removal of clues such as semen, body hair and skin tissue (he went so far as to order his victims to scrape beneath their fingernails):

> I am writing to you in the belief that you may be experiencing some remorse, ambivalence and confusion in relation to your recent outbreak. I am deeply troubled by your behaviour and feel that you need to seek appropriate treatment as soon as possible. You must know, within yourself, that your underlying urges to commit this type of offence are, as yet, unresolved, and it is clearly only a matter of time before you offend again. It may well be at this time that you feel some repugnance in relation to your cruelty towards this child [Nicola Lynas]. You may well be wavering about making contact [with police] because you fear the consequences of your actions. This is quite understandable. However, in the absence of revealing yourself and receiving some assistance for your problems, you will no doubt re-offend, and I fear the frequency of your offending and the severity of your behaviour will both increase.
>
> The fact that you have released this child and possibly others suggests that you have some insight into other people's feelings and, associated with this, the magnitude of your disturbance. To your credit, it would appear that you are able to control your fantasies and impulses for lengthy periods before acting them out. This indicates that you may well be a good prospect for treatment.

> Perhaps these fantasies have been brooding within you for many years and only recently they have become too much to contain. No doubt you realise the devastating impact that you have had upon this child, her family, and indeed our community. Perhaps this affords you some vicarious pleasure? Alternatively, strong labels that have been attached to your behaviour such as 'psychopath' may, in the setting of your confusion, be causing you some distress. You may well have read widely on areas concerning this type of offending. The cunning manner in which this offence was executed and the associated absence of clues, suggests that you are an intelligent individual capable of considerable planning. If this is the case, then you'll be aware that the likelihood of your re-offending is very high. So too is the prospect of escalating violence with your offending.
>
> It bothers me that you took considerably more time to release this child than your earlier victims. This suggests that the struggle within you was more protracted and that perhaps, at some point, you were considering not releasing this child at all. Reflect on this and be aware that next time the struggle may be even greater with you possibly panicking and acting in an even more dangerous manner.
>
> Although you have acted in an abhorrent fashion with this offence and, I suspect, others, I nonetheless intuitively feel that you want to seek assistance. In your own interests as well as those of your potential victims and the community in general, I again urge you to make contact with a psychologist and/or Insp Dannye Moloney who is handling this case. Certainly I am available at any time to speak with you, if you so desire. Be assured that in the absence of treatment your prospects and prognosis are extremely bleak. – Yours sincerely, Tim Watson-Munro.

In predicting that Mr Cruel would re-offend, and that he might panic and inflict violence on his next victim, the forensic psychologist was tragically prescient.

Nine months later, on the stormy night of Saturday 13 April 1991, 13-year-old Karmein Chan was taken from her home, a two-storey mansion with gym, pool and tennis court, in Templestowe. She was minding her two young sisters, 9-year-old Karly and 7-year-old Karen, when around 9 pm Mr Cruel, wearing his balaclava and wielding a knife, broke in and spirited her away. Karmein was barefoot and wearing only a short white nightie. The younger girls, whom the kidnapper had forced into a cupboard, heard their sister tell the intruder, 'Don't do that!' The children's parents, successful restaurateurs Phyllis and John Chan, were at work in the family's Chinese restaurant in Lower Plenty. Karmein was a charming and intelligent child, a student from the same school that Nicola Lynas had attended.

As police scoured the grounds they saw that Phyllis Chan's Toyota Camry sedan, parked at the front of the house, had been painted with the words 'Pay Back Asian drug dealer' and 'More And More To Come.' They believe this was an attempt by Mr Cruel to make the kidnapping seem the work of a drug gang.

Phyllis Chan, who would liken having one's child snatched away to 'being stabbed and then having your heart bleed inside you', made an impassioned plea to Mr Cruel: 'Please, please, release my daughter. All the family love her. Don't spoil my family. Bring her home safe ... She loves her sisters and her mum and dad. I love her really very much. Karmein, I can't miss you any more.' Said sister Karen: 'I miss you a lot of time. I am very scared in the dark and Mum and Dad miss you very much.' And Karly: 'I wake up all the time. I need you, Karmein ... Please bring Karmein back. We miss you very much with our hearts.'

Then, heart-rendingly, the desperate mother sent a public plea to the abductor, addressing him not as Mr Cruel, but as Mr Kind: 'We miss Karmein very, very much. Please let Karmein go. We know you are a caring person. We hope Karmein is safe with you. Thank you for letting her free. And we can rebuild our lives. Please hear our plea.' If Mr Cruel did hear, he did not respond.

This time, thanks to Karen and Karly Chan, who had observed the intruder closely before he locked them away, police got a more exact description of the kidnapper. He was aged 25 to 35, 168 to 177 centimetres tall, of slim to medium build. He wore grey running shoes, a green-grey tracksuit and a balaclava. His accent was Australian.

The Lynas and Wills families were lucky. Their children were returned to them. Not so the Chans. Karmein remained missing. With no word from her or the kidnapper, it was as if she had been swallowed up, had never existed. The agonies endured by her parents, not knowing their daughter's fate but fearing the worst, were terrible beyond belief as the days turned to weeks and the weeks to months. Almost a year to the day after the abduction, a human skull and some bones were found in a shallow grave by a man walking his dogs at Edgar's Creek, which traverses a State Electricity Commission site at the corner of High Street and Mahoney's Road in Thomastown. The remains were around a year old, and there were three bullet holes in the skull. This was all that was left of Karmein Chan.

In confirming that the remains were the missing girl's, Detective Inspector David Sprague, head of Task Force Spectrum, said he believed Mr Cruel may have executed Karmein after she saw his face. 'It is horrific. For a child to be killed in that fashion is incomprehensible ... Although John and Phyllis Chan may never hear the laughter of their daughter again, they can now say goodbye to Karmein and put her soul to rest as she deserves. The family will now have the opportunity to start rebuilding their lives.'

It didn't turn out that way. The marriage of Karmein's parents could not withstand the pain they endured and John and Phyllis parted.

Task Force Spectrum sifted through the burgeoning files and the statements of victims, then joined with the FBI to publish a profile of the kidnapper and murderer, hoping it might lead to someone providing information that would stop his atrocities. Mr Cruel, the investigators surmised, could be aged from the late twenties to the late forties, is possibly of slight to medium build with a small paunch, and have fair hair and eyebrows. He may wear glasses. He could be a loving husband and father, a compassionate friend and a good neighbour. He is most likely intelligent, creative and obsessively clean – perhaps washes his hands again and again. He is Australian-born and habitually uses such prim and antiquated terms as 'missy', 'worrywart' and 'bozo'. Though he took pride in his crimes, gloating over newspaper reports to his victims, he may be a nervous man, for his hands shook violently while binding one victim. He told more than one captive child that he had been subjected to sexual abuse when he was a little boy. He may dress neatly and keep a neat home. Chances are he is a respected member of the community, possibly working closely with children as a teacher, sporting coach or youth administrator, though with the mobility to move freely across Melbourne. Friends and colleagues may know him as kind and friendly. He may be a devoted family man and in that case would have been absent from his home at the time of the kidnappings. He would be sexually dysfunctional, and have a stash of pornography, probably child pornography. A sensitive person, he might have seemed agitated and distracted in the days after the abductions. The knots he tied when binding his victims were similar to those tied by farmers and truck drivers, and by musicians re-stringing guitars and violins. Based on the fleeting glimpse obtained by one victim, Mr Cruel's bedroom had a beige carpet, peach-coloured full-length curtains, a double bed with peach-coloured bedhead, a lemon lampshade with thin white stripes on an orange base. A dark blanket covered a cabinet or bookcase, possibly because it contained incriminating objects, such as photographs. In the adjoining bathroom there was a sliding shower door and a dual-flush toilet in or close to the bathroom. The driveway to the house or flat was on the right-hand side and steps led to the door. Planes could be heard flying overhead, which indicated that Mr Cruel took his victims to a suburb or town on the Tullamarine flight path, possibly Watsonia, McLeod, Coburg, Keilor, Strathmore or Plenty. (Police would duly inspect the bedrooms of more than 30 000 residences under the Tullamarine flight path.)

A poster with the legend 'Police Need Your Help' and bearing the photographs of Sharon Wills, Nicola Lynas and Karmein Chan was posted to every home in Victoria and many in South Australia and New South Wales. The reward was increased again, to $300 000. Still no takers. And despite claims that crime scenes were contaminated and vital incriminating items, such as binding tape, lost, Operation Spectrum ground on. In the course of their massive and gruelling investigation, which ended in 1994, the thirty-five operatives of the task force spent nearly $4 million conducting the probe and following up over 10 000 tips from the public. They interviewed more than 25 000 people from all over Australia, the United States, Britain and Hong Kong, arresting and charging seventy-three of them for child pornography, blackmail, firearms, burglary or rape.

But they did not catch Mr Cruel.

The *Herald-Sun* did its bit, begging readers to rack their brains, to recall the dates of the abductions – 27 December 1988, 3 July 1990, 13 April 1991 – and ask themselves if someone they knew was away or acted strangely at these times, and even if that person was a loved one to tell the police.

The murder of Karmein Chan was Mr Cruel's last known act. But even today, sixteen years later, his balaclava-clad spectre has not lost its appalling power to haunt. Perhaps he has died. He may be in prison. Maybe he has moved overseas. Or, terrifyingly, he is still in Australia, going about his daily life, interacting with loved ones and friends who would be appalled to know his horrifying secret, his fear of being caught having overwhelmed his compulsion to kidnap, assault and kill. But if the latter is the case, say police, there is no guarantee that he will not offend again.

If, however, Mr Cruel is dead, the world is a better place.

CHAPTER 12

THE ACID TEST

Martha Rendall: Serial killer
1907–08

When, in October 1909, Martha Rendall was convicted of fatally poisoning three of her stepchildren, she had no competition for the position of the most despised person in the land. As he donned the black cap to impose the death sentence in the Supreme Court of Western Australia, Mr Justice McMillan called the woman who had reinforced every fairytale-inspired prejudice about wicked stepmothers a 'moral deformity'. Rendall was also branded variously as 'evil', 'depraved', a 'monster'. Hanging was too good for her, wrote one enraged citizen to a newspaper, reflecting the mood of the populace. Why not give her a taste of her own medicine, so to speak, and pour hydrochloric acid down *her* throat, as she had done to those poor innocent kiddies in her so-called care?

Yet even Rendall's most vociferous detractors could not deny that she died with style and, disconcertingly for all those who were convinced of her guilt, proclaiming her innocence long after hope of a pardon had fled. As she stood before the noose, Rendall said quietly, 'On the last day of my life, before God I say I am innocent. I am completely and absolutely innocent of the crime for which I am dying. I pray God forgive those who swore falsely my life away.'

If she was telling the truth, and *was* a victim of others' lies, it's hoped those people whose testimony convicted her – her surviving stepsons George and William, whose tales of cruelty and murder instigated the police investigation, and a gaggle of neighbours – were plagued by guilt for the rest of their days. Was Rendall sinner or sinned against? Certainly the evidence against her, though circumstantial, was formidable. But really, no one will ever know for certain.

Martha Rendall was in her mid-twenties when she fell in love with Thomas Morris in Adelaide in 1894. From a battling Adelaide family and with two children from a previous relationship, she worked around Adelaide as a domestic cleaner and servant. Morris, a carpenter and factory foreman, was a decade or so older. He and his wife Sarah had nine children. Though Morris continued to live with Sarah and five of their children (two had grown up and moved away and two had died young), he and Rendall began an affair which soon became known to his wife, their friends and acquaintances. To escape scorn in those more stitched-up times, and perhaps to cool off the relationship, for Rendall was now urging him to choose between her and his wife, Morris uprooted his family and they moved across the Nullarbor to start life anew in Perth.

After a few months – because he was missing his lover? – Morris and his clan returned to Adelaide, where he resumed the affair. Once more Sarah took understandable exception and marital strife ensued. In 1905, in a last-ditch attempt to mend his marriage, Morris, Sarah and the children returned to Perth. But this time Rendall followed.

The Morris home became a battlefield. Sarah accused Thomas of loving Rendall more than her and sleeping with her every chance he got. Which was probably true. He in turn accused her of drinking to excess and having sex with men she'd just met. One day in March 1906, their 13-year-old son Arthur blabbed to his father that he'd seen his mother in the arms of another man. When Sarah came home that night, Morris beat her savagely and ordered her to leave the house.

During the divorce proceedings, Thomas's violence was overlooked. Sarah was deemed to be an unfit mother and custody of their five youngest children was granted to Thomas. He bundled up the youngsters and rented a small rundown cottage in Robertson Street in then working-class East Perth. The day after they moved in, Martha Rendall, now thirty-eight, joined them as common-law wife to Morris and stepmother to the children, whom she insisted call her 'Mother'. She also demanded that Thomas introduce her to new friends as 'Mrs Morris'. She told people that she and Morris were married and insisted that the bride in Morris and Sarah's wedding photo displayed on a mantelpiece was her. This puzzled many acquaintances, because dumpy, pudding-faced Rendall looked nothing like thin, sharp-featured Sarah.

To pay the rent and put food on the table for their large family, Morris often trekked to rural areas for weeks at a time to ply his trade as a carpenter, leaving Rendall to care for the children in the tiny house. In her astute work, *Murdering Stepmothers: The Trial and Execution of Martha Rendall,* writer Anna Haebich reflected, 'Money pressures, life alone with five children in an overcrowded dwelling and the effort and drudgery of housework no doubt contrasted with Rendall's dream of life with Morris. Added to this were the stresses and expense of nursing her stepchildren through serious illnesses.'

In early 1907, four of the children, Annie, Olive, Arthur and George, were stricken with diphtheria and typhoid. Local doctor John Cuthbert administered bismuth-based tinctures for their sore and swollen throats. The sick children cried and moaned in their pain, and rarely slept. The household, always unruly, collapsed into pandemonium. At the end of her tether, Rendall often lost her temper and smacked the children. Then, undoubtedly debilitated by the pressures of her unenviable situation, she also fell ill.

After a while, the sick children and Rendall responded to treatment. It was in the weeks after their recovery that things got nasty.

In June 1907, Annie Morris, aged nine, the second youngest of Morris's children, suddenly experienced convulsions, diarrhoea, severe stomach cramps and vomiting attacks. Dr Cuthbert believed her symptoms were the aftermath of diphtheria. He prescribed a tincture of opium to ease her discomfort, but on 28 July the little girl died. The official cause of death was epilepsy and a weak heart.

The following month, Dr Cuthbert was called back to Robertson Street to hear 7-year-old Olive complain of terrible pain in her mouth, throat, stomach and chest. The doctor examined her but could find no trace of diphtheria, and over the next days, with no clue as to what was causing the problem, watched helplessly as her condition deteriorated. He summoned a Perth City Council medical officer to inspect the house – the sanitation systems were given the all clear, nor could the inspector identify harmful toxins in the water pipes or wall paint. He quizzed Rendall on Olive's diet and it too passed muster. The inspector, like Dr Cuthbert, could offer no explanation for the child's illness. Olive passed away on 16 October. Official cause of death: enteric fever and haemorrhage.

Ten months later, it was 15-year-old Arthur's turn. The symptoms were the same as Olive's. Dr Cuthbert prescribed sulphurous acid with glycerine, but this panacea had no effect. Alarmed, he summoned reinforcements. Dr Robert Newton, throat specialist Dr James Kingston and pathologist and bacteriologist Dr John Cleland all examined the wasted and fast-fading Arthur and threw up their hands, clueless. Newton noticed 'a peculiar membranous condition of the throat, and portion of the back of the tongue. I had never seen anything like it before'. Arthur died on 8 October 1908.

There followed a post-mortem, which Rendall, somewhat bizarrely, insisted be conducted at home. Present were Dr Cuthbert, Dr Cleland, a Dr John Cumpston, Thomas Morris and Martha Rendall who, the medicos later reported, 'acted strangely'. When they arrived, they said, she had approached them aggressively and declared that she intended to remain in the room throughout the post-mortem to prevent them taking away 'any portion of Arthur's body'. Dr Cuthbert made the incision and found congestion and blood in Arthur's stomach and bowel. He next examined the liver and spleen, but when he attempted to probe the throat and chest cavity Rendall leaped in and stopped him, then refused point-blank to allow him to take tissue samples for analysis at the medical laboratory. *Very* odd behaviour, thought the doctors. Meanwhile Thomas Morris stood back from the bed, away from the fray. Dr Cumpston suspected poisoning and wanted to summon the coroner to finish the autopsy, but he was overruled by his colleagues. Dr Cuthbert wrote on Arthur's death certificate that he was a victim of 'cardiac failure, ulceration of the bowels and haemorrhage'.

Three children taken in rapid succession by a mystery illness was every parent's worst nightmare. At her stepson's funeral at the local Methodist church, Rendall wore black and wept, just as she had done at the funerals of Annie and Olive. The community wept too and embraced their grieving friends who, all who knew them then readily agreed, seemed to be model parents. They prayed that the remaining sons, George and William, would not follow their siblings to the grave and prayed even harder that, if some kind of epidemic had gripped the community, that their own little ones would be spared.

In April 1909, six months after Arthur's death, 14-year-old George Morris disappeared from home. His father called the police to report him missing, but his whereabouts were soon discovered. George had gone to the Subiaco home of his mother, Sarah, blurting out a dreadful story. He claimed he had fled because he was being poisoned by his stepmother Martha Rendall, who had swabbed his throat with spirits of salt (a commercial form of hydrochloric acid), a substance used in soldering metal, and poured it into his tea. He and his brother William were convinced that Rendall had done away with Annie, Olive and Arthur in the same way.

Distraught at the murder of her children, and furious that according to George they had been slain by her hated rival, Sarah contacted the police. A subsequent coronial inquiry before Mr A.S. Roe recommended that Martha Rendall and Thomas Morris be charged with Arthur's murder. Rendall received the news stoically. Morris was aghast, crying that he would never harm his children and that his beloved Martha was innocent too. In fact, he said, Martha was 'a perfect jewel'.

The trial at the West Australian Supreme Court got under way on 7 September 1909, before Acting Chief Justice McMillan. Rendall and Morris pleaded not guilty to the charge of wilfully murdering Arthur Joseph Morris. The prosecution accused Rendall of administering hydrochloric acid to the children, with Morris's blessing. No motive for the crime was offered. Although the evidence was circumstantial, said Crown Solicitor A.E. Barker, 'We suggest that the boy – and his sisters – met his death by poison criminally administered.'

Rendall, who wore a black gown and veil for the duration of the trial, maintained her composure and a haughty silence, remaining impassive as relentless allegations of cruelty and infanticide were made against her. Her demeanour was not unlike that of Lindy Chamberlain decades later and, as in her case, before a word of evidence had been aired in court the yellow press and some sections of the public had concluded that anyone so cold, so unsympathetic, someone who refused to break down, confess and beg forgiveness, was surely guilty.

The Truth bellowed, 'Astounding allegations of devilish deeds. Innocent little sufferers have their throats swabbed with spirits of salt: [the evidence] has been appalling in its awful allegations of a callous criminality, demoniacal and diabolical to the utmost degree.' The paper erroneously reported that Rendall laughed when the agonies of her stepchildren were recounted. Outside the court, citizens bayed for her blood.

As Anna Haebich accurately noted, 'Alternative explanations that her apparent lack of emotion was a public mask ... that reflected a state of rigid fear and shock at the web of horror in which she was suddenly enmeshed were not considered.'

Prosecution witnesses included George and William Morris, Sarah Morris, chemists, doctors and neighbours, those same citizens who had once offered Rendall and Morris loving support but who now, in hindsight, seemed to consider the people next door the incarnation of evil.

George Morris testified that his father had instructed him to go to the chemist and buy spirits of salt for Rendall when his sister Olive was sick.

Yes, he had seen his father use the spirits of salt while soldering a washing dish, but he was sure that he had witnessed Rendall mix the substance with the medicine prescribed by Dr Cuthbert in a cup and paint the sick Arthur's throat with it using a brush with a long wire handle. 'Arthur was always crying,' swore George, 'but more particularly when his throat was being painted.'

George told the court that on Arthur's demise he had heard his father say to Rendall, 'I have only got two [children] left now', that Rendall had replied, 'Anyone would think I was the cause of it', and that Morris retorted, 'So you are'. He had also seen Rendall beat Olive 'for the least little thing' and apply a substance to the blades of a pair of scissors used for cutting rags and poke them down Olive's throat when she was ill.

George said he had come to suspect that Rendall had poisoned his sisters and brother, and when, after Arthur died, he noticed his own tea tasting bitter and developed a sore throat he feared she was poisoning him too, and ran for his life to his mother.

As the trial wore on, the demonising of Martha Rendall gathered momentum as a small army of people who were prepared to say negative things about her was paraded before the jury by the Crown prosecutors.

Neighbour Florence Feakes recalled for the court a dreadful scene that she said took place one day when she visited Rendall and the sick Annie. Entering the girl's bedroom she found Annie weeping bitterly, and moaning, 'Take me to Mother! I want my mother!' Feakes had asked Annie where the pain was and she indicated her mouth and chest. In an unrelated but telling aside, she reported that Rendall had once pointed to a wedding photo and remarked that it was 'Mr Morris and me on our wedding day'. Feakes had thought that while it was definitely Morris in the shot, Rendall must have changed a lot because she looked nothing like the thin woman in the wedding gown.

Another neighbour, Mrs Carr, testified that she often heard children's 'pitiful cries' coming from Rendall and Morris's house next door and that the ailing Arthur once called to her from his window, 'Murder! Police! Save me, Mrs Carr!' Looking over the fence, she then had seen 'Martha doing something to his throat'. Carr said she'd done nothing because, after all, she was not the lad's mother, but had advised Rendall to take the boy to hospital. Rendall had replied that she would not allow it.

Another time, while visiting Rendall, she saw Arthur in bed. When she asked him how he felt he had groaned, 'Not much better.' She went on, 'He seemed to be exhausted and was hardly able to speak. I thought he was going to die every moment. There were large clots of blood in the room.' She had seen by Arthur's bedside a wire-handled brush, a bottle cap and an open bottle. She picked up the bottle to smell its contents. 'Good God, woman!' she had exclaimed to Rendall, 'You are not using that for that boy's throat! It is enough to kill a horse.' Rendall had been defensive and assured Carr that the doctor had prescribed the medicine. Just before Arthur died, testified Carr, Rendall had said to her, 'The boy will never get better. He is done.' To gasps from the gallery, Carr described how Rendall had thrown Arthur onto a wire stretcher on the veranda and snapped, 'There, die!'

David Lewis, who delivered bread, said he had been at Rendall's home once and seen Arthur struggling in bed, and Rendall had pointed to the sick boy's feeble efforts, cried, 'Look at him trying to get out of bed!' and laughed derisively.

Another neighbour, Jane Orton, told the packed court that she had been at Rendall's home during Arthur's illness and: 'I heard the boy giving utterance to distressed noises. Mrs Rendall did not take his illness seriously. She did not appear to be sorry for him and was very indifferent. She said the skin *always* came off his tongue.'

Dr Cleland testified that when he examined Arthur, he was shocked to hear that the wizened lad was fifteen; he would have guessed seven or eight. He noted the membranous condition of Arthur's throat but did not know the cause. He agreed, however, with prosecutor Barker that 'this membrane and microscopic structure might be accounted for after hydrochloric acid in certain strength had been applied to the mouth and gullet'. Cleland said that yes, it was possible that Arthur's death had been caused by the swabbing of his throat with hydrochloric acid. The doctor recalled the scene at the autopsy when Rendall was anxious that he did not take tissue samples for examination, and that he and the other doctors had been struck by her 'callousness'.

In his testimony, Dr Cumpston certainly thought Rendall's behaviour at the post-mortem was 'unusual. She showed no signs of being affected by the somewhat gruesome nature of the proceedings'. The condition and appearance of Arthur's body's organs, he said, were consistent with irritant poisoning.

George's 17-year-old brother, William, now told his tale of a wicked stepmother straight from the pages of the Brothers Grimm. He and his siblings had always been happy and healthy until his parents split up and the terrifying Martha Rendall came on the scene. The very day before little Annie fell ill, he declared: 'She refused to do something for [Rendall] because she was not her real mother, and she was thrashed [by Rendall and Morris], and sent to bed without anything to eat. Next day she was brought home from school sick.' Annie's condition had deteriorated over the next weeks and then she died. 'I was not allowed into her room,' said William. Rendall had told him and the other children that Annie had a weak heart.

After Annie's death and while Olive was ill, William continued, he had seen a bottle of spirits of salt in the girls' room. He had not seen the substance in the house before his sisters became sick. He said that Olive's throat was terribly painful and that she was delirious and crying. She had called for him but, as with Annie, Rendall had prevented him from seeing her. When Olive passed away, Rendall had explained that she had died from a disease 'that doctors did not understand'.

Shortly after Arthur was stricken with the same sore throat and symptoms as his late sisters, said William, Rendall had sent him to the chemist to buy sixpence worth of spirits of salt. The label on the bottle, he remembered, read 'Poison'. Arthur had told William that the medicine Rendall was making him sip from a small bottle cap burned his throat and chest, made him nauseous and caused his teeth to ache so much that he could not eat. Arthur had thought that the medicine Rendall was administering to him smelled like spirits of salt. 'A week later,' said William, 'he was dead.'

Naturally, when brother George had come to him to say that now *his* throat had begun to ache, William exhorted him to go to his mother, Sarah, in Subiaco and unload his suspicions.

In his final address, prosecutor Barker recapped the statements of the Crown witnesses and said that the crime of Rendall and Morris was 'as atrocious as anything that had yet been unfolded in a court of justice'. Then, even though the pair were on trial only for the murder of Arthur, he recalled in detail the deaths of each of the children. 'I do so,' he explained, 'to inform the jury that Arthur did not come by a natural or unintentional death. The evidence undoubtedly has a tendency to substantiate that. The throat symptoms in the case of the other children were repeated in the case of Arthur, and the other features, such as wasting, were common to all the three children.'

For the defence, Mr J.W. Clydesdale pointed out that after all the statements there was still no incontrovertible proof that Rendall administered hydrochloric acid to the children. The evidence was purely circumstantial. The prosecution had been unable to suggest, let alone establish, a motive. The Crown had not proved that Rendall and Morris were guilty beyond doubt, therefore they must go free.

Summing up before the jury retired to seek a verdict, Mr Justice McMillan opined that 'I have never had to deal with a trial that has caused me so much trouble and so much anxiety'. He hoped the jury would banish from their minds all the sensational newspaper articles that they had read, and that they hadn't let the salacious reports prejudice them against the defendants, who must be judged solely on the evidence that was presented in court. Intoned the judge:

> Morris turned his wife out to live with the female accused, with whom he is reported to have been on intimate terms in one of the other states. Even though she might be innocent of the crime of murder, there is evidence which, if true, shows that Martha Rendall has been guilty of gross cruelty to the children. But the jury is not here to try the two accused for either immorality or cruelty, but for one crime and one crime only – the crime of murder.

McMillan said that if George Morris was telling the truth, then Rendall was a monster, but 'if George was *not* telling the truth, the monster is in the witness'. If the latter, he must understand that he may be sending his father to his death.

Continued McMillan:

> The most important part of the boy's evidence is that he got spirits of salt for Rendall when Arthur was ill.The witness said the spirits of salt was put in a cup and with a brush was taken into Arthur's room and that Arthur was subsequently heard to cry out. You the jury should have no difficulty in drawing an inference from the facts if you believe the facts.

Too, said the judge, if Mrs Carr's testimony was true, 'it is impossible to find words to describe Rendall's conduct'.

The jury, after lengthy deliberation, exonerated Thomas Morris but convicted Martha Rendall.

Before Justice McMillan passed sentence he ordered her to stand in the dock and asked if she had anything to say. 'I am not guilty,' she said simply.

Then, in his gravest voice and staring sternly at the defendant, McMillan said:

> You have been found guilty of one of the most horrible crimes of which I have ever heard. You are a woman apparently responsible for your actions. Nobody has suggested that you are mad. If you are in your senses, you must be a moral deformity. Throughout the case I have been astonished by your demeanour. I can only term you an extraordinary woman. The jury has done its duty and now I must do mine. There is only one sentence provided by law for the crime of which you have been found guilty, and that sentence it is my duty to pass ... I sentence you to hang by the neck until you are dead.

As many in the community applauded the verdict ('Hanging is too good for Martha Rendall,' railed one Mary-Anne Martin in a letter to a newspaper. 'She should be given spirits of salt in the same way she gave it to the children.'), a number assailed the editors of newspapers with recriminatory, sarcastic and bitter letters disputing the verdict and decrying 'barbaric' capital punishment.

The most affecting missive of all, however, was a sad and gentle plea from the now-freed Thomas Morris. It appeared in *The West Australian* on Thursday 30 September 1909, addressed to the editor:

> Sir,
>
> I pray you will grant me a small space in your valuable paper for this, my appeal on behalf of Martha Rendall. I am away in the backblocks seeking work, having spent my last penny. All I possess, even my tools, were sold for my defence, so that I am powerless to do anything further than to write to you on her behalf. I have waited until now, hoping someone would take the matter up. I do not know who is the proper person in authority to write to, so I appeal through *The West Australian* to that person. I know that some of the evidence given against me was incorrect. Then why not the same against her? I also know now that evidence could have been called in support of our case, but was not. I left everything to the lawyers, and no doubt they did their best with the money they had. But I say fearlessly, before God, I was innocent and so is Martha Rendall. She was everything that was good and kind and attentive to my children and did everything for their benefit. I know her better than anyone else, and I say she was incapable of doing what was attributed to her. She may have appeared hard outwardly, but no woman ever had a more tender heart than she, and I say it would be a shame and disgrace to this country and humanity if the dread sentence were carried out, because I believe that sooner or later her innocence will be proved, and I feel I cannot keep silent and allow this injustice (for injustice it is, God knows) to be done to an innocent woman. – Yours, Thomas N. Morris.

If the 'proper person in authority' ever read Morris's plea, there is no record of his acknowledging it, let alone acting upon it.

Rendall's spiritual adviser, the Reverend Thomas Allen, made a special plea for clemency to the Governor of Western Australia, Sir Gerald Strickland, Premier Major-General Sir Newton James Moore, and the state's attorney-general. The Premier consulted his ministers and then the trial judge, Mr Justice McMillan. In the end, it was decided the law must take its course. Rendall would be executed on the morning of 6 October 1909.

Meanwhile, as argument raged across the nation, the doomed woman sat quietly in her cell reading her Bible and Book of Common Prayer, quietly and mechanically proclaiming her innocence to her warders and the Reverend Allen, and looking forward to Thomas Morris's next visit. When Morris arrived she would smile radiantly and they would embrace. Sometimes, when the realisation hit them that this visit would be one of the last times they would meet, they would cry.

Their last meeting was at 7 pm on 5 October. According to gaol officials, both were 'utterly broken up' as they said their final farewell. Afraid that Rendall's body would be dissolved in quicklime in a pit on the prison grounds, as routinely happened with the bodies of executed prisoners in some other states in those days, Morris asked if he could take charge of his lover's remains. When he was assured by prison superintendent W.A. George that her body would be buried in a special section of Fremantle cemetery he expressed gratitude and withdrew his request.

After Morris left, Rendall regained her composure and told Superintendent George, 'I am to meet God tomorrow morning. I am not afraid. It's a terrible thing. I will be brave because I am innocent.'

And she made a handwritten statement which George released to the press:

> ... in spite of the mental anguish which I have suffered through being found guilty of murdering Arthur Morris, and the accusation that I had done the same to the other two children, and the solemn appeals made by my spiritual adviser to confess in order to receive

> the mercy of God through Jesus Christ, and that I might be fortified on the gallows with the courage that I had made a clear statement to man and God, I most solemnly wish to say I am innocent of having done anything that injured the children in any degree. The spirits of salt were never used by me on the children. If I had done it I would confess. I believe it would be most contrary to my most solemn convictions to profess to man to be innocent when before God I should be found guilty which would be to me dying with a lie on my lips and a crime on my soul unconfessed – unforgiven.

Just before 8 am on 6 October, Martha Rendall walked calmly and unassisted from her cell to the gallows. There, she once more denied her guilt before God, and went to her death. As Superintendent George promised, her body was disposed of in a grave in an out-of-the-way corner of Fremantle cemetery reserved for the remains of convicts and suicides.

CHAPTER 13

THE SLAUGHTER OF ANITA COBBY

John Travers, First Among Five: Kidnappers and murderers

1986

On the sultry summer evening of Sunday 2 February 1986, Garry Lynch would later say, he was looking out of his bedroom window wondering why his daughter, Anita Cobby, was so late coming home from work. High in the sky, lit up by the moon, he saw a group of clouds that before his eyes scudded together to form a monstrous face. He learned later that this was about the time Anita, a 26-year-old nurse and former beauty queen, was plucked from Newton Street in the Sydney suburb of Blacktown by a carload of murderous hoons.

Garry and his wife Grace fretted through the night, but by dawn Anita, a reliable and responsible young woman, had still not turned up at their house nor telephoned to say she was staying at a friend's. All that day the Lynches were worried sick, sure now that something was seriously amiss. At 6.30 pm Garry went to Blacktown police station and reported his daughter missing. The police report contained a description of Anita (175 centimetres tall, thin, hazel eyes, dark hair, last seen wearing red and white striped jeans and a white singlet top with three buttons at the neck), and the information: 'Last seen at 9 pm, 2/2/86, walking into the entrance of Central railway station ... Fail to return home and fail to report for duty at the Sydney Hospital at 1.30 pm on 3/2/86 and failed to telephone off sick.'

The disappearance of the former model and Miss Western Suburbs in the 1979 Miss Australia Quest was solved in the saddest way on the sweltering fourth of February when her body was found in a paddock on Reen Road, Prospect, off the Hume Highway and 3 kilometres from Blacktown railway station. Anita lay in a pool of blood. She had been savagely beaten, pack-raped and her throat had been cut.

The NSW Government offered a reward of $100 000 for information leading to an arrest. Premier Neville Wran declared Anita Cobby's murder 'one of the foulest crimes of the century and the animals responsible must be brought to justice'. A task force of twenty experienced detectives was formed to find Anita's killer or killers and Australia shuddered with revulsion when the horrific details of her murder were reported. What monster, the nation demanded to know, was capable of such savagery?

A number of people in the Blacktown area had an idea. Calls trickled in to task force headquarters from members of the public, many callers asking to remain anonymous. 'I've no proof, but there *is* someone who might have committed this terrible act' was the gist of their remarks. 'You might not be wasting your time if you made some enquiries about a bloke by the name of John Travers.'

John 'Trawney' Travers was a skinny, scowling 18-year-old, a rapist and bash artist with the disposition of a tiger snake, who came from a dysfunctional family and had been getting into strife since a child. Travers had an horrific party trick. He would have sex with a sheep, slit its throat and lie with it while it died in its own blood. Then he would barbecue the beast and eat the meat.

He and his six siblings had been raised by their mother, Sharon, and father, Ken, first in a Housing Commission home at Mt Druitt and then, having been ordered to leave the government home because of their obnoxious behaviour, in a $35-a-week white weatherboard and brick bungalow in Doonside.

Ken Travers was not adverse to physically chastising his brood. John reacted stoically, refusing to let his mother and siblings know that he was hurting. Sharon said that her son was a happy baby and toddler and as a little boy played footy and rode his bike, but he had 'turned bad' around the age of ten.

Ken quit the family in 1981, leaving the children in the care of Sharon, who suffered from Cushing's syndrome, a hormonal condition whose most obvious symptom is obesity. Sharon Travers' 140 kilogram weight made leaving the house literally impossible. Her days were spent on the lounge or in bed watching television. Her bulk prevented her from cooking, doing housework or caring for her brood. There was little money. Bills went unpaid. Often when the electricity had been cut off the family would be left to sit in the cold and dark. Sometimes John saved the day when he stole poultry from neighbours' chicken coops, and killed, plucked and cooked the birds.

From his early teenage years, Travers waged a drug- and alcohol-fuelled campaign of terror in the neighbourhood. He graffitied neighbours' walls with the words 'FUCK' and 'KILL' in red. He smashed their windows with rocks and shot birds out of the sky with his air rifle. He fed live chickens to his bull terriers Slut and Arse, and laughed as the chickens were bloodily dismembered and devoured. Then he'd set the dogs on children. Most days he'd drink a bottle of whisky or a flagon of cheap wine. He smoked marijuana before he reached his teens and was busted for possessing the drug and a bong when he was just thirteen. He tried heroin, but because he had an aversion to needles preferred drugs he could smoke.

Not that his fear of needles extended to tattooing. Travers covered his body with homemade tattoos, using needle, cotton wool and Indian ink.

There were hearts, lips, a teardrop under his left eye and on his penis the legend 'I Like Fucking Cunts'. He pierced his nipples and hooked a chain through the sleepers.

Travers was expelled from Shalvey High, then ejected from Doonside High for exposing himself to a teacher, and ended up at Newman High in Greystanes, where he fared badly at every subject but tech drawing. He was forever assaulting classmates and abusing teachers. He laughed at the kids who studied and played sport, much preferring to smoke marijuana and hash in the school toilets. He left Newman High after Year 10, and was not missed.

Travers hired on at Riverstone Abattoirs, proving himself adept with blades, and quite enjoyed hacking into the carcasses, but regular work was anathema to him and he soon quit and survived on the dole. That was enough to buy dope and alcohol, junk food, and petrol for the cars he and his mates stole. He complemented his welfare payments by burgling houses and fencing the stolen goods, usually electrical appliances.

For a while he lived with his maternal grandmother, Loylene, possibly the only person he would ever love. He was devastated when she died of cancer in 1983.

Most people who came into contact with him copped his fists or his vicious tongue, but women were particular targets. He would abuse them with vile epithets, whether he knew them or not, in the street and from his car. 'They're good for fucking. That's it,' one acquaintance heard him say.

At sixteen, Travers was convicted of stealing a car and being in possession of an unlicensed and modified rifle and sent to Cobham Remand Centre. Both there, and when he was released and continued his rampage in the outer western suburbs, he was feared and despised. But his outlaw aura was attractive to many easily-led kids in the area, and soon he found himself the leader of a lowlife band which included Les, Michael and Gary Murphy and Mick Murdoch. These youths, like their leader all from dire backgrounds, outdid themselves to do Trawney's bidding and inveigle themselves into his good books. They fought for him, assaulted young women for him, nicked for him. Mick Murdoch, through attrition and, it's reported, his willingness to sleep with Travers, won the prime position as Trawney's best mate.

As Travers passed into his late teens his crimes became more perverted and despicable. He carried a large hunting knife. He raped a woman at a party and police believe that he indecently assaulted more than a dozen other women who did not report him for fear of what he would do to them if he found out. He beat up and raped gay men and was cruel to animals. After he bit the head off a kitten, his mother fretted, 'Oh well, you know what 18-year-olds are like when they get together, biting the heads off kittens, swallowing goldfish ... a lot of kids go through that stage.' She was sure, too, that her son had 'a normal attitude to sex'.

In her bestselling book, *Someone Else's Daughter: The Life and Death of Anita Cobby*, Julia Sheppard wrote that '[Travers' mates] claimed to have seen him have intercourse with chickens, lambs, pigs and sheep ...' Not a peccadillo easily forgotten, and when Anita Cobby was killed many remembered the perversions of John Travers.

In early 1985, Travers attacked and raped a young woman at Toongabbie. This time, because he feared that she, unlike his other victims, would tell the police, he fled with three friends to Western Australia. Moving into a rented house in the town of Falcon, near Mandurah, south of Perth, it was business as usual. Getting stoned and drunk, mugging and assaulting anyone unlucky to stray into his path. He pretended to befriend a 17-year-old gay youth and raped him at knifepoint in a public toilet. His mates took photos.

When Travers returned to Sydney in late 1985, he proudly showed the photographs to his aunt, who was appalled. Later on that aunt, who was to enter Australian criminal folklore as 'Miss X', would be instrumental in her nephew's conviction for killing Anita Cobby.

After Travers committed the crime that would destroy so many lives, including his own, the report of a psychologist who interviewed him in prison was aired in court. Noted Dr Hugh Jolly:

> In the period leading up to the killing, Travers lived a half-crazed, reckless sort of life intoxicated with this and that, aggressive, paranoid and very unstable ... though I would not say he was suffering a major psychiatric illness, meaning that he was not

grossly psychotic … the harm done to Mr Travers when he was a child almost certainly, bit by bit, led to the present situation … it does seem to me that Mr Travers was beaten into a situation where insecure aggression was his only coping mechanism against a [perceived] hostile world.

Dr Jolly felt that the death of Loylene, Travers' beloved grandmother and mother surrogate, was a catalyst for his crimes:

> It seems to me that her loss was the trigger to the acting of all sorts of destructive feelings … I think he hurt someone quite badly with a piece of plastic-covered pipe because he said he had to 'let it out'. From shortly after his grandmother's death, it is my opinion that Mr Travers became markedly paranoid.

Travers' atrocities mounted through the blistering summer of 1985–86. Something dark was slithering in his soul. Came the time at a barbecue in Doonside when he mounted the sheep from behind, had sex with it, slit its throat, lay beside it as it expired, and when it was finally dead barbecued it and threw the gnawed bones over the fence into a neighbour's swimming pool.

Around 9.45 pm on 2 February 1986, Anita Cobby alighted at Blacktown from the 9.12 train from Central. As always, she went to a public telephone box at the station to call her father to come and collect her, but tonight she found the phone vandalised and out of order. So she made the fateful decision to walk the 1.5 kilometres home. When Travers, the Murphys and Murdoch, all stoned and drunk and trawling for someone they could mug and rob for petrol money, saw Anita walking alone on Newton Road, Travers ordered the driver of their car to pull up beside her …

After the slaughter Travers, voice flat, eyes devoid of expression, said to Mick Murdoch, 'I cut her throat ... I think I cut a couple of her fingers off 'cause she put her hand up. It's me first [murder].' When Murdoch asked Travers what killing somebody felt like, Travers replied, 'Like nothing.'

Armed with the information from the public of Travers' reputation for extreme and depraved violence, police made him a suspect and placed him under surveillance. Another informant told detectives that just days before Anita Cobby was killed, Travers, Mick Murdoch and the Murphy brothers had stolen a green car and resprayed it grey. The men were seen driving in the grey car on the night of the murder.

On 19 February, detectives arrested Travers and Murdoch, ostensibly over the stolen car, at Travers' uncle's home in Wentworthville – they were found sharing a bed – and took them in for questioning. Les Murphy was also apprehended. Travers and Murdoch admitted stealing the car, but when the detectives put it to them they denied murdering Anita Cobby. 'I didn't slit that slut's throat,' Travers assured them.

Police found a large bloodstained knife in the house. Travers admitted to owning it but claimed the blood on the blade was that of a sheep whose throat he had cut a month or two back. Travers and Murdoch were locked up in the cells at Blacktown police station while the search continued for Gary and Michael, the remaining Murphy brothers.

Then Travers' aunt, the one to whom he had gloated over the homosexual rape in Western Australia, contacted police and said she feared that he might have killed Anita Cobby. She mentioned his violence, his predatory ways, his treatment of women as meat. Coincidentally, Travers asked if his aunt, whom he trusted, could visit him in his cell and bring him cigarettes. He tearfully confessed to her that he had raped and murdered the nurse and that the other four had raped and beaten her.

The aunt told police and returned to his cell, now wired for sound. Once more, in a 25-minute conversation, he admitted the killing, and this time it was all on tape.

When Miss X had asked Travers if he had killed Anita Cobby, he replied, 'I killed her because …'

'Because why?' said Miss X. 'Why did you have to do that? Come here, come close, come close.'

'We were all drunk and she's fuckin' seen all of us,' said Travers, growing distraught.

'What, she saw your faces?'

'Yeah, and she got all our names 'cause I just ...'

'She got your names!'

'Yeah! ... someone had to do it,' said Travers.

'... the others said you had to do it?'

'Ah, they just, fuck, I said she's got to be done and they said ...'

'Who said it had to be done? You?'

'All of us,' said Travers.

'You all agreed?'

'Yeah, and they said, "Go on, Trawney, do your bit," so I just cut her ... they weren't gonna do it so I had to.'

Miss X later told author Julia Sheppard, 'I wanted details from him about the murder: what they did, in what order they had raped her. He didn't hesitate in the slightest.' Miss X had asked Travers, 'Did you have sex with her?' and he had told her he did and the others had too. At that point, wrote Sheppard:

> Miss X remembered, 'John's face lit up, his eyes ... they were inhuman. It was disgusting. The sheer joy. He was like somebody I didn't know. It was all I could do to stay. I wanted to be sick. It was horrific and it was something I couldn't cope with. He was not human and this was somebody I cared about. He was very proud of cutting her throat. He had well and truly dominated a woman. And he told me he had made her beg for her life.

On 22 February 1986, Travers, Murdoch and Les Murphy were charged with the murder of Anita Cobby. Gary and Michael Murphy would face the same counts when they were arrested shortly afterward.

After John Travers was arrested, someone who knew him told journalist Michael Cordell:

> That was John's way of life. That was the way he grew up. He accepted the killing of lambs and that. He accepted terrorising people. John lived that life. John believed a lot of things like that. Someone once

> said to me, 'Some people are put here from another planet that are acting as humans.' And the more and more I thought about it, I swore John was one of them.

Travers, knowing he had been caught dead to rights, pleaded guilty to each of the charges read out by Justice Maxwell when his, the Murphys' and Murdoch's trial got underway at Sydney's Supreme Court on 16 March 1987. Though declaimed in legalese, the charges imparted the evil that was done that night:

> Under Section 19 of the Crimes Act, on the second day of February, 1986, at Prospect in NSW he did murder Anita Lorraine Cobby. Maximum penalty: Penal servitude for life.
>
> Under Section 90A of the Crimes Act on the second day of February, 1986, at Blacktown in NSW, he did take away Anita Lorraine Cobby with intent to hold Anita Lorraine Cobby for advantage. Maximum penalty: Penal servitude for 20 years.
>
> Under Section 96 of the Crimes Act, on the second day of February, 1986, at Blacktown in NSW, he did assault Anita Lorraine Cobby and rob her of certain property, to wit, one bag, one purse and a quantity of clothing, and immediately after robbing the said Anita Lorraine Cobby, did use other corporal violence to the said Anita Lorraine Cobby, thereby wounding the said Anita Lorraine Cobby. Maximum penalty: Penal servitude for life.
>
> Under Section 61C of the Crimes Act, on the second day of February, 1986, in Prospect in NSW he maliciously did inflict actual bodily harm upon Anita Lorraine Cobby with intent to have sexual intercourse with the said Anita Lorraine Cobby. Maximum penalty: Penal servitude for 12 years.

> Under Section 117 of the Crimes Act, on or about the 28th day of January, 1986, at Seven Hills in NSW, he did steal a Holden sedan ... Maximum penalty: Penal servitude for five years.

The Murphys and Murdoch, however, declared themselves not guilty of the first four charges on the grounds that their involvement in the beating, rape and murder of Anita Cobby was minimal and that Travers had been more responsible.

Summing up, prosecutor Alan Saunders flayed the defendants. Anita Cobby had endured 'two hours of terror, torture and degradation [by] craven cowards in an orgy of lust'. The attack had been committed 'in an unbelievably callous fashion'. Anita was 'the victim of unbridled lust culminating in the most brutal murder this state had ever known'.

On 10 June, the Murphy brothers and Murdoch, who had sniggered throughout proceedings, even when unbearable details of their crime were being heard, were found guilty on every charge. Six days later they, and Travers, were sentenced. That day the court was packed and outside a crowd had gathered to celebrate the Cobby killers getting their just deserts.

They were not disappointed. Like Travers, his co-accused would spend the rest of their lives in prison without possibility of parole. Justice Maxwell said that while it was accepted that Travers killed Anita Cobby, the others had assaulted, robbed and sexually assaulted the deceased and they had agreed that she must die because she could recognise them:

> There is no doubt that apart from the humiliation, degradation and terror inflicted upon this poor woman, she was the victim of a prolonged and sadistic physical and sexual assault, included repeated assaults, orally, anally and vaginally. Wild animals are given to pack assaults and killings. However, they do so for the purpose of survival and not as a result of a degrading animal's passion. Not so these prisoners. They assaulted in a pack for the purpose of satisfying their lust and killed for the purpose of identification. This is one of the most horrifying physical and sexual assaults I have encountered in my 40-odd years associated with the law. The

> crime is exacerbated by the fact that the victim almost certainly was made aware, in the end, of her pending death ... The circumstances of the murder ... prompt me to recommend that the official files of each prisoner should be marked 'never to be released'. If the Executive deems it proper in the future to consider their files, then I offer the advice proffered by a former and distinguished Chief Judge at Common Law, that the Executive should grant to the prisoners the same degree of mercy that they bestowed upon Anita Lorraine Cobby on the night 2 February, 1986. I do not think the community would expect otherwise.

When Justice Maxwell intoned the words 'Never to be released', Travers raised his eyes heavenwards.

Within weeks of their being gaoled, there were reports that all five had been bashed by fellow inmates. They had to be placed in protective custody. John Travers was the main target. He was frequently admitted to the prison hospital after sustaining serious injuries from being assaulted. According to crime reporter Norm Lipson, who covered the Anita Cobby case in detail, a rumour spread that 'he had barbed wire inserted in his rectum'.

Sharon Travers refused against all reason to believe that her son was guilty – 'he may think he did it, but I'm sure he didn't'. It was her feeling that the Murphys and Murdoch had got her son drunk and stoned, had murdered Anita Cobby, and when Travers regained consciousness convinced him that he in fact was the culprit.

She revealed that she, and Travers' siblings and their families, had been victims of vile abuse and occasional assaults from the public. Their life had become hell. She told how rubberneckers would cruise her street, ogling and photographing the house where the most reviled killer in Australian history once lived.

Sharon Travers said on national television that she had a feeling John would die in prison, sooner rather than later: 'I wait for a time when I wake up and turn on the telly to find out that someone's got to him. When I visit him, prisoners yell things at you when they know you are visiting. They have said, "You won't have to visit him much longer."'

As it happened, John Travers outlived his mother. Sharon died in December 1989, aged just thirty-nine. The official cause was Cushing's syndrome. Travers attended the funeral decked out in a dark suit, tie and sinister wraparound sunglasses. He was chained with a metal restraining belt, handcuffed, and guarded by four armed detectives.

From the moment they were sentenced, the killers were separated and have remained that way. All five have regularly been moved among the high-security prisons in New South Wales. But even when they are in the same gaol complex, such as Silverwater or Goulburn, authorities ensure there is no contact.

Today, Travers is incarcerated in maximum security at the Lithgow Correctional Centre, rated officially as one of the state's most dangerous criminals. He leads a mainly solitary life and is under heavy and constant surveillance. His every moment is regulated and observed by guards. Travers has come to terms with the fact that he will never be a free man and, says Norm Lipson, who has contacts at the prison:

> He has settled in to his miserable life behind bars with just one hour of exercise a day. He has been involved in a number of assaults both as a victim and aggressor and is said to have had a number of homosexual encounters. He doesn't get or want visitors. He is still said to be angry with Miss X and with his accomplices, whom he also blames for giving him up.

It seems that Travers developed a talent for art and crafts while behind bars. In May 2002 he was named as one of a number of prisoners who were earning money selling leatherwork through a gallery. Travers had a number of items for sale, including a large image of a motorbike on which he'd placed a $300 price tag. When Sydney's *The Daily Telegraph* got wind of it and published the story, his little enterprise was stopped.

For the past decade, Travers' co-offenders, Mick Murdoch and Gary, Les and Michael Murphy, have been housed at Goulburn maximum security prison. Like Travers, they are pariahs in the prison community, leading lonely lives, and have been attacked by other inmates. They are under constant surveillance and protection. They too are allowed just one hour a day of exercise. Murdoch, says Lipson, is the best behaved of the bunch.

In August 2006, the Murphy brothers were denied permission to attend their father's funeral because they were considered very high risk. However, prison officials allowed them each one extra phone call on compassionate grounds as well as access to the prison chaplain.

Like the Hoddle Street killer, Julian Knight, the Murphys enliven their days by scheming to beat the legal system. Les Murphy won some kind of Pyrrhic victory when he appealed against his two convictions for raping a 14-year-old girl at Bondi in 1981, and the magistrate ruled in his favour. He had been convicted on DNA evidence in 1997. The NSW Court of Criminal Appeal found that the judge who heard the case had erred. A new trial was ordered, but Murphy was again convicted.

In June 2001, the NSW Parliament passed the Crime Legislation Amendment Act ensuring that 'never to be released' prisoners can only be released if dying or incapacitated. But this did not deter the Murphys. In December 2006, Gary and Les began proceedings in the NSW Supreme Court to seek re-determination of their life sentences and have a parole date set. Their bid failed.

Like Travers, they'll die in gaol.

The worst of humanity, the best of humanity.

Throughout their ghastly ordeal which, of course, continues to this day, Garry and the aptly named Grace Lynch, Anita Cobby's parents, have conducted themselves with a dignity and humanity that borders on the saintly. At first Garry, who had a stroke soon after the killers' trial, wanted only vengeance for the slayers of his daughter: 'I wanted to kill them with my bare hands. Just leave me alone with them for five minutes, I pleaded to the police.' But then, with his memories of Anita and his undying love for her locked safe and inviolable in his heart, he set about getting on with his life. He embraced Grace and said, 'We're not going to sit in a corner wearing black. Right then we made a decision to live.' He explored Eastern religion and spent time on an ashram, during which a holy man, he once told this writer, reached into his mouth and retrieved 'a strange, jellyfish-like object from deep inside me. He threw the object away, and with it disappeared all my rage'.

In 1989, with his 'little mate' Anita encouraging him every step of the way, Garry Lynch began working as a community member of the NSW Department of Corrective Services Serious Offenders Review Board, evaluating the progress of more than seven hundred prisoners as they served their sentences and became eligible for parole. 'I'm an enigma to them,' he said. 'They say, "How can you, of all people, even look at a crim like me?"'

He has also devoted himself to offering compassion and support to people just like himself and Grace, the victims of crime. 'Has God chosen me to help these people? It may be so. What I've been through enables me to help others. Maybe it's a gift God has given me that makes me able to help soothe others' pain. When I speak to people who have lost loved ones, the words just come out and have a meaning. It seems to work wonderfully. It helps, too, that I'm a bit of a gasbag!'

Today, Garry is ailing. Aged eighty-nine, by 2007 he was largely confined to his home, the same home to which Anita failed to return on 2 February 1986. He reads spiritual works and lavishes love on Grace, now eighty-one, and their surviving daughter, Kathryn.

CHAPTER 14

SUFFER THE CHILDREN

Kathleen Folbigg: Serial killer
1989–1999

It's one of the attractions – and nightmares – of policing that an officer can never know how a day on the job is going to pan out. It was 1 March 1999, and one minute Detective Senior Constable Bernie Ryan was hot on the heels of the perpetrators of a home invasion in the town of Singleton in rural New South Wales. Next minute he had been assigned to the most momentous and disturbing case of his career. Around 8 pm, Ryan's mobile phone rang. It was the station. 'Drop what you're doing and go to the hospital,' said the duty officer. 'A baby is dead and it's the fourth child of this couple to die in ten years.'

Ryan, an affable father of two and keen Rugby League fan, and his colleague Mick Prentice inspected the sad little bundle that was

19-month-old Laura Folbigg's body and spent some time talking to her parents, Kathleen and Craig. During their chat, Craig Folbigg confirmed to Ryan and Prentice what the duty officer had said, that Laura was the fourth Folbigg child to die. The first three – Caleb, who had passed away at nineteen days, Patrick at eight months, and Sarah at eleven months – explained the father, had died either of natural causes or Sudden Infant Death Syndrome (also known by its acronym SIDS or by the colloquial 'cot death'); he thought that Laura had too.

Either Craig and Kathleen Folbigg were the unluckiest couple alive, thought Ryan, or something is seriously amiss here. And while he wasn't – at that stage, at least – an expert on SIDS, Ryan didn't think he'd ever heard of a child as old as nineteen months dying from it. 'The parents seemed grief-stricken,' recalled Ryan, whose friendly personality belies his no-nonsense approach to his work, 'but you have to keep an open mind.'

Kathleen Folbigg, in the interview at Singleton Hospital that night, told Ryan and Prentice that when she came home that day, Laura was sound asleep in her cot. She had taken the baby to her own bedroom and laid her in the bed and that was where, later, after she heard the infant coughing, she had found Laura dead. Yet when Ryan went to the Folbiggs' house, he saw the baby's bottle and shoes in the lounge room, on a futon. Why on earth, he asked himself, would she have taken the bottle and shoes away from the bedroom where the tot was sleeping? Probably there was a very good explanation, but it did seem a bit odd. Could Kathleen Folbigg be lying? Had she been trying, without success, to put Laura to sleep with the bottle in the lounge room? Did she perhaps then lose her temper with Laura? Did she murder the child in a rage? And though at the hospital she talked about hearing the child's coughs before discovering her lifeless body, never again in subsequent interviews did she mention it.

'These were tiny details,' said Ryan, 'but they rankled.'

The detective felt there was a need to investigate the Folbiggs further. What he would find was deeply disturbing, and would lead to the capture of a serial killer.

When Kathleen Folbigg was eighteen months old, in 1968 her father, a small-time Welsh crook named Tom Britton, knifed her mother Kath Donavan to death in an Annandale, Sydney, street. Under arrest, the drunken Britton said he murdered his de facto wife because she was a bad mother and she had richly deserved what she got. 'I told her the baby was fretting for her and not eating. She said she couldn't care less and was not coming home. I killed her, and it can't be helped.' (Not that Britton himself was a paragon as a parent. It is believed he sexually abused Kathleen.)

With one parent dead and the other in prison, young Kathleen Britton was taken in by one of her mother's sisters, but before long the aunt gave her up, unable to deal with her uncontrollable behaviour. The child was sent to an orphanage before being placed with foster parents Deidre and Neville Marlborough, who lived with their daughter Lea, who was seventeen at the time, in the suburb of Kotara in Newcastle, the thriving industrial city 160 kilometres north of Sydney. Years later, Lea recalled how Kathleen, though cute and bubbly with a big smile, could be a difficult and jealous child, and took particular umbrage when she, Lea, gave birth to a son. Lea would recall how Kathleen would stand under the peach tree where she would be sent for misbehaving and sullenly stab her toe into the dirt.

After leaving high school at fifteen, Kathleen worked as a waitress in Newcastle and at eighteen began dating 23-year-old BHP worker Craig Folbigg. They were married in 1987 and after saving hard they purchased a home in the battlers' suburb of Mayfield. Though she could be temperamental and moody within the confines of their home, Kathleen was a party girl, popular and flirtatious, when out and about. Craig was proud of her social skills. His vivacious and noisy wife was the life of any gathering. She was known for her elaborately coiffed hair whose colour changed as frequently as her moods. When she put on a little weight, Craig would gently chide her. He liked her slim. So Kathleen became an obsessive gym-goer, sweating through energetic aerobic sessions and pumping light weights to tone and strengthen her body.

Kathleen and Craig's first child, Caleb, came into the world on 1 February 1989. Nineteen days later he was dead. Craig recalls being woken in the night by Kathleen's unearthly screams: 'My baby! There's something wrong with my baby!' Doctors diagnosed SIDS. Craig was devastated by the death of his son. Not so, it seemed to him, Kathleen. She seemed cold and unmoved, and after the funeral, said Craig, she partied as hard as before.

Craig was keen that they have another baby, and Kathleen agreed. On 3 June 1990, Patrick was born. For a short time he seemed healthy, and then, without warning, disaster struck. On 17 October, aged four and a half months, he was suddenly and for no apparent reason afflicted by terrible brain damage. The little boy went blind and suffered epileptic seizures. He died the following February. Doctors who examined Patrick's body said he had choked to death when his airways became blocked during a seizure. Again, to Craig, Kathleen seemed eerily unfazed by the tragedy.

In a bid to move on from the twin tragedies they had suffered, the young couple moved house after Patrick's death, setting up home at Thornton in the Hunter Valley. Given the trauma he had experienced, Craig Folbigg was reluctant to have a third child but, he said, Kathleen insisted that they try again. Sarah was born on 14 October 1992. She survived ten months. On 30 August 1993, Craig and Kathleen told doctors and police, they had found Sarah dead in her cot in her room. Kathleen had shaken Craig from sleep with the news that, yet again, something terrible had happened. She had been on her way to the toilet, Kathleen blurted out, and had detoured into Sarah's room to check on her. When she looked into her cot she was dead. Although there were a number of abrasions on Sarah's chin, once more SIDS was the designated cause of death.

Another new house, another new start. The Folbiggs left Thornton and relocated to Singleton. Craig said that he was aghast when in 1996 his wife said they must try for a fourth child. He objected strongly, feeling that he could not face the risk of another infant death, but she was adamant. She would leave him, she threatened, if he refused to make her pregnant. The doomed Laura was born on 7 August 1997, and it was her body that Bernie Ryan saw in Singleton Hospital on 1 March 1999.

After boning up on SIDS and conducting further interview sessions with Kathleen Folbigg, Ryan was, he says, 'as suspicious as hell, in the light of the other three kids' deaths'.

His suspicions were compounded when he discovered that no coronial inquiry had been conducted on any of the children's bodies. Had the diagnosis of SIDS, Ryan wondered, been arrived at too easily? Yes, SIDS could have been the cause of death, but there were other possibilities that seemed not to have been canvassed. Ryan was also dismayed to discover that police had never asked the Folbiggs' neighbours what kind of family they seemed. Did these people appear to be happy and loving? Or was there shouting and crying? Had they ever seen evidence of physical abuse of the babies? Anything at all that could shed light on the life the babies had been born into?

Ryan and his team gathered the medical files on the deceased children and pored over them. He read everything he could lay his hands on about SIDS, and corresponded with cot death experts in Australia and overseas. 'We planned to look at it all together and see if what killed them was SIDS, some metabolic problem never tested, or foul play,' he said.

Then one evening Detective Mick Prentice saw a program on SBS-TV about an American woman who had killed her five children – children whose deaths had all been incorrectly diagnosed. He phoned Ryan and told him to turn on SBS at once. Ryan did so, and subsequently emailed American paediatric forensic pathologist Dr Janice Ophoven, who had given evidence at the woman's trial. He told Dr Ophoven that he was working on a case with similarities to the one she had been involved in and asked would she be kind enough to review the findings he and his squad had made to date. Dr Ophoven obliged.

Bernie Ryan packaged up the Folbigg children's medical records and the organs – hearts, lungs and livers – which had been kept at the hospital, and despatched them to the United States. Dr Ophoven scrutinised the information and came back to Ryan with her belief that the chances of the children's deaths being caused by SIDS 'were a trillion to one'. Now Ryan flew to America and Britain to consult with other SIDS experts, all of whom shared Dr Ophoven's opinion, and who maintained that in all their experience they had never known or heard of three or more children in a single family falling victim to SIDS.

On Friday 21 May 1999, nearly three months after baby Laura died, Bernie Ryan received an anguished telephone call from Craig. Could they meet?

Craig told the detective that Kathleen had left him, but he also wanted to get something off his chest. He confessed that he and his wife had not told the truth about the death of Sarah, their third child. Earlier on the evening Sarah died, Kathleen had yelled at Sarah when she wouldn't go to sleep. Kathleen had later put Sarah to bed, not in her cot in her room, but in a bed in their room. Craig had woken at 1 am and found neither mother nor baby in the room. He had gone back to sleep, only to be woken at 1.20 by his wife's screams. He ran to Sarah's room and found the child dead and Kathleen standing nearby.

Ryan said he hoped Craig wasn't imparting this information mischievously in a bid to cause trouble for the wife who had split with him. Craig assured him this was not the case, then handed the detective Kathleen's diary, whose pages shockingly chronicled her deeply unbalanced and highly stressed state of mind as she became pregnant, gave birth to, and cared for each of her children.

Ryan interviewed Craig Folbigg at length that evening, and made an appointment to continue taking his statement on the following Sunday, 23 May. But Folbigg cancelled. On the Saturday he had surprised Kathleen with her lover, an American from her gym, at her new flat. A scene had ensued. The enraged husband smashed on the door of the apartment and when Kathleen opened up, had shouted at her, 'Why did my daughter have to die for you to achieve all this?'

That night, she returned to their marital home and indignantly wanted to know why he had said what he did. 'I'm not the only one who thinks you did it,' said Craig. 'The police and more than likely a lot of other people around town [do as well].'

Kathleen tearfully denied any involvement in Sarah's or her siblings' deaths. 'How could you think that of me?' she wept. 'I was their mother. I loved them. It broke my heart.' Craig wanted badly to believe her and when she begged him to take her back, he did. He also retracted what he told Bernie Ryan, and cancelled his second interview with the frustrated and furious detective.

At least, Ryan thought, he still had Kathleen's incriminating diary, made even more chilling by the frolicking angels and teddy bears on its cover. And soon afterward she obtained a second diary that had been found at the Folbigg house. Ryan read through it ...

> 3 June 1990: This was the day [Patrick] was born. I had mixed feelings this day. Wether [sic] or not I was going to cope as a mother or wether I was going to get stressed out like I did last time. I often regret Caleb and Patrick, only because your life changes so much.
>
> 22 June 1996: In my most dangerous mood, I'm not nice to be around and always want to be anywhere but where I am [which was at parties with] music and men to show off to.
>
> 14 October 1996: I would like to make all my mistakes and terrible thinking be converted ... obviously I'm my father's daughter.
>
> 4 December 1996: But I've already decided if I get any feelings of jealousy or anger ... I will leave Craig and baby, rather than answer being as before. I know now that battling wills & sleep depravaision [sic] were the causes last time.
>
> 17 February 1997 [when six months pregnant with Laura]: [Craig] should be for me forever, just because a baby is entering our life makes no difference. One day it will leave. The others did ... but this one's not going in the same fashion. This time Im [sic] prepared & know what signals to watch out for in myself.
>
> 11 June 1997: My brain has too much happening, unstored and unrecalled memories just waiting. Heaven help the day they surface & I recall. That will be the day to lock me up & throw away the key ... [Sarah and Laura] are chalk and cheese. And truthfully just as well. Wouldn't of [sic] handled another one

> like Sarah. [Laura] saved her life by being different. Totally she doesn't push my button anywhere near the extent [Sarah] did. Which is good for her ... With Sarah all I wanted was her to shut up. And one day she did.
>
> 16 December 1997 [when Laura was five months old]: Must cry to release my stress somehow. I'm starting to take it out on her. Bad move. Bad things and thoughts happen when that happens. It will never happen again.
>
> 28 January 1998: I lost it with Laura. I yelled at her so angrily that it scared her ... I nearly purposely dropped her on the floor and left her ... I feel like the worst mother on this earth. Scared that [Laura will] leave me now. Like Sarah did. I know I was short-tempered and cruel sometimes to her & she left. With a bit of help.

By the time he had finished reading these and other entries, Bernie Ryan believed that Kathleen Folbigg had murdered her four children. The diaries were, he said, 'the deepest look into her soul that you could get'.

He summoned her to Singleton police station, sat her down, and put a number of questions to her ...

He asked if she could close her eyes and see the faces of Caleb, Patrick, Sarah and Laura. She answered that she could remember what Laura, the last to die, looked like but could not bring sharply to mind the others' faces.

'How do you feel for those children?' Ryan now asked.

'For them? Or how do I feel for myself?'

'For them.'

'That they are somewhere peaceful, happy.'

'Do you really believe that?' Ryan continued.

'I don't know,' mused Folbigg. 'I prefer to believe that. That's probably what it is.'

Ryan now took another tack. 'Do you know what sort of person would kill four children?'

'I have no comprehension,' said Folbigg shortly, 'and I don't even want to think about it.'

'Were you responsible for the death of Caleb?' asked Ryan.

'No.'

'Were you responsible for the death of Patrick?'

'No.'

'Were you responsible for the death of Sarah?'

'No.'

'Were you responsible for the death of Laura?'

'No.'

The evidence against Kathleen Folbigg was largely circumstantial and the cautious detectives toiled on until early 2001 to compile the detailed data that they knew they would need to convict her.

On 19 April, Ryan knocked on her door – she and Craig had broken up again, this time for good – and placed her under arrest, charging her with the murder of each of her children, and of causing the grievous bodily harm to Patrick that resulted in his brain damage, blindness and epilepsy. 'She was very calm and matter of fact,' said Ryan, 'as if she was expecting it.'

Perhaps she was, but at her trial in the Supreme Court of New South Wales she pleaded not guilty to all counts.

Crown Prosecutor Mark Tedeschi QC told the court that although Kathleen Folbigg wanted to have children, she had killed the babies because they had impeded her lifestyle. She was, he said,

> preoccupied by her own life and looks ... desperate to resume working, going to the gym, her social regime, her sporting life, her sexual life ... There were times she couldn't abide the demands of parenthood. She resolved this by killing the children. She was totally obsessed by her own needs, wants and desires.

Exacerbating the situation, insisted the prosecution, were Folbigg's inability to sleep, her insecurity, and her impatience at what she perceived as her husband's lack of support. She smothered her children with a pillow or her hand 'in a flash of hatred, anger and resentment'.

Also raised by the Crown were the opinions of experts, such as Dr Ophoven, who believed that SIDS had not killed the children, the diaries in which she seemed to admit her guilt, and how the defendant had not appeared grief-stricken after each death. One neighbour testified that Folbigg was 'straight-faced' after baby Laura's death: 'There were no tears in her eyes. There was nothing.' Folbigg's foster sister Lea Brown said that at Laura's funeral, Folbigg changed virtually before her eyes 'from crying to being a totally different person. She was happy, laughing, enjoying a party'.

Craig Folbigg told the court his wife would behave in a terrifying manner when she was angry with the children. He recalled that on the night Laura died, Kathleen had 'pinned her to her high-chair and attempted to force-feed her before dumping her on the floor with the words, "Go to your fucking father!"'

Once during the trial, when a video recording of her 1999 interview with Bernie Ryan and other detectives was screened, Folbigg, who had been preternaturally calm to that point, wept uncontrollably and tried to leave the dock. She was restrained and taken to hospital where she was sedated. The trial was delayed for almost a week while she regathered her composure.

The defence, led by Peter Zahra, told the court that the case against his client was based almost entirely on circumstantial evidence. The Folbigg children had indeed died of SIDS or organic causes. There was no foul play. 'Every one of the children was in fact ill in their lifetime before their death.' There was evidence that Kathleen Folbigg was a loving and caring mother. Too, continued the defence, just because SIDS experts had never heard of three or more babies in the one family dying of SIDS did not mean that such a tragedy could never occur.

Bernie Ryan conceded the dearth of physical evidence against the defendant, but maintained that his case was strong:

> They said Caleb had a floppy larynx. Is it possible that contributed to his death? Yeah, anything's possible. Patrick had epilepsy and

> encephalitis. Could that have been the cause of his death? It's possible. Sarah had an elongated uvula. Could that have obstructed her airway and killed her? Anything's possible. Could Laura have died of SIDS? Maybe.

Ryan felt that the unlikelihood of all of the foregoing proving fatal to the infants, one after the other, would be sufficient to convict Folbigg.

So it proved. On 21 May 2001, the jury found that Kathleen Folbigg, who maintained her innocence through the trial and vehemently continues to do so, had murdered Caleb, Sarah and Laura and was guilty of inflicting grievous bodily harm upon and the manslaughter of Patrick. After directing a withering glance at her estranged husband, she collapsed in tears where she stood in the dock. She was duly sentenced to forty years in jail, with a non-parole period of thirty years.

In delivering the sentence, Supreme Court Justice Graham Barr described Folbigg as 'psychologically damaged' and noted that she was 'unable to ask for any systematic help or remove the danger she recognised by walking away from her child. She could confide in nobody. She told only her diary'.

Outside the court, Craig Folbigg was swamped by the media. He cried with relief that the trial was over and told reporters, 'My humble thanks go to [the members of the jury] whom I have never formally met, who today share the honour of having helped set four beautiful souls free. Free to rest in peace, finally.'

From her cell, Folbigg penned an angry letter to the *Sydney Morning Herald*:

> It took four years to come up with a totally circumstantial, non-factual, hearsay case. I now face being the most hated woman around at the moment and death threats are a real consideration ... It's a sad day when a mother can be put away for merely being a normal mother, who wrote down her emotions, anxieties and frustrations in bloody books.

Answering charges that she seemed aloof and unemotional, she wrote:

> I didn't have the choice to be any other way. I would not have been useful in my own defence. The day may come when it is time to release it all, but till my battle is done in clearing my name and reputation, that day is not yet.

She savaged her former husband:

> I have already suffered greatly at the hands of Craig and his ability to deliver with his tongue and his quite amazing ability to turn simple [facts] into exaggerated and extravagant tales.

Some qualified observers considered the possibility that Folbigg may have been genetically disposed to kill her children. Melbourne University associate professor Anne Buist, an authority in post-birth psychiatric disorders, told reporters, 'We know her father killed her mother, so we know there is a genetic issue there.' Concurred forensic psychiatrist Rod Milton, who gave evidence at the trials of John Glover, the so-called Granny Killer, and Ivan Milat:

> We can't discount what the father said: 'If I let [Kathleen Folbigg's mother] live she would have killed the kid.' That raises the genetic issue ... that maybe there's some sort of genetic tendency. We're in the land of not knowing, but to exclude it would be folly. The obvious genetic implications cannot be rejected. I think she must have lacked empathy for them, otherwise I don't see how she could have killed them.

While Bernie Ryan, Folbigg's nemesis, feels for the prisoner, he feels much more for her children, who would never grow up. His relentless pursuit of Kathleen Folbigg, he says, 'has always been about the children and the search for the truth'.

After his wife's conviction, Craig Folbigg turned down lucrative offers from television programs and magazines to tell his story. He was more intent on picking up the pieces of his life. He married again in 2004.

Bernie Ryan received a commendation and a promotion to detective inspector for his dogged police work.

From the outset, Kathleen Folbigg served hard time in Sydney's Mulawa Women's Detention Centre at Silverwater. She was reviled by fellow inmates as a 'rock spider', someone who hurts children. She was allowed from her cell to exercise alone for just two hours a day. Mainly she sat in her cell reading and studying foreign languages. She took to calling herself 'the most hated woman alive'.

In February 2005 the NSW Court of Criminal Appeal reduced Folbigg's maximum sentence by a decade and her non-parole period by five years. Said Justice Brian Sully, 'The prospect that [the original terms] offer the appellant is so crushingly discouraging as to put at risk any incentive she might have to apply herself to her rehabilitation.' Justice Sully, however, harked back to the diaries that had helped convince Bernie Ryan, and in due course a jury, that she was guilty. 'The picture painted by the diaries,' he stated, 'was one which gave terrible credibility to and persuasion to the inference, suggested by the overwhelming weight of the medical evidence, that the five incidents had been anything but extraordinary coincidences unrelated to acts done by the appellant.'

As things stand now, Kathleen Folbigg will be eligible for parole in 2028. By then she will be sixty-two years old. There will be time to start a new life, but she will be too old to bear more children.

CHAPTER 15

THE BRUNSWICK BABY FARMER

Frances Knorr: Serial killer

1892

In nineteenth century Australia there could have been few worse fates than to be a destitute single mother. With no government financial support or state-administered crèches, an impoverished woman left to care alone for her baby or child after her husband abandoned her, died or was imprisoned, or who had an illegitimate baby, had no choice other than to pay to have her infant cared for during the day while she eked out a living in a factory, or for weeks and months on end in a foster home if she secured a live-in job as a domestic servant. If she was very lucky, she found a responsible family who would care for the child as if it were their own. If she was unlucky, which was more often than not the case, she would find herself dealing with unscrupulous people – many were the mothers who returned to collect their offspring and found the child bruised from beatings and emaciated and ailing from being fed adulterated food and diluted milk. If she was *really* unlucky, a needy mother would place her baby with Frances Knorr.

Knorr, an English immigrant who set herself up in Melbourne as a baby minder – or, as the calling was known then, a baby farmer – was hanged at Pentridge Prison on 15 January 1894 after being found guilty of murdering three babies left in her care. Knorr operated an illegal, unregulated baby-minding service in her rented homes for mothers needing a safe place for their infants while they were at work. Knorr would demand that the mother pay her fee, around £2 a week, in full, in advance, sometimes for several weeks in one hit. With that money in hand, she would promptly sell the baby to a desperate childless couple, passing it off as an orphan, collecting from £5 to £20 for another payday. If she could not offload her charge this way, she would strangle the baby before renting another home in another suburb and beginning the process again. A mother would return on the appointed date to collect her child and find no trace of the baby or the woman she had trusted to care for it.

Melbourne's baby-farmer murderer may well have killed many more infants than the three with whose deaths she was charged. The true figure will never be known because a number of the children who disappeared while in her care were illegitimate, and mothers of children born out of wedlock or as a result of prostitution may not have wanted to bring attention to themselves or incur a fine for having an unregistered baby by reporting the infant missing. Nor can the number of babies she sold ever be known, for the same reason.

Knorr was born Frances Lydia Alice Thwaites at Hoxton New Town, Middlesex, in 1867, the daughter of prosperous tailor and hatmaker William Thwaites, who conducted his business in London's Chelsea. She was an unstable and promiscuous young woman who embarrassed her parents with numerous and indiscriminate affairs, often with soldiers passing through town. Frances, who also called herself Minnie, migrated alone to Australia aboard the *Abyssinia* in 1887 and found work in Sydney in domestic service and as a waitress. On 2 November 1889 she wed a German waiter named Rudolph Knorr. They co-managed an eating-house for a while but it burned down. Moving to Melbourne, they worked short stints there, she as a cook, he as a waiter. They had a daughter, Gladys, in 1892.

Contemporary police records describe Frances Knorr as 'aged about 25 years, height 5 ft 2 in [157.4 cm], fair complexion, very stout build, light brown hair, very large peculiar-shaped mouth, very talkative, and speaks with a lisp'.

When employment in Melbourne became scarce, the family relocated to Port Adelaide, in South Australia, where Rudolph resorted to crime to survive. His signature scheme was to hire furniture and then sell it, but he was no more successful as a criminal than as a legitimate worker. He was apprehended and jailed for eighteen months. Frances tried to make ends meet for herself and her daughter, working as a dressmaker in a factory, but her shiftlessness, argumentative temperament and unreliability led to her being fired. So she stole enough money to return to Melbourne with Gladys while Rudolph languished behind bars.

In Melbourne she had an affair with Edward 'Ted' Thompson, a fishmonger's assistant, living with him in Pigdon Street, Carlton North. Their relationship was tempestuous, lurching between happiness and violent argument. In the end, wanting a quieter life, Thompson broke it off. Again penniless, and not knowing how else she could feed herself, let alone her baby, Knorr became a baby farmer and committed the crimes that would cost her her life.

When Rudolph was released from prison, he joined Frances in Melbourne and became her passive accomplice as she sold or murdered the infants left in her care, moving house frequently to cover her tracks.

After only a few months, possibly believing that their activities could not go undetected much longer, they decided to start a new life in Sydney. In the Harbour City they had a second child, born on 4 September 1893. They found work, as before, in eating houses. But if they thought they were home free they were mistaken, for retribution was on their heels.

A man who'd moved into a bungalow the Knorrs had previously rented in the Melbourne suburb of Brunswick was digging in the back yard when he found the body of a baby girl in a shallow grave. He called the police. Officers checked the yard of another of the Knorrs' addresses, in Brunswick, and found two more tiny corpses buried in the garden. One, that of a baby girl, had been strangled and the cord left tied tightly around her neck.

In October 1893, there was a knock on the Knorrs' door in Sydney. When the caller identified himself as Detective Keating, Frances sighed and said, 'I know what you have come for.' The policeman's knock was her death knell.

A month later, on 27 November, at Melbourne's Supreme Court before Mr Justice Holroyd, Frances Knorr was charged with the 'wilful murder of a female child, name unknown, at a house in Moreland Rd, Brunswick, on or about the 11 April last. The prisoner also stands committed, along with her husband, Rudolph Knorr, charged with the murder of a male child, name unknown, found buried in the yard at the rear of a house in Brunswick, on the 5 September last; and further, with her husband as an accessory before the fact, with a female child, name unknown, found buried in the same yard.' The deceased were referred to as babies Nos 1, 2 and 3.

The prosecutor, Mr Walsh QC, told the court that a baby – baby No. 1 – who had been observed in Frances Knorr's care between April 8 and 11 that year had not been seen after that period. Knorr, said Walsh, had moved house repeatedly, and had lied about her whereabouts to acquaintances and to the mothers of the children in her care. She had ordered a servant girl to borrow a spade from a neighbour, a Mrs Munnerley, and was witnessed digging in the garden of the house at the exact spot where the first baby's body was found. He then detailed evidence he had compiled of Knorr's baby trafficking, telling the court 'she has sold babies left in her care by trusting mothers and has murdered others she could not sell'.

The mothers of the three babies who had been murdered and buried while in Knorr's care were called. Each testified that she had entrusted her infant to Knorr and had never seen the child again, nor Knorr herself until today in court. A Mrs Crichton, the mother of baby No. 1, collapsed and was carried from the court.

Crucial to the prosecution's case against the defendant was a letter she had written to her former lover, Ted Thompson, in which she sought to persuade him to obtain false evidence that would clear her. Thompson would have none of it. In court he testified against her, explaining how she had asked him to find a compliant man and woman and pay them to testify at her trial that the baby girl in the grave had not been Mrs Crichton's but theirs. The witnesses would swear that the baby had died of consumption and been buried in the backyard by another man. She urged Thompson, 'for God's sake and for the sake of my two little ones', not to tell a soul that the evidence was false. If their ruse was discovered, she feared she would receive 'a life sentence'. She had also asked Thompson, when he had found his pair of perjurors, to write to her in prison, posing as a woman, and tell her their names.

When Thompson point-blank refused to cooperate, Knorr took another tack. In her defence address she denied having ever written the incriminating letter and claimed that the dead baby was hers and Thompson's, that the infant had died of consumption and she had secretly buried the body because she was afraid police, knowing of her and her husband's criminal records, would accuse her of foul play. She swore she knew nothing about the two other bodies. Yes, she had sold babies to childless couples, whose names and addresses she could no longer recall, but she had never murdered a soul. She gave every indication, however, that Edward Thompson might have. On one occasion, she claimed, he had taken a baby from her and returned later without it. When she asked him where the child was, she told the court, Thompson had muttered, 'You won't see it no more.'

In his summation, Justice Holroyd said that in his opinion Knorr's protestations of innocence, her explanation that the dead baby was her own, and that she had no knowledge of the fates of the other babies who had disappeared, as well as her attempt to implicate Thompson, amounted to 'the most extraordinary piece of audacious evidence I have ever heard'.

He continued, 'There is no direct proof of the killing, but the jury might, as the prosecution asked you to, come to the conclusion that the surrounding circumstances brought before you constitute such a chain that it is impossible to escape the conclusion that the prisoner is a guilty woman.' The motive, said the judge, was that 'the prisoner was a needy woman – that she was living on a very precarious system. The highest sum she appears to have got as premium with any child was £20 and the lowest about £5, and judging from her impecunious circumstances, she seemed to have spent the money as soon as she got it.'

He further noted that he could not understand why, if indeed the body was that of her own baby who had died from consumption, she had not contacted the authorities. It was no crime to have a sick child die, regardless of past misdeeds. There had been no need to bury the child clandestinely.

On 1 December 1893, Frances Knorr was found guilty by the jury, who had felt the need to retire for just thirty minutes. She received a sentence of death. Rudolph was convicted of being an accessory and imprisoned.

On hearing the verdict, Frances swayed backwards, then forwards, and slumped into her seat. She buried her head in her lap and wept. As she was supported from the dock, distraught, she screamed at Ted Thompson, who was in the gallery, 'God forgive your sins, Ted! God help my poor mother! God help my poor babies!' Knorr's request that her daughter Gladys, who was in the care of the state, be allowed to visit her each day in Pentridge's condemned block was granted.

Until the realisation sank in that the state intended absolutely to hang Frances Knorr, and would not, as many seemed to think, make her sweat it out before commuting her sentence at the last minute, Melburnians had made her an object of hate. Now, as the execution date loomed closer, the mood changed and she became an object of pity. Rudolph Knorr pleaded for clemency for his wife on the grounds that she was an epileptic who frequently suffered severe fits, that she often acted irrationally and also fell into trances for long periods. A group called Women of Victoria demanded that her sentence be commuted because 'the killing of any woman by any body of men does not accord with the moral sense of the community'.

The impending execution of Frances Knorr was denounced in the pulpits of churches all over Melbourne, and in cities and towns in other states as well, and public meetings were held where the decision to take her life was branded 'outrageous' and 'unjust'. Petitions demanding clemency were signed by hundreds of citizens and sent to the Governor of Victoria, the Right Honourable John Adrian Hope, Earl of Hopetoun, who had the power to commute the sentence. The petitions were met with silence.

The official hangman, a Mr Jones, did more to protest the execution than sign a petition. A few days before the scheduled deed, he committed suicide. Jones was the only person in the colony who was expert at Pentridge's gallows, so his replacement, a Mr Roberts, needed to be given a crash course in the machinations of gauging Knorr's weight and measuring the drop, tying the noose and drawing the bolt.

The day before the execution, a Sunday, Knorr was reported unlikely 'to face her death calmly'. Understandably, in the shadow of death she seemed gripped by a religious fervour. She marched up and down in her cell declaiming passages from the Bible, and demanded that a group of other women prisoners who had joined her to pray sing the hymn 'Abide with Me'. The loudest, lustiest voice was hers.

That evening, there was a 600-strong anti-capital punishment gathering in Russell Street. Attending were prominent Melbourne figures including a Mr Hancock, a Mrs Goldstein, a Mrs Oldfield, the Reverend Dr Strong and the Reverend Mr Edgar. A vote was taken and it was decided to march on Government House where they would express their outrage. As the throng moved through the city streets, the police, fearing violence, dispatched a large squad to maintain order. When they arrived at the gates of Government House, sometime after 10 pm, a deputation was granted entry and an audience with the Governor.

The Reverend Dr Strong told Governor Hope he conceded that Knorr's crimes were heinous, but on behalf of the great majority of the people of the state he was asking that she be granted mercy. 'The ends of justice,' he argued, 'would be served if the death sentence was commuted to life in prison.' Too, the hanging of a woman would 'disgrace the colony'. Dr Strong said he realised that they were making their plea on Frances Knorr's behalf very late, but they had not believed until today that the death sentence would really be carried out.

Mr Hancock chipped in that he knew of a case in England where the execution of a woman was called off on compassionate grounds. The

Governor frostily retorted that *he* knew many cases in the Old Country in which the hanging was carried out.

Next Hancock tried flattery, suggesting that a show of mercy would make the Governor vastly popular. Hope remained unmoved.

The Governor brought proceedings to a swift close by demanding to know if his visitors had any new petitions or new information that might cause him to reconsider his decision. They did not. 'So,' said Hope, 'no new facts have been placed before me and by constitutional order I am bound by the advice of my ministers ... If there are no new facts I hold out no hope that my ministers will give me advice different to what they have given.' The death sentence stood.

As midnight approached the deputation hastened outside and desperately gathered the names of all those demonstrators still present on a new petition sheet. But of course there was no new evidence. The petition was taken to the Governor. Soon came his message to the protestors: 'I am apprised that no new facts are disclosed in the petition presented to me, and I am unable, therefore, to depart from the advice already tendered to me by my ministers that the law must take its course.'

As dawn broke on the hot and stormy Monday of 15 January 1894, a group of around 1500 citizens opposed to the death penalty gathered to stand vigil outside Pentridge. At 9.45 am, inside the prison's sandstone walls, waiting by the scaffold were the hangman and his assistants, all decked out in patently bogus beards and glasses so as to avoid recognition, a justice of the peace, and newspaper reporters.

All morning, Frances Knorr could be heard in her cell singing 'Safe in the Arms of Jesus' and 'Abide with Me'. The strength of her voice unsettled her captors. At 9.50, walking straight and firm, face expressionless, she was led to the gallows by Sheriff Ellis, Deputy Sheriff Casey, and the governor of the jail, Captain Burrowes. Far from falling to pieces with fright as predicted, Knorr seemed now to embrace her fate. At the drop, after the noose was placed around the prisoner's neck and tightened and a hood placed over her head, there was a dreadful delay as the wardens fussed with her skirt lest it catch on the scaffold as she fell. Finally, after her skirts had been tied to her ankles, she was asked if she had any last words. She replied,

'Yes. The Lord is with me. I do not fear what man can do unto me, for I have peace, perfect peace.' The final five words were uttered boldly, defiantly. The trap was sprung, she fell 2.25 metres, and died instantly.

Frances Knorr had not been idle in her last days. She wrote to Victorian Premier Patterson with suggestions on how to better regulate baby farming. She wrote a last farewell to her mother in England, and left a Bible with an inscription to her husband Rudolph. And she wrote a full confession to Governor Hope, detailing who, how and why she had killed. The Governor released only a paragraph of the letter:

> As I feel that I have not expressed myself clearly, I now desire to state that upon the two charges known in evidence as No. 1 and No. 2 baby, I confess to be guilty. Placed as I am now, within a few hours of my death, I express a strong desire that this statement be made public, with the hope that my fate will not only be a warning but also act as a deterrent to those who are perhaps carrying on the same practice. – Frances Knorr.

Four years after the execution of the so-called Brunswick Baby Farmer, in 1898 the Infant Life Protection Act became law. The names of children placed in foster care of any description had to be kept in a central roll book. The date on which they were admitted to care, when they were returned to their parents, their progress while in care, any illnesses, were all to be noted. Local councils were required to monitor all foster homes, and police paid regular and unannounced visits. If a child died while in care an inquest was mandatory. Nurses and carers had to be registered and it was essential that they be of good character, with no criminal record or history of emotional instability.

CHAPTER 16

THE DISCIPLE AND THE DEVIL: THE TRURO MURDERS

James Miller and Christopher Worrell: Serial killers

1976–77

Christopher Worrell was killed in a car crash on 19 February 1977, and the 23-year-old Adelaide man was buried four days later in a small churchyard. Worrell's grieving mother had ordered for his grave a headstone which read 'Untold Love and Joy He Brought to All'. And if the actions of Worrell's grief-crazed best friend, James Miller, could be thought to represent the feelings of his other friends, this epitaph must have seemed appropriate to the few mourners present. For as Worrell's casket was being lowered into the ground, the 38-year-old Miller leapt wailing into the open grave to embrace the coffin and leave upon it a photograph on which he had written: 'Chris, please try and understand. I love you as a mate and always will. Hoping to see you soon. Please forgive me – Jamie.'

The congregation must surely have wondered what bond shared by the deceased and Miller could inspire such devotion. When, two years later, they found out, they were horrified.

Worrell, who was movie-star handsome, long-haired and capable of immense and persuasive charm, was exposed as a psychopathic serial killer who had murdered seven women in seven and a half weeks in December 1976 and January and February 1977. And Miller, balding, slight, with nondescript features and myriad insecurities, was Worrell's accomplice and erstwhile lover, who had helped him snatch his victims from the streets and shopping malls of Adelaide, waited – in his own words, 'gutless, like a coward' – as Worrell assaulted and strangled them, and then helped bury them in wasteland around the tiny town of Truro, 100 kilometres north-east of Adelaide.

Miller grew up with the nickname 'Killer', not because of his homicidal tendencies but because he was an excellent fast bowler at school at Ferryden Park Primary in Adelaide's north-west. His fleeting success at cricket gave the young Miller possibly the only triumph of his life, for this product of a fractured family, one of six siblings, was so badly behaved that by the time he was eleven he had been relocated to Magill Reform School. Miller became a troubled teenager, self-pitying, sly and nefarious, and friendships eluded him. When not employed as a casual labourer, he resorted to stealing to survive and was convicted as many as forty times for theft and fraud.

Miller met Worrell in Adelaide Gaol in 1974. The former was serving three months for robbing a gun shop and the latter, who had been an RAAF recruit and council worker, had been incarcerated for six years for rape – the judge had called him a 'depraved and disgusting human being' – and armed robbery. The pathetically impressionable Miller was beguiled by Worrell's tales of his criminal life, especially by his claim that he had already murdered two women hitchhikers he'd met while driving from Perth to Adelaide. Miller fell deeply and hopelessly in love. To commemorate their relationship, the pair cut their wrists and became blood brothers.

On their release, Worrell and Miller rendezvoused and took up residence together in a flat in Ovingham, worked side by side on Unley Council's labouring gang, and caroused at night. The unlikely duo were inseparable, despite Worrell's unpredictable and increasingly intense moods and temper tantrums and the fact that sex between them petered out after Worrell made it clear that, outside prison walls at least, he preferred women to men. To the besotted Miller, a confirmed homosexual, a platonic relationship with the man of his dreams was better than no relationship at all.

Miller later said that he was driven mad, but complied, when his mate made him drive his 1969 blue and white Valiant station wagon around the suburbs while Worrell chatted up women on the street and, when successful, as he almost always was, ordered him to drive him and his conquest to an isolated location. There, his role was to make himself scarce while Worrell had sex in the back seat or in the bush.

Miller later told police that his designated role as chauffeur continued even after Worrell began murdering the women he inveigled into the car. Worrell never explained to a soul his progression from Lothario to serial killer. Had he, as he claimed to have done, killed before and this was simply more of the same? Or was what followed the result of some psychotic brain snap?

On 23 December 1976, the men were cruising the streets of Adelaide when Worrell ordered Miller to pull over. He had seen 18-year-old Veronica Knight outside the Majestic Hotel. With his most winning smile, Worrell asked the unemployed Knight if she wanted a lift, and she said she did. But instead of taking her to the Angas Street Salvation Army Hostel where she was living, Miller drove them all to the Adelaide Hills. There, said Miller, as was his usual practice, he left Worrell and Knight in the car and walked away into the bush where he sat for maybe an hour.

But this time when he returned, he claimed, he found the girl dead, tied up and sprawled in the back of the station wagon. Worrell told Miller he had raped and strangled her, but when Miller called him a 'fucking fool' the younger man had flown into a rage and held a knife to Miller's throat, threatening to kill him if he didn't shut up. The terrified Miller, meekly following Worrell's instructions, had then driven to Truro where, in the bush by a track known as Swamp Road, they took $200 from Veronica's clothing, dumped her body and covered it with foliage.

If Miller had turned Worrell in to the police right then, six lives would have been saved. But, terrified of Worrell's violence and so in love that he could not bear to lose his friendship, he did not, and for this he – and many others – would pay dearly.

Worrell and Miller's next victim was 15-year-old Tania Kelly, a student from a girls school in Stonyfell. The teenager, described by friends as a 'striking beauty', had hitchhiked from her home at Victor Harbor and was taken in by Worrell's smooth chat when he approached her in Adelaide's Flinders Street. Miller drove the two to his sister's house – after they made sure there was no one at home – and waited in the car while they went inside. About thirty minutes later, Worrell came out and, according to Miller, told him to accompany him back into the house. There, Miller would say, he saw Kelly's strangled body. 'I told Chris he should see a doctor to help him understand why he was doing what he was doing and he told me to mind my own business and that he'd kill me if I didn't help him dispose of the body,' Miller later claimed. They drove to Truro and buried the corpse.

Juliet Mykyta was a brilliant high school student who was earning Christmas holiday pocket money by selling jewellery from a roadside stall in central Adelaide, outside the Ambassador's Hotel in King William Street. On 21 January, around 10.20 pm Worrell leaned out of the passenger window of the Valiant and offered Mykyta a lift. Miller drove them to Port Wakefield Road and watched in the rear-vision mirror as Worrell overpowered the 16-year-old and tied her up. Once again Miller left the car. After a bit he heard cries and turned to see Worrell fling Mykyta to the ground outside the car, kneel on her stomach and strangle her with a piece of rope. Miller would insist that he ran to the girl's aid, but Worrell faced him down and once more he slunk away. The girl was buried at Truro.

Four more murders followed in rapid succession. After his arrest, Miller asserted that on 6 February, as he looked on, cowed and useless, Worrell tied up, sexually assaulted and killed shop assistant Sylvia Pittman and concealed the 16-year-old's body at Truro. On 7 February, nurse's aide

Vicki Howell, 26, suffered the same fate. Worrell raped and slew 16-year-old Connie Iordanides, unemployed, after he and Miller took her from a bustling street in the centre of Adelaide on 9 February. Deborah Lamb had the misfortune to be hitchhiking near Adelaide's City Bowl around 1 am on 12 February when, according to Miller, he and Worrell drove by. 'Where are you going?' Worrell had asked the unemployed Lamb; when told Port Gawler, he'd grinned and said, 'Well, get in.' At the beach there, 45 kilometres north of Adelaide, Miller shuffled off while Worrell tied Lamb up and choked her to death with her pantyhose, then helped Worrell bury her in the sand. It is possible she was still alive when interred.

There would undoubtedly have been more murders had the killing spree not been ended by Worrell's death.

On 19 February 1977, a week after Deborah Lamb's murder, Worrell and Miller and their friend Deborah Skuse were travelling from Mt Gambier to Adelaide in the Valiant. Worrell, who for once was at the wheel, was drunk and driving dangerously after consuming a number of cans of beer. Just north of the town of Millicent, according to Miller, Skuse told Worrell to slow down. Worrell had screamed at her, 'Shut up!' Distracted, he lost control of the station wagon, which began to fishtail wildly. A tyre blew out, and the car left the road and rolled over a number of times. The occupants were flung out. Rescuers found Worrell and Skuse dead in the dirt, and Miller, who had been in the back seat, alive but nursing a badly injured shoulder and sobbing softly as he stared disbelievingly at Worrell's body.

After he had jumped raving into Worrell's grave at Worrell's funeral, the distressed Miller could not resist unloading to his late friend's girlfriend, whose name was Amelia. 'There's more to it than you know about,' Miller had told her. When she asked him what he meant by that, Miller ushered her to a spot where they could not be overheard and told her about the murders. 'They had to be done in so they couldn't point the finger at us,' he confided. He said that he and Worrell had a joint pact to 'pick up girls and murder them', and that one had been strangled with a guitar string. The girls, he said, had been 'rags ... [they] weren't worth much'. He offered to take Amelia to where the victims were buried, and then added that Worrell had told him he had killed a girl in Western Australia before he and Worrell had met. Amelia told no one of what she'd heard.

The tortured Miller now led a wandering, homeless existence, dossing down in fields and doorways and bus stops, or overnighting at St Vincent de Paul and Central Mission facilities. Who can guess at the grim nightmares that disturbed what sleep he found?

Amelia, too, lived with demons, but kept her silence about Miller's confession until the remains of some of Worrell's victims were found in 1978 and 1979. In May 1979 she finally contacted the police, who promptly arrested Miller. After admitting his involvement, he took detectives to where those bodies that had not been found were hidden. Under Deborah Lamb's body, buried in the sand at Mt Gawler, police found her small, heart-shaped plastic brooch, on which was written the poignant inscription: 'God's only law is love'.

Discussing the murders of the girls, and the certainty now that they had been victims of a serial killer, one detective who had been involved in the search for the bodies mused to reporters that the young women, many of whom were plucked from the street at night and seemed to have willingly accompanied a stranger to their doom, were:

> victims of modern society as surely as victims of their killer. Modern lifestyles and values have created an environment where family life and protection are eroded by pressures on parents to allow their children to compete with their peers. Young people have no fear – they won't see the dangers on the streets around them – they think there's good in everybody.

The mother of victim Julie Mykyta, Anne-Marie Mykyta, concurred. There was a photograph, published widely in June 1979, of a detective carrying from the Truro killing fields Julie's plastic-encased and decomposed remains. The image captured for many the grinding sadness of the lovely and much-loved young woman's wasted life. However, one newspaper reader, Joanne Baxter, aged fifteen and so only a year younger than Julie, was outraged by the photo, saw it as being in 'poor taste' and an invasion of the Mykyta family's privacy. Anne-Marie Mykyta took issue. In an open letter that was published in papers around the nation she wrote:

> Dear Joanne,
>
> I am sorry that the report of the finding of my daughter's body and the picture of the policeman carrying her offended you. But what would you have? Do you want Julie to be just another statistic, hidden away in the paper, or perhaps not reported at all, so that nobody will be subjected to 'poor taste'? Julie was a person, a girl very full of life, as were Veronica, Sylvia, Vicki, Connie, Tania and Deborah. They were real girls just like you. And they died – just as you could die – not because they hurt anyone, or angered anyone, but because they were on the street at night ... I don't want Julie's death forgotten – not just because she was my daughter, but because she was a victim of our society. And, I fear, not the last victim. Every time I hear of a girl raped or injured, my daughter dies in my heart again.

Anne-Marie Mykyta later wrote a book about the ordeal of losing her daughter to evil. Published in 1981 by McPhee Gribble, it is called *It's a Long Way to Truro*. In one harrowing section, she writes of the dark days after her daughter's disappearance and before her body was recovered. She would dream of Julie '[wandering] along grey, dank tunnels of rough rock, while something trailed after, coming closer and closer. Then the crying would start: "Mum ... Mummy ... I need you ... where are you ... Oh, I'm so frightened."' The proceeds of this honest and soul-baring book went to a foundation Anne-Marie had started, the Julie Mykyta Memorial Scholarship for gifted children.

In February the following year, Miller stood trial in Adelaide Magistrate's Court on seven counts of murder. He pleaded not guilty. 'I am innocent of these murders and I will prove it. I swear I will,' he said. Also produced was a statement Miller had made to police in which he said:

> I admit that I helped dispose of the bodies and I admit that I was with Worrell before the girls were murdered, but I certainly did not think they were going to be killed, and I certainly did not take part or help in their killing at all ... I realise I have behaved very weakly and badly in not physically stopping Worrell and not reporting the matter to the police as soon as the first death occurred. I realise I should not have disposed of the bodies after they were killed. By not telling the police about Worrell I am probably guilty of some offence, but I am not guilty of murder because I did not want any of these girls to die. On each occasion I was horrified and frightened when a girl was killed ... I did not plan with Worrell or discuss with him in any way about picking up girls for the purpose of killing them.

Defending Miller, Mr K.P. Duggan QC told the jury that he was 'just waiting for Worrell and there was no joint enterprise as far he [Miller] was concerned. Miller found himself in one of the oldest relationship problems in the world, that of involvement in the wrongdoing of someone else. He was trapped in a web of circumstance. Although Miller admits that he handled the situation incorrectly, he maintains that he is not a murderer.'

The Crown begged to differ. Prosecutor Mr B.J. Jennings insisted that Miller and Worrell had 'lived, worked and indeed committed murder together ... Have no doubt that these young women were murdered because they were going to point the finger at the young man who tied them up and sexually abused them. They could also point the finger at the older man who ignored their plight and their terror. If a man assists another by driving him to a place where a girl is going to be raped and killed, then he is guilty of murder.'

On 12 March 1980, Miller was found guilty of six murders. The killing of the first victim, Veronica Knight, was deemed to be the work of Worrell alone, because with no precedent it was accepted that Miller might not have known of Christopher Worrell's murderous intentions. Miller was jailed for six life terms.

He immediately appealed, reiterating that he was not guilty of murder. The Court of Criminal Appeal dismissed his petition. Justices Walters and Wells remarked that on the basis of the facts aired at his trial, Miller certainly did know that Worrell planned to kill the women: 'It seems to us that if there was a joint undertaking that embraced the choice of murder, then that is what the two men contemplated, and for every murder that was carried out [Miller] must be guilty.'

Miller continued to gripe that his conviction was unfair. In October 1994, having spent fourteen years in gaol, he was interviewed in Yatala Labour Prison, north of Adelaide, for an article in *Who Weekly* magazine written by this author. 'I'm not a killer', he protested, 'just a petty crim. If Chris Worrell had lived, they would have charged him with murder and me [with being] an accessory after the fact. Because he died, they want me to wear the rap ... so they charged me with murder.' He was, however, burdened with guilt over the part he did play in the serial killings:

> Even if I got out of jail tomorrow, [those girls] would still be on my mind every day of the week. Even though I didn't commit the murders, I feel responsible for what Chris did. If I had gone to the police after the first murder, all [those] kids would still be alive and I feel a lot of grief about that.

Yet, he allowed, his feelings for Worrell had made the decision to turn him over to the police a difficult one. 'It would be pretty hard for you to go up to a cop and say, "My son committed murder", if you knew you would be putting your son in jail for 14 or 15 years. Well, Chris and me were close.' Too, as much as he loved Worrell and didn't want to lose him, he was also terrified of his friend's 'Jekyll and Hyde' character, and genuinely feared that Worrell would kill him if he tried to betray him.

As much as he found Worrell's death in the car crash unbearable, it had been, said Miller, 'an act of God. [The killing] just couldn't keep going on.'

After serving twenty years Miller applied for freedom again in 2000, and again his appeal was rejected. This time the Australian Supreme Court ruled that because he expressed 'regret and shame' for what he had done and there was a low risk of his ever re-offending, he should be let out at some stage in the future, but not for at least a further fifteen years, by which time he will be seventy-four years old. 'I recognise the risk that he will die in prison,' said Justice Doyle. 'However, justice requires such severe treatment for such grave crimes.'

CHAPTER 17

PORTRAIT OF EVIL

Leonard Lawson: Rapist, murderer
1954–1961

Back before videogames and YouTube, Australian children's addiction of choice was the humble comic book. Along with Superman, Batman, Hopalong Cassidy and Richie Rich, one of the most popular was a homegrown Western, Action Comics' *The Lone Avenger,* created in 1946 by 19-year-old Sydney artist and photographer Leonard Lawson. *The Lone Avenger* featured a masked cowboy hero who rode his 'faithful steed Midnight' and pitted his wits and fists against a succession of evil-doers. But, in the end, the most perverted fiend Lawson ever created was himself.

Lawson, who lived with his parents in the Sydney beach suburb of Manly, was not a particularly impressive figure. He was slightly built, sported a nerdish moustache, was neat, quiet and well-spoken. The only obviously unsettling note about the talented young artist and photographer was the thick horn-rimmed spectacles which disconcertingly magnified his eyes to nearly twice their size. But beneath his placid façade, Lawson was beset by acute psychosexual obsessions: he fantasised about spying on women, usually young women, forcing them to submit to him, raping and killing them. To the best of anyone's knowledge he was able to rein in his demons until 7 May 1954, when his sick dreams became a savage reality.

That day his assignment was to rendezvous with five young models aged from fifteen to twenty-two, from the elite June Dally-Watkins modelling academy, and drive them to bushland at Terrey Hills, near Sydney's northern beaches, where he would photograph them. But when they arrived at their destination, instead of a camera Lawson produced a sawn-off rifle and a sheath knife, and tied the hands and feet of the terrified girls. He covered their mouths with sticking plaster to prevent them screaming for help. Then he ordered his victims to watch as he raped two and indecently assaulted the others.

Lawson left in his car, but the girls freed themselves, located a telephone and called Chatswood police station. Their attacker was quickly arrested. Although a psychiatrist claimed that Lawson's 'mental condition was not all it could be', in fairly short order he was convicted and sentenced to hang for his heinous crime.

Fortunately for Lawson, soon after his sentence was handed down the NSW Government passed a law abolishing capital punishment for all crimes except treason and piracy. In one stroke of the legislators' pen, Lawson's death sentence was commuted in 1955 to life imprisonment. Serving his time, he lapsed into mild-mannered mode and was regarded as a model prisoner, polite and acquiescent, never a moment's trouble for warders or other inmates. His life term was consequently, in a move that would have tragic consequences, reduced to fourteen years and in fact, with remissions for good behaviour, he was freed after serving only seven years and twenty days.

Lawson was back on the streets of Sydney on 27 May 1961, his long-suppressed demons raging. He launched into frenzied sex with prostitutes and had a number of one-night stands with women he picked up in cafés, parks, beaches and bars. And then on 20 June, fuelled by his warped fantasies of causing harm to teenage girls, he drove to Sydney Church of England Girls Grammar School (SCEGGS), which is set on 200 hectares of gentle green farmland at Moss Vale in the southern highlands of New South Wales.

There, this seemingly genial and self-effacing man introduced himself to the headmistress, Jean Turnbull, passing himself off as an author who was writing a novel which was set in a girls' college just like SCEGGS. Turnbull invited her esteemed visitor to attend chapel and join staff for lunch afterwards. In appreciation, Lawson presented Turnbull with one of his paintings, a portrait of Christ.

Lawson was back at the school a month later and once more, after dining with the teachers and girls, he prayed with them in the chapel. As he bade them farewell, he thanked them for their hospitality and promised he'd return at the earliest opportunity. Tragically, he would keep his word.

In early October, Lawson was prowling for female prey on a Manly street when he saw Jill Bower and her attractive, dark-haired 16-year-old daughter Jane, a former Mosman school student, and now a trainee artist at the Empire Art Company in William Street, East Sydney. Jane's boss would describe her as 'the most universally liked girl in our office. She was the prettiest girl, kind and sweet and the least likely person a terrible thing would happen to'.

Lawson introduced himself to the Bowers, explaining that he was an artist and he would be honoured to draw Jane's portrait. After they'd gone on outings and dined together, and come to trust the avuncular Lawson, not suspecting for a moment that he had been sentenced to death for rape and sexual assault, the Bowers, devout churchgoers, agreed. The artist and his model began their sittings in his Collaroy apartment.

Lawson became obsessed with Jane Bower and decided he must have sex with her whether she wanted it or not. Preparing for the worst-case scenario, a knockback, Lawson went to Collaroy Beach and filled one of his socks with sand to make a cosh, then bought several ropes and cut them into more than eighty metre-long pieces.

At 5 pm on 6 November, Lawson collected Jane from her office. That afternoon at work she had washed her thick, wavy brown hair so it would look its lustrous best for the evening's scheduled sitting. Lawson and Jane then collected Jill Bower from the David Jones department store in the city. The three returned to Jill and Jane's home in Manly, where also lived Jane's siblings Belinda, 11, and Billy, 13, for an early dinner. Lawson was at his most winning. Then he took Jane to his apartment where she would sit as he continued her portrait.

They arrived shortly before eight o'clock. While he was drawing the girl with his crayons – he'd got as far as a fair likeness of Jane's face with hair flowing to her shoulders – Lawson suddenly dropped his benign front and tried to wheedle her into having sex with him. Jane was outraged and scared and tried to talk him out of it. Her resistance drove Lawson into a frenzy.

He would later tell what happened next: 'I went and got the sock and hit her on the head with it. She was sitting on the lounge with her back towards me when I came out of the bedroom and hit her. Then I tied her hands and feet with the lengths of rope I had. Then, when I saw she was unconscious I untied her feet.' Lawson undressed Jane Bower and raped her. Having done that, he said:

> I came to my senses and realised what I had done. I could see that my freedom was slipping away and I thought the only thing I could do was kill her. I got a piece of rope and put it around her neck and held it tight. She started to struggle and was half dead and half alive and I could not stand her suffering any more so I got a hunting knife and drove it into her chest. She stopped suffering then. After I put the knife into her I carried her and put her on the bed. Then I cleaned the knife and wrote the inscription on her with an eyebrow pencil. I wrote across her stomach, "God forgive me, Len." Then I put some stuff in a bag, turned out the lights, got into my car and drove away. I stopped at a phone box in Collaroy and rang Jane's mother and told her that Jane was ill, that I had arranged for a neighbour to look after her while I was away and that I would come

> down to Manly, pick her up, and bring her back to my flat to look after Jane. I only wish now that I could turn back time. I've killed the girl I loved more than anything else in the world.

But Lawson was not done yet. He loaded his .22 calibre Remington automatic rifle, filled the pockets of his jacket with forty-eight .22 cartridges and four more packets containing 167 bullets, and stuffed his lengths of rope in an overnight bag. Then he drove to Moss Vale, to the Sydney Church of England Girls Grammar School.

Next day, Tuesday 7 November, was Melbourne Cup Day. At 7.30 am, Jane Bower's cousin, Graham Troy, at the behest of her mother, who was distraught that Jane had not returned home or telephoned, peered through a window of Lawson's flat and saw her ravaged body sprawled across a bed. He called the police.

At the same time, at Moss Vale, in the intimate chapel of the exclusive girls' school, one hundred and fifty pupils and teachers were saying morning prayers. Just before 8 am, Lawson, wielding his high-powered rifle, stormed in.

Headmistress Jean Turnbull, recognising the intruder as the author who had been a guest at the school a few weeks before, approached him and demanded to know what he thought he was doing. Lawson, wild-eyed, shrieked that he had killed someone already – 'I might as well be hanged for a lamb as a sheep' – and he was going to hold the students hostage until Olympic runner Marlene Mathews, reigning Miss Australia Tania Verstak, and a nun who had visited him in prison were brought to him. He planned to trade the three women for safe passage out of Australia. If Mathews, Verstak and the nun were not delivered, he warned, he would kill nine girls. Turnbull, a brusque and formidable woman, hefty, with cropped hair and known to the pupils as 'Bull', tried to calm the raging man, and invited him to join them in prayer. But Lawson was in no mood to converse with the Lord. As the brave headmistress attempted to reason with him, at the same time attempting to calm the students now petrified with fear, Lawson continued to rant his demands and wave his rifle wildly.

'Don't harm my girls,' she pleaded. 'They are more important than we are ... What about our Leaving Certificate girls? They are having their English examination this morning.'

'I don't care about that!' yelled Lawson.

Turnbull, sounding cooler than she felt: 'Well, we might as well go on with our service.'

Lawson bridled: 'I consider that *I* am more important than your service!'

Now the headmistress, though her heart was pounding, adopted a confidential tone. 'The girls will stand up for the Canticle, sit down for the lesson, stand again for the Creed and then kneel down for prayer,' she whispered to him, 'so don't be alarmed if they move all at once.'

Turnbull left Lawson's side and took her place in the pulpit at the front of the chapel. She pretended to write in her prayer book, in reality scrawling two notes saying there was a man with a rifle in the chapel and that the police should come at once. While Lawson was distracted, making a girl tie the chapel door shut with one of his pieces of rope, Turnbull passed one note to a teacher, who hurried outside with it, and herself dropped the other out the window.

Lawson now joined Turnbull at the pulpit and gave her a note that *he* had penned. She read the foolscap sheet, all the time trying not to betray panic or distress. 'To whom it may concern,' Lawson had written in the spidery block letters that would have been familiar to anyone who had read the voice bubbles and captions of *The Lone Avenger*:

> Read this carefully, before any attempt is made to contact the police. Lives depend on it. By now the police will be hunting me for murder, so I am going to hold the girls as hostages for a few hours. No harm will come to them if you obey my instructions to the letter. I am heavily armed – my most effective weapon being a high-powered automatic rifle which holds 15 shots in the magazine and which I can fire almost as fast as a machine gun.

Knowing that her ability to appear unflustered might be all that could prevent a massacre, Turnbull retorted, 'Are you sure you are not bluffing? Do you want to get material for your book?'

Beside himself, Lawson keened, 'No, I'm not bluffing! If any attempt is made to contact the police before twelve o'clock noon, two girls will be shot dead. I am *not* bluffing. I have killed once, so now I have everything to gain and nothing to lose by killing more. It's the same penalty I must face. The police will be handed a note instructing them to bring three people here so I can talk to them. When that is done, I shall quietly give myself up and no one will have suffered any physical harm whatsoever – as long as, in the meantime, no one tries to enter this room or approach any closer than one hundred feet of this room without my permission. Every time I see anyone within that distance I will immediately shoot one girl through the head. If I need anyone or anything I will give a "hey there" and a mistress will stand on the pathway between the chapel and the office and I will give her further instructions. I will be constantly on the alert so make sure there is no one in the office block or closer to this room than one hundred feet. Anyone who comes closer will be the direct cause of an innocent girl losing her life. I am not a killer by nature or desire, but if forced to do so by anybody foolish enough, then I won't hesitate. If I see hide or hair of the police before twelve o'clock then I'll make you regret you ignored my instructions. I am sure you don't want any girls dying because of your stupidity.'

Just at that moment Lawson saw through the window detectives Gilmore and Mathers charging up the path to the chapel. 'Here are the police. I'll shoot you all now', he screamed, and began firing wildly. Jean Turnbull leapt on Lawson and grappled with him, trying to point the gun barrel to the ceiling. He continued to shoot, five deafening explosions. One bullet shattered a door, two smashed into walls. Another tore into Turnbull's hand. A fifth pierced the heart of Wendy Luscombe, just fifteen, an irrepressible and popular girl who excelled at tennis and hockey, killing her instantly.

Jo Taplin, 14, had been sitting beside Wendy in the pew in front of the chapel's first door. When the shooting started, recalled Jo to reporters, Wendy had saved her life by pushing her under the seat onto the floor.

Wendy then fell alongside her, saying, 'Jo, he has shot me.' Lawson's bullet had entered the schoolgirl's chest and exited from her back.

In a mighty display of valour, for which she was later awarded an MBE, Jean Turnbull continued to wrestle with Lawson, and was joined by staff and students. Some of the students were seen to whale away on Lawson with fists and feet. The detectives crashed through the broken door. Lawson was overpowered and handcuffed. 'I didn't mean to do it. I didn't mean to do it,' he moaned again and again.

Sally Davis was in the chapel with her schoolmates on a day she will never forget. 'I remember vividly that a dog strolled into the chapel and we all laughed,' she recalls. 'Then the atmosphere of hilarity became one of fear and terror when the man came in with a gun and we realised he was holding us up.'

Davis recognised Lawson as the visiting author who had lunched at the school:

> He sat at the headmistress's table among the teachers. He had come to SCEGGS on the recommendation of F.J. Thwaites, a fellow who published his own novels and wrote radio programs, who told the headmistress that Lawson was a writer friend of his who was writing a novel about a girls' boarding school, and asked that he be entertained to lunch.
>
> Madame Sherman, an elderly French teacher, approached Lawson and said, 'These children have lives ahead of them. If you must kill someone, kill me instead.' But of course that was no good to him. He wanted young hostages so he could escape the country after having killed the girl in Sydney.
>
> [Wendy Luscombe] was in my class, and then she repeated. She was a happy girl with flaming red hair and freckles. I didn't see her fall. I was hiding under the seat with about four other children piled on top of me.

To this day Davis doubts that Jean Turnbull did the right thing in wrestling with Lawson. 'No one knows for sure,' she says sadly, 'but perhaps if there'd been no melee Lawson's gun would never have gone off.'

Lawson was bundled into a police car and driven to Sydney, where he made a statement to police. Detective Sergeant Bateman questioned him about the murder of Jane Bower. 'It is too terrible,' moaned the double murderer, and burst into tears. When he regained his composure and was again able to speak he offered only, 'I knew Jane for five weeks ... She was one of the sweetest, most virtuous girls I have ever known. I have done a horrible and terrible thing ... I panicked, but the only course I could see to save myself was to kill her.' He told Bateman that when he was raping and killing Jane, he lost all reason – 'blacked out' – and five minutes later, 'I was perfectly normal and worried about what might have happened.' The hardest thing he had ever had to do, he sobbed, 'was clean things up. I carried Jane in and put her on the bed and after I had put her pants back on I wrote that thing on her stomach.'

At Sydney's Central Court, on 15 November 1961, Lawson was remanded to face two counts of murder and one of attempted murder. An angry crowd gathered to watch as he was escorted into the building. Made to look even more diminutive by the outsized green gabardine coat he wore, he seemed dazed. When told by the magistrate that there would be no bail, Lawson, who had spent the hearing with eyes downcast and a rueful expression on his pasty face, looked up, sighed and said softly, 'I think it would be a waste of time in the circumstances, sir.'

Police now had possession of a note that Lawson had written to his parents sometime between the killings of Jane Bower and Wendy Luscombe. In it, he indicated that his plan was to take his own life, his contrite, hapless tone sounding for all the world like the ramblings of a character in one of his comic strips:

> Dear Mum and Dad, I have done a shocking and dreadful thing. Whatever this monster that moves inside my body did, it did with a vengeance this time. It was something entirely beyond my control – it was so fantastic it must be hard to understand but,

> whatever it is, it sends sanity out of the window, and then, just as quickly, after it is over, I come back to hard, logical sanity, which is a dreadful experience. I cannot express the horror I feel at what I have done. Jane was one of the finest, sweetest and most virtuous girls I have ever known. I thought the world of her mother Jill ... I can imagine what this is going to do to her. As far as Dad and all the others who have had faith in me, I am completely distraught at the unhappiness I have caused over so many years, and now this – oh God, forgive me. I am completely sane and rational now, and I have to kill myself, for as long as I live, I will only bring misery and unhappiness to all associated with me. Time will heal the hurt to you, and you and Dad have many wonderful friends ... Try to forget that you ever had a son. In my normal state of mind now I want to live and it is going to take a lot of courage to pull that trigger, but it is the one and only decent thing for me to do. Do not mourn me for I do not deserve any more thought than a mad, crazed animal because that is what I am when this dreadful brainstorm takes control of my mind. I cannot ask your forgiveness – not for this. All I can say is that I have never known such shame or fear of the unknown than I feel at this moment knowing I have only a few hours left to live. Goodbye, Mum and Dad. You are fine, decent people and you never did anything to bear a son like me. Your broken-hearted son, Len.

On 13 December, Lawson arrived under heavy guard at Moss Vale courthouse for the inquest into Wendy Luscombe's death. As he was entering the building, Ron Luscombe, Wendy's father, broke from the crowd and assaulted Lawson, who cowered under the attack. Before the shaken and shaking killer could be dragged to safety, Luscombe connected with a few hearty swings. Luscombe turned to the press and public and shouted that he wished he could have inflicted more damage.

At his trial at Sydney's Central Criminal Court in April 1962, the court heard from psychiatrist Dr O.R. Schmalzbach, who had examined Lawson at Long Bay Gaol on 19 March. Schmalzbach blamed Lawson's 'psychological development' for his crimes, invoking his sex fantasies, his predilection for imagining scenes of violence and rape involving young girls. 'His psychiatric condition is one which can be called an obsessive-compulsive personality with phases of depression and possible sadistic tendencies.' Central to his psychiatric condition was Lawson's ritual, in his attacks, of binding the wrists and ankles of his victims. Afterwards, said the psychiatrist, Lawson's recollections of the atrocities he committed were 'vague and dreamlike'.

On 4 April 1962, a jury took just eighteen minutes to find Lawson guilty of murdering Jane Bower. Judge McClemens sentenced him to life imprisonment. He was never convicted of the murder of Wendy Luscombe because, with the defendant already imprisoned for the rest of his days, the Crown took the decision not to prosecute the second murder charge.

The information that Lawson had served just seven years of the first life sentence he had been dealt – a sentence that had itself been commuted from the death penalty – after he attacked the five models in 1954 had been suppressed at the murder trial for fear it would prevent his receiving a fair hearing. When he was convicted of Jane Bower's murder, the shocking news was released, and sparked furious condemnation among the public, in state parliament and in the media. If Lawson had remained behind bars, Jane Bower and Wendy Luscombe would still be alive. The lives of the girls' loved ones would not have been destroyed. The children and teachers at SCEGGS would not have been traumatised. There were calls for a Royal Commission into Lawson's early release. Whoever gave approval had blood on his hands, cried the media. There were demands that the death penalty be restored and for a law to be enacted ensuring that in future a life sentence meant exactly that.

This time, Lawson would not be released early. He would spend the rest of his days in prison. Not that that would save Sharon Hamilton from harm.

In Parramatta Gaol, Lawson's sado-sexual fantasies continued unabated and he suffered from deep bouts of depression. As with his first term behind bars, however, Lawson was able to maintain the masquerade that he had mastered his demons, winning the trust of prison officials, warders and fellow inmates and convincing them that he was meek, obedient and harmless. He was granted privileges, such as being allowed to paint and draw and watch television whenever he felt like it, and he was even appointed president of the Robin Hood Committee, a prisoners' group that staged entertainments for fellow inmates.

On 18 June 1972, the Robin Hood Committee welcomed a dance troupe to the gaol. After the show, the entertainers were invited to tea and biscuits in the prison's arts and crafts room, which Lawson had made his headquarters and where many of his portraits of notable Australians were displayed. Among the dancers was 23-year-old Sharon Hamilton. She found herself chatting to one charming prisoner, who told her he had painted the portraits on the wall. She told him that the one of the late US President John F. Kennedy was 'very beautiful'. She saw the signature and asked flirtatiously if he was the famous author Henry Lawson, and the prisoner had laughed and said, 'No, I'm *Leonard* Lawson.' Hamilton then ventured to the personable artist that she had heard that there had been trouble among the inmates at other concerts but this had been such a pleasant occasion that surely nothing could go wrong today. Lawson muttered, 'You never know, you never do know,' grabbed her around the chest and thrust a makeshift dagger against her throat. 'Don't anyone move or I'll let her have it!' he shouted, sounding again like a character in *The Lone Avenger*, as a trickle of blood spilled from a small wound in his captive's neck. Suddenly a fellow inmate rushed forward and punched Lawson in the face. He staggered backwards and was subdued. Hamilton broke free. Lawson later tearfully claimed that the attack was a ploy to make officers gun him down because he could not bear to spend any longer in jail. Five years was added to his life sentence.

Sharon Hamilton was treated for wounds to her neck and hand from Lawson's repeated jabbing and from her attempts to prise the shiv from his grasp. For a while she resumed her career as a showgirl. But she was as surely a victim of Leonard Lawson as Jane Bower and Wendy Luscombe. Severely disturbed by the incident, Hamilton suffered severe anxiety and made a number of unsuccessful suicide bids. She repeatedly saw doctors and psychiatrists. Her condition worsened to the point where she could no longer dance. She sued the NSW Government for damages and lost earnings caused by its inability to control Lawson, and in 1976 was awarded $99 380 in compensation for the attack. In February 1978 Hamilton died from a self-administered overdose of barbiturates.

Twenty-two years later, in 1994, Lawson applied for day leave from Grafton Gaol. He cited his excellent behaviour since his attack on Sharon Hamilton, his dedication to his art, as evidenced by the skilful portraits painted from photographs of President Kennedy, Melbourne's Archbishop Mannix and the entertainers Jack Davey and George Foster. He had donated many of his pictures to charity, and received a Good Citizen award from the mayor of Grafton for his good works. The application was turned down by Justice Jeremy Badgery-Parker in the NSW Supreme Court on the grounds that, once freed, there was 'a very good risk' that Lawson would endanger the community. Lawson was hardly surprised. Realistically, given his record, day release was never going to happen, and in a reflective moment he confided to a reporter that while freedom was enticing 'the rhythms of the city and its women would get to me'.

With all hope of release gone, Lawson became institutionalised. Prisoner 101700 rarely left his cell, just sitting sketching or following his new passion, videotape recording and editing of television programs. An innocuous enough pastime, thought prison officials, until they made a random check of his cell and found a compilation videotape he'd cobbled together and hidden: the tape interspersed footage from the children's show *Sesame Street* with explicit and confronting scenes he'd taped from R-rated films on SBS. The carefully contrived juxtaposition of innocence with graphic sex and violence shocked those who saw it. Also in his stash were a number of pornographic videos he had somehow acquired. Lawson's video collection was confiscated; it remains of interest to criminal psychologists to this day.

These video nasties, coupled with an incident when he'd tried to make physical contact with a woman dentist, saw Lawson reclassified from a C2 (low security) inmate to C1 (high security) and transferred from the relatively cushy minimum security wing at Grafton to 2 Wing in the main prison. The warden also recommended that he be moved to tough and forbidding Lithgow Correctional Centre. In despair at that prospect, Lawson, by now seventy-six years old, frail and ailing, with a heart condition, hypertension, depression and rapidly narrowing arteries, warned that the relocation would kill him.

So it might have proved. On 26 November 2003, three days after he moved into Grafton's 2 Wing to share cell 242 with Allan Baker, reviled murderer of mother of three Virginia Morse in 1973, Leonard Lawson, double murderer and serial rapist, who had spent forty-eight of the past forty-nine years in custody, awoke and showered, and poured himself a bowl of cereal. He never got to taste it. He clutched his chest and fell to the ground. Allan Baker pressed the alarm button in the cell and a nurse was summoned. She performed CPR and frantically checked for vital signs but found none.

CHAPTER 18

SINS OF THE SON

Sef Gonzales: Mass murderer
2001

For an exhibition of sheer audacity, Sef Gonzales' bravura performance at the funeral of his murdered parents and sister is hard to beat. On 20 July 2001, the 20-year-old Sef stood at the altar of the Holy Spirit Catholic Church at North Ryde in Sydney's north-west, dressed in his flash, urban-cool dark blue shirt and charcoal tailored suit, before three coffins containing the stabbed and bludgeoned bodies of Teddy, Mary-Loiva and Clodine Gonzales. In turn, he delivered into a forest of microphones arrayed in front of him, as if at a press conference, a eulogy to each of the deceased. When he came to his father who, just days before he had stabbed so hard and so often that he all but severed his spinal cord, he mourned, 'I loved to lie on Papa's chest, as a child, listening to his heart beat. At that early moment [it] instilled in me all the strength I needed to face life ahead of me.'

Then in a sweet, clear voice, Gonzales paid soulful tribute to his lost loved ones, singing the cheesy Mariah Carey power ballad 'One Sweet Day':

> *Sorry I never told you all I wanted to say*
> *Now it's too late to hold you 'cause you've flown away, so far away*
> *Never had I imagined living without your smile*
> *And I know you're shining down on me from heaven*
> *Like so many friends we've lost along the way*
> *And I know eventually we'll be together*
> *One sweet day.*

As with almost everything else in the life of Sef Gonzales, the performance was a lie. The words and music which moved to sobs scores of mourners at the service, and thousands of others who heard it broadcast on radio and witnessed it on TV news, were part of an elaborate charade to deflect blame for the murders.

The Gonzales family had come to Australia from the Philippines in 1991, when Sef was eleven. The boy almost didn't make it. When an earthquake demolished his wealthy property developer and solicitor father's Queen Victoria Hotel in their hometown of Baguio City, 250 kilometres south of Manila, in 1990, little Sef had been buried deep in rubble, pinned by a wooden beam. 'Papa! Papa! Papa!' he screamed. As aftershocks continued to tear at the site, Teddy Gonzales risked his life to drag his son out of the debris with his bare hands and haul him to safety. The boy threw his arms around his father and cried.

As Sef Gonzales grew into a teenager in Australia, he continued to hug and kiss his father. His mother, too. But it was all for show, for in his heart he had come to despise them.

The problem was that Teddy and Mary-Loiva, who had made a wonderful success of their new life, buying first a home in Blacktown and then their palatial and spacious dream home with its altar to the Virgin Mary at the top of the stairs in North Ryde, demanded so terribly much of him. Devout and steeped in the old Filipino ways, they were very strict, stricter than any of Sef's Aussie mates' parents. They required – no, demanded – that their son be as God-fearing as they were, perfectly behaved, ever-respectful, that he shun decadent Western ways. That he befriend only those of whom they approved. That he excel in every exam at school and go on to a glittering career at university to become a heart surgeon, or a solicitor working alongside Teddy in his thriving Blacktown immigration law practice.

Which drove Sef into a fury. No way, man, that his parents' lifestyle was for him, man. He believed himself way too cool to be spending his precious time praying or burying his head in textbooks. His parents did not know it, but he far preferred to chill out in shopping malls with their fashion shops, juice bars and cinemas, bop with the grooviest kids at techno dance parties, power around Sydney in souped-up cars and be a hip-hop singer. Outside the home he wore baggy home-boy pants and T-shirts that accentuated the toned biceps and six-pack he'd acquired at the gym. Out of his parents' sight he gelled his shiny black hair into a spiky crewcut and indulged his penchant for dousing himself in aftershave lotion, the more odoriferous the better.

Gonzales' dilemma was that while he wanted to be his own person, he was also desperate to get his hands on his share of his parents' $1.5 million property and investment fortune. The last thing he wanted to do was jeopardise his inheritance. So he calculatingly lived a double life. He played the loving and dutiful son, pretending to revere and respect his family while keeping his street life a secret and wishing them out of his life.

Those who saw the baby-faced kid in the bosom of his family would have described him as sweet-natured, soft-spoken, kind, self-effacing and charming, and incapable of disappointing, let alone hurting, Teddy, Mary-Loiva and younger sister Clodine. The reality was very different. Sef Gonzales was vindictive, vengeful, manipulative and scheming, and totally capable of causing terrible harm.

Resentment of his parents' authoritarian edicts, not to mention their robust health, which consigned any inherited windfall to the distant future, became hatred. And Gonzales began playing over and over in his head daydreams in which he collected his inheritance, and Clodine's share as well, sooner rather than later.

Like many a sociopath, Sef Gonzales convinced himself that he was special, and that greatness and privilege were his due. He was above the rules. Laws that applied to ordinary people did not bind him. How much of the image he created for himself he truly believed will never be known, but away from his home, swaggering and posturing while leaving a pungent trail of aftershave fumes in his wake, he lived it to the hilt.

The dream life of Sef Gonzales, playing on a big screen in his head complete with Technicolor and Dolby sound, starred himself as Boy Wonder. He told acquaintances a litany of lies, and such was his talent for sincerity and plausibility that most believed his ludicrous claims. He may even, at times, have believed them himself.

He was, he boasted, a gangsta with bullet scars who required 24/7 protection in the form of armed bodyguards. He was a rapper and hip-hop singing star who, if he chose to do so, could take his choice from a number of lucrative record deals which had been offered to him by major American labels. He was such a stud that when he went to brothels the women he had sex with wanted to pay *him*. He was a fashion tycoon and a million-dollar model for Calvin Klein. He set up his own tribute website with styled beefcake photos of himself where people who existed only in his imagination lauded him. 'What a man!!!' drooled one. He owned a TV production company. He was a very good chance to win a medal for tae kwon do at the impending Athens Olympic Games.

Why, all that could prevent all this glory was the cancer with which he had been stricken and which he was bravely fighting.

It seems that few if any of his real-life pals suspected he was a fabulist. Said one, 'He seemed very genuine. When I think of it now, he fooled so many people and I remember the shock I felt when I found out about the lies. He was a master of deception. That's why he was able to fool so many people. The things he said came out so genuinely it was hard to question them … even when he was boasting he seemed modest.' Recalled another, 'I always respected him for his dedication and motivation. I thought keeping in touch with him would help me learn something and mature a bit more.'

Though Sef seemed to have little trouble faking it with friends, in time Teddy and Mary-Loiva Gonzales began to see through the butter-wouldn't-melt charade he affected at home. Sef continued to assure his family that he loved them, that Clodine was cute, that Teddy was his mentor and hero, but he was not, they were realising, the responsible, diligent, devout and devoted young man he pretended to be. They caught him out when he falsified his high school exam results (he had offered to fabricate Clodine's as well but she refused and told their parents, incurring his wrath) and there were many bitter arguments as Teddy and Mary-Loiva called him on some of the things they had been hearing about him. They carped endlessly about his girlfriends and how he embraced what they considered the worst aspects of Western society, the music, the clothes, the slang, the attitude.

They were equally tough on Clodine, who was sent to Melbourne to live with an aunt and complete high school there after Mary-Loiva took exception to her boyfriend.

Tempers really flared when Sef failed to attain sufficient marks in the Higher School Certificate to study either medicine or law. He was reduced to taking science at the University of New South Wales in 1999 and 2000, in the hope that his marks would allow him entry to the university's Faculty of Medicine later. When that ploy failed because of poor results, he enrolled at Macquarie University where, again, he tried the back-door route to the degree that Teddy and Mary-Loiva wanted him to attain. He embarked on a Bachelor of Arts course with law subjects he hoped would gain him admission at some stage to the Faculty of Law. But he had no more success at Macquarie than at New South Wales. His performance in examinations was woeful. Often he didn't even turn up, phoning in on the morning of the exam claiming, usually, to be suffering from a respiratory tract infection and thus unable to attend.

His parents laid down the law, saying they would slash his allowance and take away his beloved Ford Festiva if his results did not improve. The prospect of catching a bus hardly jibed with his self-image of the rich and famous wunderkind. Unfortunately, when they made their threat Sef already knew that he had failed his third year finals and that it was only a matter of weeks before they found out about it.

Not long afterward, Teddy and Mary-Loiva levelled the direst threat of all. If Sef did not change his ways they would disown and disinherit him. This, they made abundantly clear, was not an idle warning. They had never been more serious. Faced with the loss of his birthright, the daydreams of Sef Gonzales became a murderous plot.

In February 2001, Gonzales bought a quantity of lethal seeds through the Internet, planning to poison his family with them. When the seeds arrived he steeped them in warm water and stored the potion in a film canister underneath his bedside table. Then, in a bid to make the poisoning seem the random work of a madman, he typed a letter to a food company: 'Three of your products have been poisoned. By now they are on supermarket shelves. This is what you get for treating employees like garbage. Good luck finding infected cans before someone dies. Go to hell!!!' He also wrote anonymous letters purporting to be from the mystery poisoner to the Federal Police and the Australian Quarantine and Inspection Service.

On 3 July he laced his mother's food with the poison. Mary-Loiva was rushed to Sydney Adventist Hospital at Wahroonga suffering excruciating abdominal pain, vomiting and diarrhoea. To allay suspicion, Sef also claimed to be stricken, telling a doctor that he believed he and his mother had most likely contracted food poisoning at a restaurant they had attended together on 30 June. But when Mary-Loiva recovered and was discharged next day, her son realised he would need to try another tack.

The catalyst for the carnage that Sef Gonzales perpetrated on his family came two days after the failed poisoning attempt, when Mary-Loiva decreed that he must stop seeing a woman, four years older than himself, with whom he had fallen in love. Though the object of his affection already had a boyfriend, Gonzales wooed her with grandiose lies, promises of engagement and a necklace engraved with the letter G. For a time she went out with her ardent suitor. All seemed to be going well until he introduced her to his parents. Mary-Loiva, as she had been toward Clodine's boyfriend, was cold and distant throughout the meeting, and ordered Sef never to see her again. If Sef defied her, she threatened again, he would be cast out of the family and could forget all about his inheritance. The young woman, possibly with some relief, returned to her boyfriend.

Sef fell into black despair. His parents and his sister, he decided, must die. That way he would get the entire inheritance today, not in forty years, and he would be free to live the life he wanted, and maybe even win back his true love. A no-brainer, baby.

The bare facts of 10 July 2001 are these. In the chill of the morning Teddy and Mary-Loiva Gonzales drove to Teddy's legal practice in Blacktown in separate cars. She worked there as office manager. Clodine, who had turned eighteen the day before and would soon return to school in Melbourne, remained at home studying. Sef drove to Macquarie University, then returned home. In the early afternoon he went to his father's office, where he had been earning money as a part-time paralegal. He attempted to fix a broken computer and made some phone calls relating to cases. Between 3 and 3.30 pm he drove home, arriving around four o'clock. He parked his Festiva in the open carport at the front of the house and went inside.

Around 4.30, as thunder boomed overhead and lightning writhed through the sky, Sef, armed with a baseball bat and two large knives he had plucked from a knife block in the kitchen, approached Clodine from behind as she sat studying at the desk in her bedroom and smashed her on the head with the baseball bat, as many as six times. When she fell to the floor he first choked her, then stabbed her repeatedly in the neck, chest and abdomen until she was dead.

No one knows how Sef Gonzales spent the next ninety minutes or so as he waited for his mother to come home. When Mary-Loiva walked through the front door, he struck. It was heard in court that he 'inflicted multiple stab wounds and cuts to Mrs Gonzales' face, neck, chest and abdomen. Mrs Gonzales' windpipe was completely transected, that is, the upper half of the windpipe was completely severed from the lower half'.

Then it was Teddy's turn to die. Driving home from the office, he called the house. No one picked up. Strange. He walked through the front door at 6.50 pm. A horrified courtroom would later hear how Sef 'attacked Mr Gonzales with one of the kitchen knives while Mr Gonzales was still close to the front door. [He] inflicted multiple stab wounds to Mr Gonzales' neck, chest, back and abdomen. One of the stab wounds penetrated his right lung, another penetrated his heart and another partially severed his spinal cord. Vastly more force was used ... than was necessary to kill Mr Gonzales.'

Sef changed his blood-drenched clothes for clean ones. To make the killings appear racially motivated, he now spray-painted the words 'FUCK OFF ASIANS KKK' on the kitchen wall.

Around 7 pm he left the house, disposed of some of the clothes he had worn – they still have not been found – washed himself clean of blood in the grounds of a local primary school, and drove to the home of his friend Sam Dacillo, who lived nearby. The evening before he had arranged to meet Dacillo and together they would go to dinner in the city.

Dacillo later said he did not notice anything untoward about his mate's conversation, appearance or demeanour that night – maybe, he conceded, he looked 'a little sick', but that was it – as they ate at the Planet Hollywood movie-theme restaurant in George Street, then made the machines whiz and whirr at a video arcade across the road. During their night out, Gonzales carefully established an alibi by telling the unwitting Dacillo that he had spent the afternoon and early evening driving around Blacktown seeking an old friend.

At 11.45 pm Gonzales pulled up in the carport at 6 Collins Street. If he expected to find the house a crime scene, one at which he could feign shock and surprise at what had happened to his family in his absence, he was disappointed. The house was as dark and quiet as when he had left it. There was nothing else for it, he would have to 'discover' the bodies himself and notify police.

At 11.48, he dialled 000. 'Somebody shot my parents, I think, they're all bleeding, they're on the floor!' he screamed down the line at the operator. 'They're not breathing, what do I do?' Police and ambulances were despatched.

Meanwhile, Gonzales ran across the road and banged on the bedroom window of neighbour John Atamian. When Atamian responded, Gonzales, crying and groaning, told him that he had arrived home to find his family had been killed. Another neighbour, Shane Hanley, heard the commotion and came to investigate. When Gonzales repeated that his family had been slain, he and Hanley went into the death house. Hanley saw the corpses and saw Gonzales straddle his parents, wailing 'Papa! Papa!' and 'Mummy! Mummy!', trying to resuscitate them and staunch their wounds.

For the next few days, Gonzales was a ubiquitous media presence, pleading for whoever had massacred his family to give themselves up. A week and a half after the slaughter, he stood in the Holy Spirit Catholic Church in dark shirt, tie and suit, his hair gelled and spikey, offering eulogies to those he had slaughtered.

All who knew the Gonzales family were shocked. They had seemed a picture-postcard family. Said Catholic priest Father Kevin Dadswell, who remembered them from when they lived in Blacktown, 'They were a very devout family, a very close-knit family ... a really nice family.'

In the aftermath of the killings, as police, led by Detective Inspector Mick Sheehy, searched for the culprit, Gonzales took his flint-hearted detachment to grotesque levels. He repeatedly pleaded in the media for the killers to come forward. He publicly mourned his slain family. 'It is difficult to explain the love and ties in my family,' the seemingly distraught young man said, 'but if you were to picture the four corners of the world, in my world we were the four. The three corners of my world are now gone.'

Oddly though, as more than a few noticed and would later recall with a shiver, while Sef's face was crumpled with grief, and his sobs seemed to come from some place deep within, no tears streaked his cheeks.

In his first interview with police on the night of the murders, Gonzales claimed to Detective Sheehy and his team that he had seen an intruder running from the house after he had discovered the bodies, and that a prominent Philippines businessman had recently emailed threats to his father. Did the officers think this man might have been responsible? A week or two later, he showed police an email he had been sent, surely by the killer, saying that hitmen had murdered Teddy, Mary-Loiva and Clodine and that he, Sef, was supposed to be a victim himself. 'It's a blessing you were not there,' the email concluded.

Some months later, he reported to police that he had been assaulted and his apartment had been invaded by people he suspected of being the murderers.

But while police gave Gonzales no indication that he was under suspicion, what they were learning about him as they investigated the background to the murders, as part of their routine inquiries, was causing them considerable disquiet. Things like the paint stains on the sleeve of the jumper he wore on the night of the slayings that was the very same paint that the killer had sprayed on the kitchen wall. Yes, he could have brushed against it when he arrived home and found his family dead, but still ...

They discovered that just three days after the murders, on 13 July, Sef Gonzales had contacted Teddy's accountant, one Mr Stafford, enquiring about a self-managed superannuation fund through which his father handled some of his finances, and wanting to know exactly how much inheritance money would be coming his way. He also demanded to know if any other relative had put in a claim for a portion of the estate.

And, while the legal red tape over the inheritance was being finalised, Gonzales laid down deposits, first on a $170 000 Porsche and then a Lexus SC430 costing about the same, telling the salesmen that he would pay the balance when his inheritance came through. He pawned his mother's watch and sold both his parents' cars, pocketing the proceeds, then rented a luxury eleventh-floor apartment in a block in Chatswood and furnished it with items from the family home. He pestered an aunt in the Philippines for handouts in lieu of his inheritance pile.

He partied hard, worked on his muscles at the gym, told more outlandish tales to his friends, and blathered on non-stop about his singing career. He claimed that so impressed had Columbia Records been by his rendition of 'One Sweet Day' at his family's funeral that they had signed him to a lucrative recording contract. He continued to fork out on aftershave. After the September 11, 2001, terrorist attacks on Manhattan, he told mates that he had attended the funeral in New York of a victim who had been a friend and also paid the airfare of the victim's mother from

Sydney to the United States so she could pay her last respects. He called such charity organisations as the Starlight Foundation, said he was *the* Sef Gonzales, and virtually demanded to be invited to their fund-raising functions. Oh, and on the drawing board too was a musical production he would stage at Macquarie University, 'Sef G's Street Kids on Stage'.

Police, in fact, were astounded when they learned of his fantasy life. They knew full well that while he did front a hip-hip group, Definite Vibez, he wasn't a singing star, or a Calvin Klein model, or an Olympic martial artist. Nor did he own a television company. Nor have cancer. What sort of person would tell such outrageous lies, they wondered.

None of the foregoing was incriminating, mused the investigators, but it was scarcely the typical behaviour of a bereaved son. They applied for, and were granted, an order to tap his phone. Inexorably, they gathered a formidable mass of information and caught him out in lie after lie. Gonzales became the prime suspect.

In early questioning, Gonzales had told police how at the very time Mary-Loiva, Teddy and Clodine were killed he had been driving around Blacktown trying to find the home of a mate. But two people had since come forward to report seeing his car in the carport that afternoon. Between 4.10 and 4.30 pm, Mariella Pavone, a client of Teddy Gonzales, dropped a package of documents in the Gonzales' letterbox and observed the green Ford Festiva, registration SEF 80G. And shortly after 6 pm, as Mary-Loiva and Clodine lay dead, Sef's aunt, Emily Luna, called at the house. She too saw the vehicle. She rang the front doorbell. No response. She saw a movement inside the house and rang again, but when no one opened the door she assumed it was her eyes playing tricks and left.

Informed of Pavone's statement, Gonzales backtracked. Yes, he *had* driven home after searching for his friend in Blacktown, but had not gone into the house and so had not seen the corpses. He had received a text message from Sam Dacillo and driven straight to Dacillo's to keep their dinner date.

Detectives then informed him of Aunt Emily's recollection that she had seen his car in the carport after 6 pm. Okay, okay, he conceded, he supposed he had better tell the truth. His car *was* in the carport when Aunt

Emily called, but he was not at the house. He was ashamed to say it, but he had left his vehicle there when he arrived home at four and caught a taxi to a brothel in Chatswood. He hadn't mentioned this before because he didn't want his extended family to know that he frequented prostitutes so he had made up the tale that he had been driving in Blacktown. He named the woman he had been with at the brothel. Then, he said, he had caught a taxi home, picked up his car, again without going into the house, and driven to keep his date with Dacillo.

Police checked with the sex worker – who had proof that she had been on holidays for the week of 10 July. Faced with her statement, Gonzales toughed it out, said she must be mistaken. Detectives listening in then heard him telephone her and attempt to coerce her into changing her story. They also had tapes of Gonzales calling the brothel, in worried tones asking if they kept records of clients or had surveillance cameras on the premises. A signed letter from a taxi driver saying that he had driven Gonzales from North Ryde to the brothel at Chatswood was also revealed as a fake. Gonzales blustered on, digging himself into an ever deeper hole. Maybe he had the sex worker's name wrong. Maybe he had been discombobulated by the death of his family and gone to a brothel other than the one he had named.

Police examined the hard drive on his computer and found that he had visited such sites as 'How to Kill' and 'White Man Killer', and found evidence of his searches for the poisonous seeds. They located the hidden film canister containing the seed and water mixture in his bedroom. Confronted with this, Gonzales spluttered that he had been so upset over the break-up with his girlfriend that he purchased the seeds to take his own life. Police would later find that the keys on his typewriter matched those in the letters the mystery poisoner sent to the food company, the Federal Police and the Australian Quarantine and Inspection Service. Not only that, his fingerprint was found on the letter sent to the Australian Federal Police.

On 13 June 2002, the investigators of Strike Force Tawas decided that they had enough evidence to convict Sef Gonzales and, eleven months after the slayings, charged him with three counts of murder.

At his trial in the Supreme Court of New South Wales, Gonzales declared his innocence, even though he knew that if he pleaded guilty and displayed remorse he might receive lesser sentences: 'I lied about one or two things to friends. I was put on trial for being a lousy person. I have deep remorse for people I lied to but [they] can't make me plead guilty to murder.'

He applied for access to his inheritance to fund his legal defence, but his bid was opposed by his grandparents and rejected by the Supreme Court because the family estate was yet to be finalised.

Psychiatrist Professor David M. Greenberg interviewed Gonzales and told the court he 'could not make the diagnosis that just prior to his family's murders he was suffering from a major depressive disorder', and that there was 'insufficient evidence to diagnose Mr Gonzales as suffering from a personality disorder at this time'.

While in custody Gonzales was a sweeper at Silverwater Correctional Centre and his behaviour was, reported staff, 'polite and unproblematic'. One prison authority who interviewed him prior to sentencing said he presented 'as a quiet person eager to engage in discussion surrounding the offences. However, it would appear he does so with the expressed intention of arguing his innocence and to avoid taking responsibility for the offences. He expressed feelings of sadness and grief in relation to the death of his parents and sister, and betrayal in relation to the withdrawal of support from his extended family and friends.'

The Crown submitted to the court that there had been a high degree of brutality or violence in the commission of the murders, that they had been premeditated and planned and although they had been committed in one criminal episode there had been distinct intervals of time between them; that Gonzales had obtained seeds with the aim of poisoning his family, had callously gone out with Dacillo on the night of 11 July to create an alibi; 'had acted out of the base motives of ridding himself of threats to his way of life and of obtaining an inheritance from his parents'; that he had laid false trails with the intention of misleading police, had not pleaded guilty or shown any contrition, and did not suffer from any mental condition 'that might have mitigated his criminality'. The murders had been committed after careful planning and in cold blood.

Sef Gonzales was found guilty of the murders of Teddy, Mary-Loiva and Clodine Gonzales on 20 May 2004. When the verdict was delivered, he emitted a loud gasp, then laid his head on the wooden shelf of the dock. After a while he raised his head and looked at the ceiling, his mouth forming words which most assumed were prayers. For himself or his family, no one knows. But probably the former, for in the cells later that day he was hectoring his legal team about the possibility of an appeal.

In sentencing the defendant, Justice Bruce James said:

> [that] in order to characterise any case as being in the worst case category it must be possible to point to particular features of very great heinousness... the noun 'heinousness' ... being variously defined as meaning atrocious, detestable, hateful, odious, gravely reprehensible and extremely wicked.

Gonzales' crime fulfilled each of these definitions:

> I consider that the murders show features of very great heinousness and that there are no facts mitigating the objective seriousness of the murders and hence the murders fall within the worst category of cases of murder at common law ... On the three charges of murder I sentence the prisoner to concurrent sentences of imprisonment for life, each to date from 13 June, 2002.

This time, Gonzales showed no emotion. After the sentence was brought down he simply left the dock, his face expressionless. Outside the court, his aunt Emily Luna sighed, 'It's actually a very sad day because we love Sef very much. I'm just glad it's over.'

After his arrest and conviction, Sef Gonzales was deserted by his friends and many in his extended family. Every week since he has been imprisoned, however, he has received a visitor who sits and talks quietly with him. Father Paul Cahill was the Gonzales family's parish priest in Blacktown; he has known the prisoner since he was a tiny and cherubic 11-year-old altar boy.

In August 2007 Gonzales asked the Court of Criminal Appeal to overturn his conviction and the three life sentences, citing police errors and an unfair grilling in the witness stand as his reasons. He took exception to the detectives' assurances, in the days and weeks and months after the killings, that he was not a suspect when all the while they were compiling evidence against him. And he complained that the relentless questioning of Crown Prosecutor Mark Tedeschi QC was so objectionable that it constituted an unfair trial. Tedeschi at one stage had called Gonzales' evidence 'absolutely pathetic'. If the appeal were successful, the conviction could be quashed and a retrial ordered.

Father Cahill, who had beseeched his parishioners to pray that Gonzales received a fair trial, supported the now 27-year-old's appeal, telling the *Sydney Morning Herald*:

> I have believed him all along. I have accepted what he has said. He has pleaded not guilty and I think there is a lot of light and shade in what is there ... it depends how people look at it. I will continue to be a support person. As a Catholic priest it is my responsibility to continue to support him and be there for him if he needs me. My area is a spiritual one and he needs assistance – as we all need assistance.

The appeal failed. On 27 November 2007, appeal judges Justices Roger Giles, Elizabeth Fullerton and Roderick Howie ruled against Gonzales.

In a bizarre postscript, in 2004 real estate agents Peter and Erica Hinton of L.J. Hooker North Ryde sold the Gonzales family home to a couple for $800 000 without disclosing that it was the scene of a triple murder. When the buyers, Mr and Mrs Lin, learned of this dark history they asked to be released from the contract and sought a refund of their $80 000 deposit. As devout Buddhists, they believed that a house in which murder had been committed was haunted and would visit misfortune upon them. L.J. Hooker resisted until public and media pressure caused them to tear up the deal. Disciplinary action was taken by the Commissioner for Fair Trading against Mahevi Pty Ltd, trading as L.J. Hooker North Ryde, and the Hintons, citing misrepresentation of the sale of the property and failure to act honestly, fairly and professionally. The agency and the agents were penalised a total of $41 800.

CHAPTER 19

THE KIMBERLEY KILLER

Josef Schwab: Serial killer

1987

After a lifetime of hard toil, Marcus Bullen figured he'd earned the right to kick back. So the 70-year-old former deputy mayor of Fremantle, Western Australia, invited his son Lance and daughter-in-law Joan to join him and his wife Winifred in the Top End of the Northern Territory to bask for a bit in the warm, dry winter days that follow the end of the wet season there. June, Marcus knew, was a fine month for pitching a tent and reeling in barramundi that never taste so good as when they're cooked on an open campfire. The sojourn had been everything Bullen had hoped. In a postcard to a friend back in Fremantle, he wrote, 'So far, having a lovely time.'

As the holiday neared its end, on 9 June 1987 father and son waved cheerfully to their wives and drove off from their campsite on the Victoria

River, near the small town of Timber Creek, 350 kilometres south of Darwin and 220 kilometres south-west of Katherine, planning to head upriver to check out new fishing spots. They didn't expect to be gone long, maybe an hour or two. About 10 kilometres from their camp they stopped their Mitsubishi Sigma station wagon and got out to survey the flow of the water.

Suddenly a small, wild-eyed man wearing camouflage gear and wielding a .223 Armalite assault rifle burst from the scrub. The Bullens stood transfixed by shock and confusion as the marauder, possessed by a weird manic fury, reeled and jerked around them like a demented marionette, screaming at them to lie face down in the dirt. When they complied, he shot both men a number of times in the back.

The gunman stripped the corpses and buried them in shallow graves in the sand at the river's highwater mark. His hope, it is thought, was that the crocodiles that infest the river would dispose of them. Next he set fire to their Mitsubishi, having stashed the men's clothes inside. That done, he returned to his own vehicle parked in the bush a short distance away, and continued his journey, west across the border into Western Australia. Police later said that they believed the killer had stalked the Bullens for some days before striking.

By the time dusk fell, Winifred and Joan Bullen were deeply worried. Marcus and Lance had been gone all day. They were good and responsible men and would never have purposely caused their wives undue concern. At such times you think the worst, and no doubt they did. Could the Mitsubishi have broken down? Could they, please God no, have fallen victim to crocodiles? Winifred and Joan drove to Timber Creek and notified the police that their spouses were late returning from a fishing recce. Next morning, when the men still had not returned, a police search party went looking for them. The searchers found the burnt-out wagon and there, still buried in the sand, the murdered men. Lodged in mud at the death site was a spent .223 cartridge and in the dirt a clear bootprint that did not match the footwear of either deceased.

As word of the slayings spread by bush telegraph around Timber Creek and further afield, detectives were contacted by several people who reported seeing a white and orange 1971 or 1972 Toyota 4Runner four-wheel-drive with a small, dark-haired man at the wheel in the region around the time the Bullens were shot. They filed the information.

Investigators started probing the lives of Marcus and Lance Bullen to identify anyone who might have harboured a grudge against them, perhaps someone whom Marcus had wronged during his time in public life. The truth, when finally it became known, was a lot more scary. Their murderer was a serial killer, shooting dead innocent strangers at random with no more motive than that it thrilled his deranged mind to do so.

Julie Warren and Phillip Walkemeyer were two of the most popular young people in the northern West Australian town of Kununurra. They planned to marry on the banks of the Ord River on 25 July 1987. They would have made a good match. Warren, a 24-year-old New Zealander, was vivacious and fun-loving and, said Carol Rolland, her workmate on the checkout counter at the Kununurra supermarket, 'a gentle, loving person'. Walkemeyer, 26, nicknamed 'Quagmire' because it rhymed – at a stretch – with his surname, was employed by the Department of Aviation at Kununurra's airstrip. 'A jovial happy man', according to Carol Rolland, he was president of the town's squash club and a keen runner.

Early in June, the lovers set off with their friend, Terry Bolt, 36, a father of three and an air traffic controller at Derby, on a fishing and camping trip into the wilds of the Kimberley region in Western Australia's deep north. They set up camp on the banks of the Pentecost River on Hope Valley Station, 100 kilometres west of Kununurra and 300 kilometres west of Timber Creek across the Northern Territory border. Like the Bullens they sought peace and relaxation. And, tragically, like the Bullens they found death.

On Sunday 14 June, the friends were chilling out around their campsite, laughing, joking, having a few drinks after a day's fishing with two Kununurra mates who had joined them for the day. They would have talked about Julie and Phillip's engagement party on the following Saturday night, for which Walkemeyer had bought a large keg of beer.

Around dusk the daytrippers bade farewell and disappeared over the scrubby rise to the east towards home. As the two men drove away they saw parked by the roadside a vehicle, white with orange flashes on the sides. Thinking nothing of it, they continued on their way.

The gunman, wearing camouflage gear and boots, descended on Warren, Walkemeyer and Bolt like a wolf come to feed. His footprints, found later, indicate that he approached stealthily at first, creeping through the bush, careful not to alert his prey. When he got to the clearing where the trio were camped he hit the ground running, shouting, and rapid-firing a Ruger Mini 14 .556 semi-automatic rifle with a 30-round magazine. The terrified campers tried to flee but inevitably were cut down. Julie died first, from a single bullet wound to her back. Her companions were also shot in the back, not once but many times.

As he'd done with the Bullens, the killer stripped the bodies. But this time, instead of burying the corpses he rolled them into the river. He helped himself to his victims' bankbooks, jewellery and watches, put their clothes in Walkemeyer's Toyota Hilux four-wheel-drive, drove it into a nearby creekbed, set it on fire and cleared out.

When Warren and Walkemeyer failed to show up at the supermarket and the airstrip next day, and calls to their homes brought no response, alarmed colleagues contacted the police. Although it was possible that the campers had simply been having too much fun to return to work, the murders of Marcus and Lance Bullen the week before compelled authorities to initiate a search. The two Kununurra friends who had spent part of Sunday with the missing trio reported the white, orange-flashed Toyota 4Runner they had seen when they left the campsite. Police were quick to note that a similar vehicle had been spotted in Timber Creek around the time the Bullens were killed. Then a truckie came forward. He said that on Sunday afternoon he had been driving on Hope Valley Station and saw thick black smoke in the distance. He went to investigate its source. Nearing the smoke, he saw coming towards him from the direction of the fire a white 4Runner with orange flashes on the sides. He pulled off the narrow road to let the vehicle pass and noticed that its driver was a small man who looked to be in his mid-twenties, with pale skin and short dark hair. The truckie continued on to the blaze, and found a Toyota Hilux in flames. Now the driver of the 4Runner was the prime suspect.

Next day, 15 June, Julie Warren's body was found floating in the Pentecost River. Walkemeyer's and Bolt's remains were recovered the following day 3 kilometres downstream from where Warren was found. Her friend Carol Rolland said sadly to reporters from the *Northern Territory News* that Julie's family were scheduled to arrive in Kununurra from New Zealand in a couple of weeks for their daughter's wedding, but now 'they'll have to come for a funeral instead'.

Said another friend to the *News*, reflecting the town's fury at the savage murders, 'Julie and Phil were top people. They were very much in love. All they wanted to do was get away from the town for a while. A lot of the men in town are out with rifles looking for the person who did it. They want to get him, all right.' One mate recalled Phillip Walkemeyer shuddering when he was told of the Bullens' murders and suggesting they could have fallen foul of a drug-runner. Walkemeyer's mother, Maureen, told reporter Warwick Sinclair, 'Julie was his first love. They were loved by God and totally devoted to one another. Tonight I know they are in heaven together. My son was a gentle giant ... a beautiful person [who] loved people, camping and fishing. That's why he loved the north-west. It is a peaceful place. I knew he was happy here. Phillip died in God's arms. It would have been a beautiful wedding.'

A forensic squad unearthed a quantity of Ruger cartridges at the Pentecost River campsite, and a bootprint that matched exactly the one found on the riverside where the Bullens had met their death.

Certain now that the person responsible for the five murders was a serial killer, one of the most extensive air and ground searches in Australian history was commenced. A squad of seven highly trained, heavily armed Tactical Response Group (TRG) police was despatched from Perth. They set up headquarters in Kununurra, joining a team of crack Northern Territory and West Australian police. Road blocks were set up in the north of the Territory, in Western Australia and even down into South Australia. Police halted every car to check that the Kimberley Killer, as he was now nationally known, was not inside, then warned the occupants to take extreme caution and not to stop for a soul. Warned Mike Speechley of Perth's Royal Automobile Club, '[The killer] appears to be out there. If you have to go, go in company. And be very, very wary of strangers.' Added Detective Sergeant John Carnie, one of the officers leading the manhunt, 'I would advise tourists to be on the alert for any strange vehicles or strange movements, to make sure that any firearms are secured and be on the lookout.' Soon the highways of the Top End were almost totally deserted.

Reggie Tatya, an Aboriginal tracker from Broome, was hired and flown from his home to scour the countryside around Home Valley Station. 'I carry a gun. I'll shoot him first,' Tatya declared. Not that he didn't have a Plan B should he encounter the killer. 'I can also hide behind trees,' he said.

People in the towns and on isolated homesteads alike lived in mortal fear that the Kimberley Killer would come calling. They deadlocked their doors, treated strangers with uncharacteristic suspicion and hostility, and armed themselves to the teeth. They kept their weapons oiled and loaded and ready for use in their homes and cars. Kununurra gun-shop owner Diana Oliver was typical of the terrified residents in the wake of the murders. She would tell how she kept a loaded 12-gauge shotgun on her kitchen table and instructed her kids how to use it if they had to. Said taxi-driver Mark Adrian, who carried his shotgun under the front seat of his cab, 'If I see the bastard I'll shoot first and ask questions later. I must be prepared. I could easily be called by the killer to take him somewhere.'

Said one police officer, 'We are in the dark. All we know is that we have a dangerous, cold-blooded murderer.'

Apart from not having a clue to the killer's identity, let alone his motivation, the greatest problem the searchers faced was the sheer vastness of the difficult terrain where, if of a mind to, a fugitive could hide forever. As one officer wearily remarked, 'It's real needle in a haystack territory.'

In a 17 June editorial, the *Northern Territory News* called for Federal Government aid, perhaps involving the Australian Army, to supplement the sorely stretched resources of the West Australian and Northern Territory police:

> No one undervalues the good efforts of the police, particularly in the Northern Territory. Assistant commissioner Neil Plumb and Det Supt Colin Pope are thorough professionals on top of the job. But they, and their West Australian colleagues, simply cannot be expected with their relatively scarce resources to cover the thousands of hectares of some of the most rugged and inhospitable terrain in the world. There is little doubt the police will capture the murderer in time. But time is the essence. It is critical the killer should be caught quickly otherwise he will kill again. He has shot five people dead in seven days. There is no reason to imagine he will stop there and every reason to believe his ghastly trail of killings will go on. Expense must be no obstacle ... An all-out effort is needed today and every day until this killer is caught. Nothing but his capture will satisfy the public.

The end came more quickly than anyone expected.

On Friday 19 June, at around 8 am, helicopter pilot Peter Lutenegger was flying low over Jubilee Downs on Plum Plain, 10 kilometres west of the rugged little Kimberley town of Fitzroy Crossing, 80 kilometres south-west of Kununurra. Lutenegger was mustering cattle for a big rodeo in Fitzroy Crossing the following day. Down below he saw a white vehicle partially hidden under branches and a tarpaulin in a grove of trees. Well aware, like everyone else in the Top End, that the murder suspect probably drove a white vehicle, he swooped close, the wind from his blades blowing the tarpaulin aside. Lutenegger could make out a man inside the vehicle. And as he hovered the man, who sported a red bandanna around his head, Rambo-style, was bare-chested and bare-footed, and wore army-style fatigue pants, clambered out and brandished a rifle at the chopper. Lutenegger flew out of range and radioed the police. Within an hour, a small army of detectives, along with the TRG wearing flak jackets, camouflage clothes and armed with high-powered sniper rifles, was converging on Jubilee Downs in small planes.

Any thoughts the TRG held that the man holed up in the white vehicle might be just an innocent camper were quickly dispelled when, as the aircraft approached, he fired at them with his Armalite rifle, a volley hitting one plane. Police already on the ground and closing in all recalled hearing the sound of the bullets thudding into the wing – *smack! smack! smack!* They feared the plane was crippled and would crash, and were relieved to see it wheel away to safety into the blue.

There was no place, however, for the TGR to hide. The gunman knew he was trapped and made a last stand. He blasted round after round at the officers, who skittered from ant hill to tree trunk, all the time moving closer, cutting off possible exit routes. The ant hills exploded and some of the smaller trees were sheared in half by heavy fire. Miraculously, no policeman was wounded, though their gear took hits.

In an effort to disable their quarry, the TRG lobbed hand-grenades of teargas and gunpowder in his direction. The grenades exploded and the heat and shrapnel set off the little mounds of ammunition the gunman had piled around him for easy access, and set fire to the scrub. The man raced through the flames and acrid smoke, shooting wildly as he ran.

The gunman continued to pepper the police, who returned the compliment. One police bullet shattered the wooden stock of the gunman's rifle and blew off his right thumb. Though bleeding heavily, the man rushed to the back seat of his vehicle and replaced the destroyed Armalite with the Ruger with which he had slaughtered Warren, Walkemeyer and Bolt. He unleashed another hail of bullets before another round of fire from the TRG hit him in the stomach and he fell. He lay still as the police cautiously approached. Then, like one of those characters in horror films who refuses to die, the Kimberley Killer leapt to his feet and levelled his rifle at the police. 'Open fire!' shouted Inspector Bob Brown. At the command, an officer shot the man through the heart. He fell dead, face down in the dust as his blood pooled around him.

Stockman Alan Simpson saw it all. 'The police gave him a body wound first and he lay doggo. Then he got up, shot in the stomach, and he just kept coming. The police opened up and eliminated him.'

The TRG leader, Inspector Brown, said later to the producers of *The Kimberley Killer*, a television documentary made as part of the *Crime Investigation Australia* series some years afterwards:

> Before every operation, you're nervous, but confidence in yourself, your team members, your training and your equipment overcomes this. Normal people wouldn't do what we do. They'd walk off or run away. The TRG aren't in a position to do that. No one took a backward step. [What happened to us that day] only happens in wartime … Killing him was the only possible result because he was very much determined to kill one of us. Of that I have no doubt.

Brown distinguished himself following the shootout by running to the white and orange 4Runner and driving it out of the burning scrub. In doing so he preserved important incriminating evidence, including the shooter's passport, the boot which had left a print at both murder scenes, and belongings stolen from his victims.

The Kimberley Killer *had* been eliminated. But, as one detective said as he looked down at the ruined body, 'Who the hell was he?' In the following days, that question was answered.

The 4Runner's registration number was traced: the vehicle had been hired from the Avis branch at Brisbane airport on 23 April by a newly arrived German tourist named Josef Schwab. He had never returned it. The passport in the car was Schwab's and although the pleasant-faced, clean-cut young man pictured in the document bore little resemblance to the bearded, crop-haired, sunburned and bloodied corpse that lay in the morgue at Derby Regional Hospital, he was definitely the deceased.

The terror over, the tourists came out of hiding like cockatoos at dawn. And as the roads filled with travellers again, and the riverbanks thronged with anglers and made barramundi once more an endangered species, the investigators, slowly, with the help of Schwab's family, Interpol and various other sources, compiled a portrait of the Kimberley Killer.

Josef Schwab was born in Bavaria on Christmas Day 1960 and grew up in Starnberg Lake in the town of Poecking, 20 kilometres south of Munich. He was by all reports a quiet fellow, albeit with a fondness for firearms. His uncle, Andre Schwaiger, was a crack shot and so proud of his marksmanship that he nailed a plaque commemorating his success in a shooting contest to the front of his house. An introvert who preferred his own company, Schwab had been in trouble for stealing a car. (His fingerprints, sent from Germany, were used to positively identify him.) This wasn't his first visit to Australia. He'd come here in 1981 and made his home for a time in Adelaide, where he is remembered for his enthusiasm for driving out into the bush and shooting wild pigs.

Schwab's father recalled, 'It was Josef's greatest dream, a dream of freedom, to go to Australia.' And his mother said, 'He wanted to support himself as a cabinetmaker when he first arrived in Australia but the best job he could find was nailing together crates. He earned little money and came home in 1984.' He tried to go into business for himself, but failed, then worked as an armed security guard for the United States Consulate in Munich. He flew back into Australia from Bangkok on 23 April 1987.

On landing in Brisbane, Schwab hired the 4Runner, then bought four guns, including the Armalite rifle and the Ruger, and hundreds of rounds of ammunition, from a Brisbane gun dealer for $1000. It seems he had come back bent on mayhem. He drove from Brisbane through Mt Isa to Darwin, shooting donkeys, pigs and kangaroos on the way. He stayed at Darwin, then moved on, south-east to Katherine and west to Timber Creek, where he stalked and slew the Bullens. West again to the Kimberley. More killings – Warren, Walkemeyer and Bolt – and then, mercifully, his own death.

The last his mother and father had heard from him was a cheery postcard sent from Darwin on 21 May. In the deepest shock, neither was able to suggest a reason for their son's murderous rampage. The people who came forward later to say they had come in contact with Schwab – from the Avis dealer at Brisbane airport to service station employees and café owners of the Top End – invariably described him as polite, friendly, good-looking and with a charming smile.

Well and good. But why did Josef Schwab do what he did? It's clear that his dreadful acts, to stalk and kill randomly for killing's sake and not for gain – we can surely discount the meagre belongings he took from the bodies – were those of a demented individual. But questions abound. Why did he kill? Why did he kill in the highly ritualised manner – stalking, shooting in the back, stripping his victims of clothes, disposing of their bodies – that he did? Did some event in his life trigger his atrocities or were they, like the crimes of Martin Bryant, John Glover and Julian Knight, the result of a slow and relentless accumulation of failure, frustration and humiliation that eventually manifested in massive and terrible bloodshed?

Did Schwab kill more than the five victims we know about? Possibly – many people who go missing in the Top End are never heard from again. He could have slain any number of these and buried them easily and anywhere. We'll never know.

The chance of answering any of these questions died with Josef Schwab. As Sergeant Jim King, police media officer at Perth police headquarters at the time of the murders, said, 'Why did Schwab do it? We'll always be in the dark.'

CHAPTER 20

THE PORT ARTHUR MASSACRE

Martin Bryant: Mass murderer
1996

When the firing began, everyone at the old jail and restaurant complex at Port Arthur on Tasmania's Tasman Peninsula that Sunday, 28 April 1996, thought it was a local historical society re-enactment of the convict days. In seconds, as people began falling, fatally wounded by gunman Martin Bryant, they knew that they were horribly mistaken and ran for their lives. In ninety seconds, Bryant, a thin 29-year-old with long blond surfie locks tumbling around a cherubic face, shot dead twenty people in Port Arthur's Broad Arrow Café, then went outside to the car park and surrounds and shot dead another twelve. Some thirty-seven people suffered non-fatal gunshot wounds. Most of Bryant's victims were daytripping tourists, hoping for a little fun with their history.

Once, most Australians believed, such massacres only happened in other countries, but these days, some twelve years after Martin Bryant's homicidal rampage, no one really believes any more that our world is safe.

Just after 1 pm, Bryant, wearing jeans, sneakers and a dark duffle coat, and carrying a large Prince sports bag, took a seat in the Broad Arrow Café. After a bit, he unzipped his bag and took a Colt AR15 semi-automatic assault rifle with thirty .223 calibre bullets in its magazine from the bag and rose from his seat. Casually, unhurriedly, he strolled through the room from table to table, picking off patrons. Moh Yee William Ng and Sou Leng Chung, visiting from Kuala Lumpur, died first, then Kate Scott, 21, after her friend Mick Sargent was wounded in the head.

Abandoning the carnage in the café, Bryant sauntered out to the car park where he had left his yellow Volvo, and opened the boot. He had clearly come bent on destruction, for in the boot were a loaded 12-gauge shotgun, a .308 calibre FN FAL semi-automatic rifle with a full magazine, and another magazine for the Colt AR15. He snapped the latter into the death weapon, almost too hot to hold because of the number of shots he'd already fired, and recommenced the killing. He was heard to yell, 'No one gets away from me!'

The murder of the Mikac family epitomised the horror of the day. Bryant stalked Nanette Mikac, who worked as a guide on Port Arthur's popular ghost tour, and her daughters Madeleine, 3, and Alannah, 6. Bryant ordered Nanette to kneel. She beseeched him, 'Please don't hurt my babies.' Face calm, his demeanour detached, Bryant shot Nanette and Madeleine dead. Alannah ran behind a tree. Like a jackal stalking its prey, Bryant moved to the tree where Alannah cowered, and killed her too.

The death toll continued to rise: Zoe Hall, Winifred Aplin, Sarah Loughton, Pauline Masters, Andrew Mills, Peter Nash, Anthony Nightingale, Mary Nixon, Ronald Jary, Mary Howard … innocent people, good people, people who were loved and would be terribly missed, caught in Martin Bryant's lethal and random cross-hairs.

During the slaughter, it seems that Bryant spared just one person. Robyn Lawler in 2004 would tell Andrew Denton on his *Enough Rope* program on ABC-TV that her brother Ashley found himself gazing down the barrel of Bryant's gun that day. As he looked into Bryant's dead eyes, Ashley was certain that his end was seconds away. His sister said he saw his life flash before him. Suddenly Bryant lowered his gun and waved at Ashley, as if to say, 'Oh, hi.' Lawler then told Denton how, in 1993, her brother had been one of those who pulled Bryant from the wreckage of the car crash that killed Helen Harvey, Bryant's benefactor. Bryant had recognised his Good Samaritan at Port Arthur and repaid him by letting him live.

Twenty minutes after he fired the first shot, with thirty-two people lying dead at Port Arthur, Bryant commandeered a BMW, forced Glenn Pears into the boot, and drove to the Seascape guesthouse, 2.5 kilometres away, where he had murdered the elderly proprietors, Sally and David Martin, earlier in the day. He now made the total number of deaths thirty-five, by shooting Pears. Police, by this time in hot pursuit, laid siege to the Seascape, believing that Bryant was holding the Martins hostage. Holing up for eighteen hours, Bryant eventually set fire to the guesthouse and tried to flee. He was captured and, suffering serious burns to one side of his body, taken to Royal Hobart Hospital. After treatment he underwent lengthy police and psychiatric examinations in a bid to learn why he had done what he did. While he had severe intellectual difficulties, he was pronounced sane and ordered to stand trial.

A remarkable and perceptive interview with Bryant conducted on 4 May 1996, six days after the slaughter, by Paul E. Mullen, director of Victorian Forensic Psychiatry Services and professor of forensic psychiatry at Monash University, and quoted in part below, leaves little room for doubt that Bryant felt alienated and persecuted by society. Yet many people in this world are victimised and rejected, and they don't feel compelled to slay thirty-five people to make amends.

Bryant was born on 7 May 1967, the elder of Maurice and Carleen Bryant's two children. He was a troubled, and troubling, child. His speech and motor skills did not develop as quickly as other children's. He was small for his age. He glowered and sulked, tortured domestic animals, set himself on fire and cut down trees. He was eerily unemotional. At infants and primary school he was a slow learner and could not relate to classmates, who called him 'Stupid Marty'. He was friendless. He tormented some children, hitting them and urinating on them, and was himself terrorised by others. 'I was hazed and knocked around all the time, no one wanted to be my friend,' he told Professor Mullen. Once, when he was nine, he attempted to sell jewellery he had made outside the Broad Arrow Café at Port Arthur, but the staff had gruffly sent him packing.

Bryant's father hoped against hope that his son would be like 'an oak tree and mature eventually' but that didn't happen.

By his late teens, Bryant, who had an IQ of 66 (the national average is around 100) and a mental age of eleven, still could not read or write, and had been diagnosed as severely intellectually handicapped, and suffering from paranoid schizophrenia and a personality disorder. He was granted a disability pension.

In 1991, the then 24-year-old Bryant became a live-in odd-job man on the farm at Copping, some 40 kilometres east of Hobart, of eccentric and kindly Tattersalls Lottery heiress Helen Harvey, in her late fifties. The farmhouse was host to scores of cats, dogs and pigs. Harvey, unlike anyone outside his immediate family whom he had ever met before, cosseted him, and lavished money on him. Copping locals considered him 'weird but harmless'.

The following year Harvey was driving her car, with Bryant in the passenger seat, when the car collided with another vehicle and she was killed. Bryant suffered head and back injuries, but his pain must have been eased when he learned that Harvey had left him her fortune, which included a mansion and more than $500 000. His mother organised for Perpetual Trustees to manage his windfall, but he still had sufficient funds to buy a Volvo and a surfboard. He also acquired some property. One place he set his heart on was the Seascape guesthouse. He wanted to buy it for his father but was outbid by David and Sally Martin. He stormed from the auction, having convinced himself that the Martins had maliciously bought the Seascape to thwart what he erroneously believed was his father's dream – to own the establishment.

Maurice Bryant apparently committed suicide in 1993. He had split from Carleen. His body was found at the bottom of a lake.

The two rocks of Bryant's life, his father and Helen Harvey, were gone, dead within a year of each other.

Bryant travelled, usually alone but occasionally with a girlfriend, to America and Europe and Asia. Later, during an interview with a psychiatrist he became angry when he recalled how he had often tried to engage fellow travellers in conversation but had invariably been rebuffed. He enjoyed the long international flights because the person strapped into his or her seat beside him *had* to talk to him. Professor Mullen noted that:

> Mr Bryant became quite animated in describing some of what he regarded as the more successful interactions with fellow travellers on the journeys to and from Europe and the United States ... Next to the journeys themselves, Mr Bryant listed the sex video shops in Amsterdam as the greatest pleasure he had derived from world travel.

Other delights in Bryant's life were frequenting prostitutes, scuba diving, watching TV, drinking (sweet, sticky spirits, liqueurs and wine, Guinness stout), which became heavier and more frequent from mid 1996, and listening to Cliff Richard records and the soundtrack of *The Lion King*. His favourite films were the ultra-violent *Under Siege, Child's Play, The Protector* ... and *Babe*.

He was also entranced by weapons and accumulated a stash of firearms magazines. One neighbour remembers him musing, sometime late in 1995, 'Nobody ever wants to listen to me, or go with me. I'm getting fed up with this. I'll think of something, and everybody will remember me.'

Some young women found Bryant attractive at first but then, always, they shied away, repelled by his moods and being made to watch *Child's Play* over and over again. He broke up with and then reconciled with one girlfriend shortly before the disaster at Port Arthur.

Professor Mullen reported after he examined Bryant in the wake of the massacre:

> [Bryant] talked of the extent to which he thinks about the distress and the rejections in the past. He said that he tries to live day by day, but acknowledges that frequently thoughts about past rejections, and what he recalls as his victimisation at school by bullies, intrude. He has become more caught up in these thoughts about past indignities over the past year. He said he became increasingly unhappy and angry because he had no real friends. He said, 'all I wanted was for people to like me'. Their failure to respond to his overtures led him to feel 'that I'd had a gutful'. This culminated in the months before the tragedy in a sense that there was no future for him, that he would always remain lonely and rejected and that he would be better off dead.

> [He] acknowledged that he has always been somewhat self-conscious and shy. He has throughout his adult life felt as if people looked at him in the street, talked about him behind his back, and laughed at him. He feels that they make derogatory comments about his appearance and how he is dressed. This, in recent years, has been combined with a conviction that people wanted to hurt or harm him. He sometimes believes that particular people he sees in the street are bent on physically attacking him. These sensitive and persecutory ideas are not organized into any system of belief that there is a plot aimed against him. It amounts to a degree of over-sensitivity and a general conviction in the malevolence of others rather than being suggestive of delusions of persecution.

When invited by psychologists or police to talk about the mass killings at Port Arthur, Bryant always replied that if he had done anything there he had no recall of it, and couldn't say what had led to the shootings, if indeed the killings had even occurred. The only gripe he had, he reiterated, was that people had been unkind to him all his life and at times he had harboured feelings of revenge which led to him imagining himself strangling and shooting. Only to Professor Mullen, it seems, did he admit any culpability, replying to the question as to why he chose Port Arthur to get even for past slights by saying: 'A lot of violence has happened there, it must be the most violent place in Australia; it seemed the right place.'

So it's possible to conclude that in the weeks leading up to the Port Arthur tragedy, Bryant was enraged by the persecution he believed he had suffered, distraught at the loss of Helen Harvey and his father, riven by his romantic crisis, and beset by a need to take revenge on the Martins and the people who had chided him for selling trinkets at Port Arthur when he was a boy, and by extension those who visited Port Arthur. Professor Mullen told a reporter that he believed Bryant was contemplating suicide in the months leading up to Port Arthur, but when he read of the massacre at Dunblane, Scotland, on 13 March 1996, where sixteen schoolchildren were slain by a deranged shooter named Thomas Hamilton, he decided to emulate that. People, such as his neighbour, recalled Bryant saying, shortly before descending on Port Arthur, 'I'll do something that will make everyone remember me.'

On 28 April, he drove to the old convict site, with its ruined jail buildings, parkland, lake, car park and Broad Arrow Café. As usual, it was thronged with visitors and staff. Finally, he may have thought, as he sat in the café and unzipped his bag, people would take notice of Martin Bryant.

When interviewed by detectives in a holding cell after his arrest, Bryant was vague and distracted. At one point he made the bizarre observation that, on the whole, he'd rather be at a Kentucky Fried Chicken store. He denied having been at the Port Arthur site, but the officers kept pressing ... The cat and mouse exchange between police and prisoner was surreal ...

> Detective: Well, I'll tell you what's happened.
>
> Bryant: Mmmm ...
>
> Detective: There have been twenty people in that Broad Arrow Café ...
>
> Bryant: Mmmm ...

Detective: … who were shot and killed and there were a lot of others injured.

Bryant: Right …

Detective: There were also a number of people in the car park who were killed as a result of being shot. There were four people that were taken out of that BMW who were shot and killed. There were two children and their mother on the way to the toll booth …

Bryant: Oh God, it's awful isn't it?

Detective: … and a girl in a white Toyota Corolla that I just showed you. And we believe you're responsible.

Bryant: You reckon I'm responsible … I only went surfing that day.

Detective: We've got all the time in the world, Martin.

Bryant: Obviously I have too, so what does it matter?

Detective: What matters is we'd like to know why you've done [this], what you've done, mate. It's simple.

Bryant: What have I done? I mean, I know I've done the wrong …

Detective: I've just told you what you've done.

Bryant: I've done the wrong thing by stealing a car …

Detective: Are you understanding what I just said to you? Because I've just told you what you've done.

Bryant: What have I done?

Detective: You've killed thirty-five people ...

Bryant: Ohhh …

Detective: … and injured several others …

Bryant: Mmmm …

Detective: … and a lot of people have identified you … killing those thirty-five people.

Bryant: All I know is other people have said to me, asked a couple of times whether I was at Port Arthur and I've said no because I wasn't at Port Arthur that day.

Detective: You took one of the guns out of your bag and opened fire in the café.

Bryant: Why would I do that?

Detective: I don't know, you tell me …

Bryant: Why would anyone do a thing like that?

Detective: Well, you tell us. That's what we want to know, Martin. Why.

Bryant: What ... what ... would ... I wouldn't hurt a person in my life.

Detective: You're in a little bit of trouble, Martin, aren't you? Would you say?

Bryant: I dunno, I s'pose I am. I'd like to get hold of some bail money.

Bryant seemed crestfallen, but cheered up at the prospect of getting Kentucky Fried Chicken for dinner.

There have been few more popular pieces of legislation than that put in train when, with the nation shocked and in mourning, Prime Minister John Howard took what he termed 'an opportunity to grab the moment and think about a fundamental change to gun laws', and began measures to ban rapid-fire rifles and shotguns and make gun licences and registration of all firearms mandatory. There was also a guns-buyback program in which owners of rapid-fire rifles and shotguns who handed in their weapons were financially compensated. Around 700 000 guns were turned in and destroyed. When the Prime Minister announced his plan, he was clearly wearing a bullet-proof vest beneath his coat.

Bryant was deemed fit to stand trial on thirty-five counts of murder, twenty of attempted murder, four of aggravated assault, three of causing grievous bodily harm, eight of wounding, one of arson and one of unlawfully setting fire to property. He originally pleaded not guilty, but when he appeared before Tasmania's Supreme Court in Hobart on 7 November 1996, he changed his plea to guilty. Throughout, as he repeated the word 'guilty' to charge after charge, he giggled and snickered.

In sentencing him, Tasmania's chief justice William Cox said, 'Taking into account of the medical evidence and of his lack of insight into the magnitude and effects of his conduct, apparent in all his appearances before this court, I have no reason to hope and every reason to fear that he will remain indefinitely as disturbed and insensitive as he was when planning and executing the crimes of which he now stands convicted.' The chief justice turned his gaze on Bryant, and continued, 'Martin Bryant, on each of the thirty-five counts of murder in this indictment, you are sentenced to imprisonment for the term of your natural life. I order that you not be eligible for parole in respect of any such a sentence.

'On each of the remaining counts in the indictment, you are sentenced to imprisonment for twenty-one years, to be served concurrently with each other, and with the concurrent sentence of life imprisonment already imposed. In respect of each sentence of twenty-one years, I order that you likewise not be eligible for parole. Let him stand down.'

Bryant's lawyer, John Avery, later explained Bryant's change of plea to *The Bulletin* magazine:

> It was never quite as simple as asking, 'Did you do it, mate?' We talked at length about what he said he did. It was through a process of talking, not grabbing him by the throat and forcing him, to bring him around to changing his plea. I wanted him to come to the decision. The evidence was absolutely overwhelming. He was entitled ... to have his guilt proved so it was my job to explain to him the implications – on himself and the families of the victims – of pursuing the not guilty. He certainly recognized that pleading guilty would be seen to be a better outcome for everyone, including himself, but I would not go so far as to say that it was out of any remorse. He didn't have the ability to show remorse.

Avery also said that Bryant's 'only regret afterwards was that he didn't shoot more people. This was not a situation that got out of hand. It went pretty much as he intended'.

Martin Bryant was returned to Risdon Prison, where he had been kept under heavy guard since the shootings.

And that's where he remains. But the thin surfie has gone. Nowadays Bryant, because he will not participate in any physical activity, is a grossly overweight ('he's whacked on at least 30 kilos and is as fat as a seal,' one former inmate told this author) 40-year-old with cropped dark brown hair.

From the outset he did himself no favours with prison staff. He was narcissistic and boasted about the carnage he had caused. Once, reportedly, he urged a prison staffer to bring her small children to his cell so he could meet them. He then mimed pointing a pistol at the children's heads, and said, 'Click, click.' Equally horrifying, another time he applied to be a sperm donor.

For the first few years of his incarceration in the gaol's high security hospital wing, Bryant did make an effort to interact, spending time in the prison library and playing chess and table tennis with other inmates. No more. His life in solitary confinement in Risdon is one of almost total silence. Prison officers told reporter Norm Lipson that he chooses to be mute and that it has been around two years since he has had a conversation with another soul. He does not watch television or listen to the radio.

Sources within Risdon describe Bryant, with vast understatement, as 'a strange character' who, before he chose not to speak, at one minute could conduct a mature conversation and the next be squeaking and babbling like an infant. He is kept in solitary confinement because, as the former inmate told this author, 'If they put him in with mainstream prisoners, he'd be dead within fifteen minutes. Bryant shot children at Port Arthur, and blokes who hurt kids are despised.'

Indeed, Bryant has been bashed on a number of occasions after his guards took their eyes off him for just a moment. On 21 June 2003 he was reportedly punched in the face by one inmate, and two weeks later had cleaning fluid hurled in his face by another.

For the past three years Bryant has refused visits. Once he allowed his tragic mother Carleen entry to his spartan cell with its vinyl mattress and lidless steel toilet, freezing in winter and suffocatingly hot in summer, but now he has barred her, and everyone else. Carleen Bryant told *The Bulletin* that the last time she saw her son:

> [he was] like a zombie ... He won't speak and just stares into the middle distance. I can sit in front of him for 15 minutes and he says nothing ... My poor Martin. He couldn't have shot all those people down at Port Arthur. He didn't have the brains to do it.

According to a psychiatrist who has observed the prisoner, he seems 'lost in a profound depression'. He is dishevelled and makes little attempt at cleanliness. A psychologist told *The Bulletin*, 'He is an overweight, shambolic wreck. If the community wanted a severe punishment for Mr Bryant, then they have it. What he has now is far worse than the death penalty.'

It seems as though Bryant is just waiting to die. Indeed, he is constantly on suicide watch, having attempted to take his own life five times in the past five years, most recently on 25 May 2007, when he slashed his wrists but was treated before he bled to death. On other occasions he has overdosed on sedatives, tried to choke himself by cramming bandages down his throat, swallowed a metal toothpaste tube and attempted to slash the femoral artery in his groin with a razor blade. On a number of occasions he has been found with blades secreted on his body. In the wake of the most recent suicide bid, he is checked at 15-minute intervals.

Bryant continues to receive scores of letters, mostly from women, but they remain unopened. Inmates at Risdon, apparently, are taking bets on when Martin Bryant will finally successfully end his life ... for they feel certain he will.

Euthanasia expert Dr Philip Nitschke in June 2007 put the case that since Bryant wanted so badly not to be on this earth, as evidenced by his series of suicide attempts, and given his particular circumstances, he should be allowed to die. Nitschke said the state had no interest in rehabilitating Bryant and that the sole purpose of his incarceration was 'punishment, and punishment without hope of release is tantamount to torture. As a society we should admit that we are sanctioning torture here and in those circumstances we should allow him to die or provide him with the means to obtain a peaceful death.' Meanwhile, as experts argue, and victims' loved ones, survivors, politicians, police and the general public regularly visit

Port Arthur to sadly mark the worst mass murder in Australia's history, it is clear that the scars inflicted by Martin Bryant have not healed. Recently, Andrew Hansen and Chris Taylor of the ABC-TV comedy show *The Chaser* presented 'The Eulogy Song', which scathingly mocked recently deceased celebrities, and included the line 'It pays to throw away the facts and have a rose-coloured look ... When he dies Martin Bryant will look like a saint.' They could have had no inkling of the hurt and angry reactions their joke would arouse.

The performance elicited an eloquently furious response from journalist John Hamilton of Melbourne's *Herald-Sun,* who reported from Port Arthur and covered Bryant's trial:

> Andrew Hansen and Chris Taylor, you are both a bloody disgrace. Your vile, tasteless song on *The Chaser,* slamming the dead, struck a new low for television, for the ABC's public accountability, and for pure sick-making gross offensiveness ... There was nothing funny about the Port Arthur massacre, Andrew Hansen. You sang the words written by Chris Taylor. Nothing to see through rose-coloured glasses. Nothing saintly about Martin Bryant. Alive or dead, he should always be remembered as mad, bad and possessed by the devil, an evil being who killed 35 people and who has ruined the lives of hundreds of others. You see, Andrew, you smug, self-satisfied 'comedian' tinkling away at your piano, looking for cheap laughs from a compliant studio audience, I was at Port Arthur 11 years ago. I was with a group of reporters who shook their heads and quietly wept as the horror unfolded. The police tour of the crime site took 2½ hours. It culminated in a superintendent leading us to a place where there were green rugs and a piece of light-blue plastic sheeting held down by three orange road cones and a piece of broken branch from a gum tree. I remember it as yesterday. The blood trails trickled down the hill towards Port Arthur, then petered out. 'A mother was here with her two little girls, one aged 3 and one aged 6,' said the policeman. 'The gunman shot the mother and the young one and the 6-year-old tried to hide behind that tree

but he chased her and shot her.' His words hung on the air. Tiny birds cheeped somewhere in the bush but they sounded still afraid and distant. Then, Andrew, I was in the Hobart courtroom seven months later when Martin Bryant appeared.

Funny? Well, he thought so. This is what I wrote then: 'Martin Bryant stood in the wooden dock in his sharp light blue suit. He smiled. He smirked. He sniggered. And he giggled. But it was at the ... 28th count of murder that he began to laugh out loud. Bryant stood there, hands in pockets, long tendrils of blond matted hair hanging down on each side of his flushed face, hanging like some rough woven hempen plaits around the face of a painted sailor doll. The judge's associate ... had been reading the charges for eight minutes when she reached the name that he recognised, the name that provoked the laughter. Nanette Mikac, wife and mother. "How say you, are you guilty or not guilty?" asked the judge's associate. "Guilty," said Martin Bryant, bobbing down as usual to mouth the words into microphones on the bench in front. He stood there, smiling, smirking, one hand now at his face, shielding his laughter as she read out the next two counts of murder, the children's names. "Count 51, Madeline Grace Mikac." – "Guilty," he laughed. "Count 52. Alannah Louise Mikac." – "Guilty,' he laughed again. By the 61st charge, one of attempted murder, Bryant was banging a hand on the rail in time with his glee and barely able to get the word "guilty" out.'

Andrew Hanson and Chris Taylor, you should now both appear on television and give an unreserved public apology to all those affected by the Port Arthur tragedy. No smiling, smirking or sniggering. Say sorry – and bloody well mean it.

CHAPTER 21

GONE TO GOWINGS

Darcy Dugan: Serial prison escapee, armed robber

1940s–1980s

With a name like Darcy Dugan, he could only have been a villain. In a brazen and outrageous 30-year criminal career, the serial prison escapee, robber and conman epitomised ruthlessness, cunning and gutter-smarts. He hurt and duped many in his time, but somehow there was always something likeable about Darcy Dugan – his cheeky incorrigibility and cheerful acceptance of punishment when he was caught, the way he hammed it up in the spotlight. When he died in 1991 at the age of seventy, having spent thirty-five of those years in gaol, he was mourned as a modern-day Ned Kelly or Robin Hood. Without him, went the accepted wisdom, Sydney was going to be a less lively place.

Dugan and his brother Tom grew up in the Sydney working-class suburbs of Newtown and Ultimo. Their father was Dick Dugan, who worked as a tiler and who, in spite of Darcy's myriad transgressions, idolised his son until the day he died. As if the boys were living out some Warner Bros crime flick of the 1930s, brother Tom led an exemplary existence while Darcy was very early beguiled by the criminal life. Putting his motto of 'never buy a thing when you can steal it' into practice, he led a gang of young thieves who broke and entered in the inner suburbs. Reform school became his second home. Each time on his release he re-embraced the outlaw life and offended again. Breaking the law came as naturally to the young thug as eating and breathing.

Soon Dugan was too old for boys' homes and was sent to prison to serve his time.

In his twenties he boasted 'No prison will ever hold me', and set about proving it. While incarcerated for robbery in the 1940s, he made seven escape attempts, managing to bust out three times and being caught on each occasion by the tough and ferocious Detective Sergeant Ray Kelly, who over the years would become Pat O'Brien to Dugan's James Cagney, and whom Dugan called 'The Jinx'.

In his first escape, from Long Bay Gaol on 25 January 1946, Dugan was on the loose for three weeks after he removed the steel grille of a prison van which was transporting him and crawled through the opening. On 4 March 1946, Dugan sawed through the thin wooden roof of prison tram No. 948 that was shuttling him from Darlinghurst Court back to the Bay. He surrendered a day later.

In August 1949 he audaciously climbed a perimeter wall at Long Bay and leaped 7 metres to the ground. This time he enjoyed ten days of freedom.

He made many other bids to flee prison which failed. He tried to hurl himself through a plate-glass window, was a prime mover in a mass breakout plot at Grafton Gaol, and schemed to blow up a wall at Parramatta Gaol and vanish in a high-powered car he would have waiting in the street outside.

In September 1949, Dugan was sentenced to a further ten years' imprisonment for the August escape attempt.

Completely unfazed, on 10 December 1949, Dugan and a fellow inmate named Bill Mears broke out of Sydney's Central Police Station when they cut through the bars of their cell with a hacksaw blade, scuttled across the roof of the building, slid down a 10 metre drainpipe into a lane, and scaled a 4 metre gate before running to George Street and hopping aboard a tram to freedom. Before he fled into the protective arms of an underworld only too happy to shield him, Dugan scrawled on the cell wall for the benefit of warders, 'Gone to Gowings!' (the tagline of a long-running contemporary advertisement for a popular men's wear store). They shook their heads and grinned.

Despite an intensive manhunt led by the dour, bespectacled Ray Kelly, who looked more like a bank clerk than a cop, and the offer of a £500 reward for information leading to their arrest, the escapees remained free until 14 February 1950, during which time they caused havoc. Having kept their heads down over Christmas and New Year, on 9 January Dugan and Mears trained their revolvers on Randwick shopkeeper John Thompson and relieved him of three watches, two wirelesses, a wallet, an overnight bag, sunglasses, a fur coat, a carton of cigarettes, two bottles of whisky and two of beer, fifteen petrol coupons, a pair of binoculars and £190 in cash.

Four days later, on 13 January, they robbed the Commonwealth Bank in Ultimo of £30. During the robbery they wounded the manager, Les Nalder, who would spend the rest of his days as an invalid, and fired at bank employees Roger Joseph and Alexander Robinson. A teller named Allan Grant was bashed.

Dugan and Mears targeted a shop at Balmain on 3 February. A man called Sid Tuck was wounded, and Fred Simmons, Walter Forbes and Harry Sale were fired upon.

During all this, somehow Dugan had time to write a letter to the tabloid *Daily Mirror*, assuring readers that he was having 'a lovely holiday'.

Dugan and Meers were finally captured on 14 February in the northern beaches suburb of Collaroy. After a tip-off from, it is believed, a neighbour that the escapees and two attractive women were partying in a fibro holiday house at 44 Alexander Street, a team of detectives closed in on the house at dawn, guns drawn. Through a window they could see Dugan and Mears sharing a bed, both dressed in pyjamas. The police banged on the door, one of them yelling, 'We are police! Hands up, Dugan and Mears!' Mears woke in a hurry and stood against a wall, hands in the air. Dugan, who had grown a pencil-thin Errol Flynn moustache while on the run, dived under the bed. He was hauled out and both were promptly handcuffed. The women were nowhere to be seen. Dugan and Mears seemed such nice men, agreed the locals. The smaller one (Dugan) had romped with the neighbourhood children on the front lawn of the house, making them, declared a Mrs McKillian, 'scream and laugh with joy'.

The 'Gone to Gowings' graffito and the story about romping with the kids were responsible for the widely held 'tough guy with a heart of gold' image of Darcy Dugan. From then on he was thought of as a good bloke, a lovable rogue who, for all his faults, was touched by humanity. Darcy's dad helped to embellish the myth. On Darcy's arrest, Dick Dugan, a good-natured 78-year-old knockabout with a ready grin and teeth like tombstones, blamed Mears for leading him astray and said he would spend what little money he had on a good defence lawyer for his son. 'Even if I finish up broke, I will see that everything is done to defend Darcy,' said Dick. 'I'll have a heart-to-heart with him … a father talking to his son, and I know Darcy will appreciate it.'

Despite his father's and his lawyer's best efforts, later that year Darcy Dugan was sentenced to death for the attempted murder of Ultimo Commonwealth Bank manager Nalder. The sentence was afterwards commuted to life in prison.

Apart from a half-hearted bid to escape in 1953, and the time he was attacked by a prisoner wielding a chair – not his fault – Dugan proved an exemplary inmate. 'They haven't broken his spirit, but they've tamed him,' Dick Dugan told reporters in 1955, then added that his son's behaviour was so good that surely he would be released in a few years.

Then, he continued, eyes growing misty at the thought, together they'd start a new life in South America.

Prison authorities, whose memories were short, rewarded the serial escaper for toeing the line in prison by transferring him from Grafton Gaol (commonly, and deservedly, known as 'The House of Fear') to the less stringent Parramatta Gaol, and giving him a job in the carpentry shop. Which was exactly what the wily Dugan hoped they'd do.

He bided his time at Parramatta for two years, then made his move. On 12 January 1957, Dugan, now thirty-seven and prematurely grey-haired, was found to be missing from his cell. Alarms rang and the gaol was locked down as police and warders scoured the site. Once more the redoubtable Ray Kelly was called for.

After being present and accounted for at the 8 am roll-call, Dugan had gone to the carpentry shop, where he climbed into a wheelbarrow and concertinaed himself into a tight package, then had an accomplice cover him with sawdust and wheel the barrow out to a sewage-pump shed in the gaol's vegetable farm. There Dugan lowered himself into a hole in the shed's concrete floor that he had been digging for the past five months. His plan was to wait for night to fall and give him the cover he needed to dash to the prison walls and escape.

Dugan's attempt was thwarted late in the afternoon. Kelly and a squad of armed police had swarmed all over the prison and after an eight-hour search found him cowering in his hole. He went quietly when they rousted him and relieved him – who knew how he'd acquired them? – of £31 in cash, a crystal radio set with an earphone, a knife, eleven pieces of fruit, suit pants and a casual shirt, a jumper, two handkerchiefs, a pen, a shaving brush and razor, and pages he'd ripped from a street guide of Sydney.

In an editorial a day or so later, the *Sydney Morning Herald* echoed the fears of a distinctly edgy community when it mused about the tough lot of the warden of a gaol in which is housed:

> a criminal as tough and cunning as [Dugan, a] notorious escapee who is always likely to make any system of prison supervision look silly if given half a chance. But that is the greater reason for ensuring

> that the fractional opportunity is not afforded. Whatever the Comptroller-General of Prisons or the Parramatta authorities may say, the public has a right to ask for the most searching inquiry into the conditions in which Dugan was able to gather the assortment of articles and the money found in his possession ... No intelligent person wishes to see our prisons controlled with the harshness of a concentration camp ... but when dangerous criminals – especially those with a fixation on escape – are lodged in gaol the security measures should be such as to ensure that they stay there. A great deal of arduous police effort in bringing wrongdoers to justice has too often been poorly rewarded, and the community exposed to needless anxiety, by laxity of control within the prison walls ... When found, Dugan had a small radio. With a little more patience he might have ended up with a television set.

As Dugan languished in a maximum security cell back at Grafton, his father conceded that the trip to South America might now be off. 'My son has been foolish in destroying the good conduct record he has built up,' he mourned to a reporter from the *Herald*. '[I had hoped] that I could meet him out of gaol again before I die. But surely he will get a long sentence this time. I saved to give Darcy and his brother Tom a good start in life. Tom has gone straight – he is a cleanskin – but although it's a terrible thing for a father to admit, Darcy has a kink and he is a criminal.' Then, conveniently overlooking bullet-punctured and wheelchair-bound Les Nalder, old Dick asserted 'but I defy anyone to say that Darcy ever injured any person'.

Six years of relatively trouble-free prison time later (if such indiscretions as another abortive escape bid in 1958, a fight with a fellow prisoner, being caught trying to smuggle letters to a woman, and hiding a radio in his cell can be overlooked), and once more Dugan's winning ways had prison authorities extolling his good attitude and hard work as a bootmaker, carpenter and tailor. 'Darcy's all right. He has complied well with the discipline and obeyed the rules,' said one Grafton warder, and then added, without a hint of irony, '... the main problem with him [is] his attempts to escape.' Why, so well-behaved had Dugan been, so reformed a character was he, that if he continued to keep his nose clean, there was every chance he would be paroled in 1965, by which time he would have served fifteen years of his life term.

In November 1964, Dugan was transferred to the minimum security Brookfield Afforestation Camp near Tumbarumba in southern New South Wales. Brookfield was a halfway establishment where prisoners 'decompressed' from the prison system in preparation for their release. Said one official, 'It's better that we see how he is going to react now, rather than when he gets back into society ... We have to taper [imprisonment] off because you can't take a man straight out of a cage where he's spent years of his life and give him immediate total freedom. You have to do it gradually.' Dugan's father Dick and brother Tom excitedly began planning the great day when their son and brother would be with them once more.

Unbelievably, despite knowing that total freedom was just weeks away, Dugan blew it all. He was incorrigible. He simply couldn't help himself. A prison was something you broke out of. So he did. Night after night, driving a car he had stolen and hidden for his personal use in a forest on the grounds of the camp, and sometimes in company with Ian Henke, a fellow prisoner, Dugan relieved petrol stations, bowling clubs and golf clubs, pubs and shops in the vicinity of money, cigarettes and food before returning to his bunk. When police investigated, they homed in on the prisoner most likely – and in Dugan's cabin they found the trapdoor through which he climbed to head off on his nefarious sorties without being spotted by guards.

Dugan's release was rescinded and he was transferred under heavy guard to a maximum security cell at Goulburn Gaol. 'Oh, well,' he reportedly sighed.

Reporters, knowing Dick Dugan was always good for a quote, made a beeline to his room in a ramshackle Ultimo boarding house. Darcy's bitterly disappointed, now 90-year-old father did not let them down. 'It's a frame-up,' he said, weeping. 'He wouldn't be so foolish as to try something so close to getting out. I had money for Darce, and a job. It was the wish of my life to see him come through the front door, and put my arms around him and kiss him. Now I'll never do it.'

Dick Dugan was right: he never would. The loving, steadfast old man passed away in August the following year. His son, by then an inmate again of Parramatta Gaol, was allowed to attend the burial at Rookwood Cemetery. Trim and fit-looking, with his grey hair neatly brushed back, Dugan wore a dark suit with a white pocket handkerchief for the occasion. He would have looked like any urbane executive were it not for the handcuffs and the police escort. Tom, his brother, joined him at the graveside and they chatted for five minutes before Dugan was led back to the prison van and returned to his cell.

Then, on 14 September 1967, after seventeen years, seven months and four days in gaol, Darcy Dugan, now aged forty-seven, was freed. NSW Justice Minister John Maddison said he was convinced that Australia's most notorious prisoner was finally a changed man. He was more mature than he had ever been in his life, and he had a whole new set of values. He had promised to go straight, and the government and Corrective Services chiefs believed him.

Dugan himself weighed in. When he walked out of the prison, and before taking up digs at the home of a childhood friend outside Sydney while he found his own flat, he vowed that his days as a lawbreaker were over. All he wanted now was to be left alone, to fade into anonymity and be a law-abiding citizen. 'I just want to be one of the mugs,' he declared, then crowed that his life had been so colourful that he was seriously considering writing his autobiography – which would be sure to be a bestseller ...

For all his protestations of wishing to disappear from the limelight, Dugan willingly became a media darling. He was well advanced with his memoirs, and orchestrating a bidding war among the tabloids for a series of articles on his time behind bars. He might even become a reporter himself. Or – why not? – a salesman. And, having seen the damage that narcotics can do while in prison, he felt his drug counselling services might be in demand.

In November, Sydney radio station 2GB personalities Andrea and John Pearce staged a publicity stunt whereby Dugan dined with legendary policeman and chief of the CIB Ray 'The Blizzard' Blissett, and top *Sydney Morning Herald* reporter Max Suich, at the trendy Weinkeller restaurant in Pitt Street. Dugan played along. He boasted over lunch of how he had become a keen punter at the races and he had a system that worked. 'And, to tell you the truth, I've been chasing the ladies. I went through a 17-year drought!' He reminisced with Blissett about life on the streets of the inner city in the lawless old days. Preening and posturing as the *Herald's* photographer snapped away, Dugan said he had no respect for newspaper reporters and police officers (Blissett and Ray Kelly excepted, of course), but would have made a good cop himself, 'maybe tougher than Kelly'. Over dessert he offered Blissett some tips on how to have a happy retirement.

At Christmas Dugan was among a clutch of prominent identities, including Andrea, the Reverend Ted Noffs, Barry Humphries, Joe the Gadget Man, *Vogue* editor Sheila Scotter, New South Wales Premier Robert Askin and Colonel Crint of the pop group The Regimental Band of the Foot and Mouth Deserters, who were asked by a newspaper to tell their Christmas wish. 'I want to enjoy Christmas with an attractive companion. And I don't want a hangover,' was Dugan's witty response.

One who offered the hand of friendship was the Reverend Ted Noffs of the Wayside Chapel in Kings Cross. Noffs was seriously impressed by Dugan's expressed determination to make a positive contribution to society, and by the way Dugan eagerly accepted when Noffs asked him to volunteer his services helping the city's underprivileged, and in distributing Austcare envelopes to aid world refugees.

Largely thanks to his championship by Noffs, Dugan, who had never before acted (at least not on a stage), was cast as a warder in the Ensemble Theatre's September 1969 production of *Fortune and Men's Eyes*, a grittily realistic and so controversial play set in a prison, at the Anzac Auditorium. The play, directed by Max Cullen, received good reviews, as did Dugan. 'Mr Dugan, though an amateur vocally, acts with a chilling plausibility,' wrote prominent theatre critic H.G. Kippax in the *Sydney Morning Herald*.

Dugan was the toast of Sydney. It seemed he was everywhere. On stage, on radio and television, being interviewed on everything from his total rehabilitation to his Melbourne Cup tips to the dangers posed by homosexual prisoners to young offenders in the prison system. He was doing good works with the dispossessed. He was a regular, sprucely dressed, eyes sparkling, a quip on his thin lips, and usually accompanied by an attractive woman, at restaurants and city picture shows.

While all this was going on, Dugan, unbeknown to his society and media friends, was also busy with another project. Robbery with menaces.

The first anyone knew that Dugan was playing his supporters for fools was when a small army of police armed with rifles and teargas dragged him from his rented home in Rozelle, in Sydney's inner west, at 9 pm on 17 November 1969. In Sydney's Central Court of Petty Sessions 'Darcy Ezekial Dugan, 49, social worker', was charged with five counts including armed robbery, assault and possession of an unlicensed pistol. Thirteen more charges were levelled in the days and weeks to come. Twelve accomplices were also charged with a series of counts, including armed hold-ups and assaults committed at Bondi Junction, Alexandria, Granville, Ashfield, Double Bay, Bellevue Hill, Paddington, Rozelle, Dulwich Hill, Mosman and Sydney city between April and September 1969. Among the goods found at Dugan's home and those of his cohorts were many thousands of dollars in cash, expensive paintings, cameras, walkie-talkies, a movie projector, gold rings and other jewellery, cars, a sleeping bag, a rug, tools and building materials. One especially nasty charge was that Dugan pistol-whipped one Keith Hoppitt and robbed him of $2350. He had also assaulted Ronald Silverton, the proprietor of Kleemo's jewellery store in Pitt Street, Sydney, and stolen from the store diamond rings, opals, sapphires, rubies, brooches and $350 in cash: total value $39 000. Dugan was waging a campaign of violence by day while posing for society photographers and treading the boards at the Anzac Auditorium by night.

Just as Dugan's father had believed in him and stood up for him no matter how incriminating the evidence, now the Reverend Noffs took his side. Supporting Dugan's application for bail, Noffs told the court that he had employed the defendant as an assistant welfare officer at the Wayside Chapel and that his duties had included educating released prisoners and young offenders that 'crime does not pay and [placing] his own antecedents before them'. Noffs had always found Dugan 'dedicated and conscientious in his work and [he] never resorted to subterfuge'. He said Dugan had told him, when he terminated his work at the Chapel on 31 January 1969, that he was leaving to complete his autobiography and rehearse for his role in *Fortune and Men's Eyes*. Noffs said he was confident that Dugan had been sincere with him and that he found it impossible to believe that he had been consorting with criminals, as the prosecution asserted, and merely pretending to be a law-abiding citizen. He would be welcome back at the Wayside Chapel at any time in the future.

At his trial in December, a witness for the defence said she had been with Dugan, whom she had met at the Wayside Chapel, when he went to Kleemo's two weeks before the robbery. He had told her he was keen to buy an engagement ring for his girl, someone named Margaret. The pair entered Kleemo's and Dugan had asked Ronald Silverton if he could see some engagement rings priced between $500 and $700. Silverton obliged. Dugan had looked at the rings, then left.

Silverton himself then took the stand and identified Dugan as one of a group of masked men who had stormed into his shop at 9.30 am on 22 August. Dugan's mask had slipped and he recognised him not only as the man who had been browsing there a fortnight before, but as the famous Darcy Dugan, so familiar a face on television and in the newspapers. Dugan had said, 'This is a stick-up. Stay perfectly still', and levelled a .45 calibre automatic pistol at Silverton while the others cleaned out the jewel cases and shelves. Dugan had prised open a locked drawer with a crowbar and emptied it of rings and loose stones. The robbers then fled into Pitt Street. Other witnesses testified that they had noticed Dugan, whom they recognised, lurking in a suspicious manner across the road from Kleemo's from around 9 am, before he was joined by a group of men and went into the store.

When he was committed to stand trial, Dugan erupted in court, claiming that the jewellery had been planted in his home by police and that the unsigned record of interview they had tabled, in which he confessed to the crimes, was bogus. 'I'd need to be bloody mad to have signed that!' he railed. A police officer testified that when diamonds were found in Dugan's carpet-sweeper on 17 November, Dugan had accused the officer of planting them there, and had threatened to kill the policeman 'if it takes me 30 years!'

At his trial in Sydney Quarter Sessions, which began on 27 April 1970, Dugan pleaded not guilty. His request that the highly respected Judge Monahan, chairman of the District Court judges, preside over the proceedings was turned down by Monahan himself who, incredulous at Dugan's cheek, noted that it was not the prerogative of the defendant to choose the judge.

In his defence, Dugan denied any wrongdoing and damned the charges against him as a 'giant frame-up' perpetrated by police who hated him for speaking out against law enforcers since his release.

Nevertheless, on 7 May after an eight-day trial, Judge Prior declared Dugan guilty as charged and on 22 May sentenced him to fourteen years. The prisoner nodded respectfully and walked quietly down to the cells. Fair cop.

He spent the next few years in prison making a nuisance of himself. He appealed to the Supreme Court against his conviction, and the appeal was thrown out. In 1971 he sued the very institutions which had courted him so assiduously – radio stations 2GB and 2UE, Channel 7, Mirror Newspapers, *The Sun* and the *Sydney Morning Herald*, Associated Newspapers – for a total of $21 million, but Mr Justice Yeldham ruled that a convicted felon still serving a life sentence could not sue for damages at law.

In 1977 Dugan, then aged fifty-seven, was treated for a deteriorating kidney. He was released from the prison hospital in time, however, to make a notable appearance at the NSW government's Royal Commission into Prisons. He swore there that he had been beaten by warders and prison staff many times and been doused with boiling water while incarcerated at Grafton Gaol. He had been singled out for extra punishment because he had refused the edict that 'intractable' prisoners were forbidden to look prison officers directly in the face and must avert their eyes when in their presence. 'I would not allow them to humiliate me in this way,' he said. 'One night Officer L was standing in front of the wing when I was marching to my cell and my eyes passed over him. He immediately attacked, saying "Look down, you bastard!" The same thing happened on three successive nights but I was determined I was not going to lower my eyes for him.' So Officer L had blackened Dugan's eyes by punching him repeatedly in the face. Dugan also claimed that he had been bashed on ten consecutive nights by an Officer J. In spite of the punishment he had continued to look the guards in the eyes. In time, he said, they had tired of persecuting him, 'though not other prisoners'.

Dugan told the Commission that the only way he had remained sane while locked up for so long was to read four pages of the dictionary every night and an encyclopaedia.

Homosexuality, which, incidentally, Dugan 'detested', was rife in prisons, he told the Commission. 'It spreads like a disease, cultivated in ideal laboratory conditions ... Kissing, cuddling and hand-holding goes on all the time.' In the prison tailorshop at Cooma Gaol he had seen 'thirty or forty homosexuals [carrying on] their love affairs in full view of everyone'.

At the age of sixty, Dugan was released from Maitland Gaol on 28 May 1980, deemed to be too old now to be a serious risk to society. Besides, he was *really* ready to settle down this time. As proof, in July he wed Jan Simmonds, 40-year-old Canberra journalist and slimming club proprietor and sister of the notorious criminal Kevin Simmonds, who hanged himself in Grafton Gaol in 1966. His faithful ally the Reverend Noffs officiated at the Wayside Chapel. 'I've got myself one in a million!' beamed Dugan, natty in a light blue suit on whose lapel reposed a huge carnation.

The Dugans did not live happily ever after. Fourteen months after their marriage, on 12 July 1981, Dugan, yet again unable to curb his criminal instincts, held up an Ashfield service station. He wore an army hat, a mask and dark glasses, and brandished a .25 pistol and a knife at the proprietor. Alas for Dugan, the 'proprietor' was a detective who had been tipped off six days before that the old crook was plotting the heist. When Dugan cried 'Hold up!', Detective Sergeant Dennis Gilligan yelled right back, 'No, Darce. Police! Drop your gun!' At that, other officers who had been hiding in a storeroom crash-tackled Dugan from behind, sending him sprawling to the floor.

In court, charged with armed robbery, Dugan claimed he'd been set up. Added his wife, '... by an agent provocateur!'

When a reporter asked him how he felt, Dugan smiled wearily and sighed, 'Mate, I'm stuffed.'

And, in a way, he was. Not just because he was found guilty and sentenced to three and a half years in prison, but also because his body was failing. He had severe kidney and heart disease now, and in 1984 was felled by a stroke. Frail, rheumy-eyed and with skin like parchment, Dugan was a low-security prisoner at Malabar Training Centre. On 8 November 1985, he walked out of the prison gates for the last time. Nattily dressed, white-haired and sporting a spiffy goatee, he was met by Jan Dugan who, although their marriage had not survived his most recent imprisonment, was standing by him. As the pair walked to a vehicle, onlookers remarked how shaky the old lag looked.

Dugan went to live in a boarding house in Glebe that had been established to ease prisoners back into the outside world. He saw his brother Tom every few weeks, and stayed in touch with Jan. He tried to go dancing at his local pub – he had always loved to dance – but his stroke-affected legs just wouldn't whiz him about as they used to. To anyone who'd listen he'd say in a weak and raspy voice that he was writing a book, was really writing it this time, and as well as being about his life and times it would be an exposé of the iniquities of the NSW prison system.

In January 1987, police raided the halfway house searching for criminals and stolen goods. By mistake, they smashed down the door to the room where Dugan lay bedridden. The invasion, said his friends, brought on a heart attack.

He survived another four years, racked by more strokes, more heart attacks and respiratory disease. The latter got him before the others could, as he lay semi-comatose in a nursing home. He was a couple of days short of his seventy-first birthday when he died but he looked much, much older.

They buried Darcy Dugan in Rookwood Cemetery, in the same plot that his father Dick's cheap casket had been lowered into twenty years before, and later the mourners held a rambunctious wake at the rakish Bourbon and Beefsteak Bar in the heart of Kings Cross. Present were cops and robbers, showbiz types, journalists, prison guards and people who had crossed paths with Dugan when he worked at the Wayside Chapel. Max

Cullen, who'd directed him in *Fortune and Men's Eyes*, was there, and so was writer Rod Hay, who would pen a well-received biography of the villain. Jan Dugan read a quotation from Shakespeare. Some people danced to Glenn Miller's 'Moonlight Serenade'. Everybody laughed and cried and drank too much. And they swapped stories, both tall and true, about Darcy Dugan, the greatest escapologist, they reckoned, since Harry Houdini.

REFERENCE SOURCES AND BACKGROUND

1 The Graeme Thorne Kidnapping, 1960

The Daily Mirror, **1960**: June 1, July 7, 8, 9, 10, 11, 12, 13, 14, 15, 16, 19, 20, 21, 22, 23, 25, 27, August 17, 19, 20, 22, 26, September 15, 27, 28, 29, October 10, 11, 12, 13, 14, 15, 17, 18, 19, 20, 21, 22, 24, 27, 28, 31, November 18, 19, 21, 22, 23, December 5, 6, 12, 13, 14, 15, 16; **1961**: March 20, 21, 22, 23, 24, 27, 28, 29, 30; **1968**: October 7.

2 The Vampire Killer, 1989

Additional reporting by Norm Lipson
Court transcripts
The Nine Network
The Seven Network
ABC-TV
Network Ten
Ron Hicks, *The Vampire Killer*, Bantam Books, Sydney, 1992
The Courier-Mail, **1989**: October 24, November 8; **1990**: January 31, February 1; **1991**: February 1, 2, 5, 6, 7, 8, 9, 12, 13, 14, 15, 16; **1992**: August 1, 21; **1996**: March 12, May 25, 27, September 23; **2003**: September 10, 11; **2006**: June 26.

3 The Granny Killer, 1989–90

Additional reporting by Norm Lipson
Court transcripts
The Seven Network

ABC-TV
The Nine Network
Network Ten
Fox-8
Larry Writer, with Steve Barrett and Simon Bouda, *Garden of Evil: The Granny Killer's Reign of Terror*, Ironbark Press, Sydney, 1992.
Larry Writer, 'Face to Face with Evil', *Who Weekly*, May 18, 1992.
The Daily Telegraph, **1989**: March 2, 5, May 10, 11, November 3, 4, 24, 25, 26: **1990**: March 20, 21, 22, 23; **2005**: September 10, 11.
The Sydney Morning Herald, **1989**: March 2, 3, 6, May 10, 12, November 3, 4, 24, 25, 26, 27, December 16; **1990**: March 20, 21, 22, 23; **1991**: November 20, 21, 22, 23, 26, 27, 28, 29; **2005**: September 10.

4 The Law of the Razor, 1920s–1930s

Court and police records from NSW Government archives and the Justice and Police Museum, Sydney.
George Blaikie, *Wild Women of Sydney*, Rigby, Sydney, 1980.
The Story of Camberwell, Southwark Council, London, 1972.
Alfred McCoy, *Drug Traffic: Narcotics and Organised Crime in Australia*, Harper & Row, Sydney, 1986.
John Ramsland, *With Just but Relentless Discipline: A Social History of Corrective Services in New South Wales*, Kangaroo Press, Sydney, 1996.
Dennis Whitburn, *Penthouse History of Crime in Australia, Part V: The Law of the Razor*, Horwitz Sydney, 1988.
Larry Writer, *Razor: A True Story of Slashers, Gangsters, Prostitutes and Sly Grog*, Pan Macmillan, Sydney, 2001.
The Daily Mirror, January 6, 1932.
The Daily Telegraph, November 22, 1936; February 1, 1964.
People, March 15, 1950.
Smith's Weekly, September 23, 1950.
The Sydney Morning Herald, **1914**: June 11, October 14; **1927**: March 28, July 13; **1929**: August 3; **1932**: March 20; **1933**: September 16; **1970**: November 25.
The Sun, May 16, 1929.
Truth, **1927**: June 12, July 17; **1928**: January 1, 15, September 16, 23, 30; **1930**: January 12, April 6, June 29, October 19; **1932**: January 31, February 7, March 6, August 7; **1934**: November 25; **1936**: October 4; **1956**: April 29.

5 The Hoddle Street Massacre, 1987

Additional reporting by Norm Lipson
Court transcripts
The Nine Network
The Seven Network

ABC-TV
Network Ten
The Age, **1987**: August 10, 11, 12; **1988**: October 29, November 11, *The Age Good Weekend magazine*, December 3; **2003**: October 8, November 10, 25; **2004**: October 19.
The Sydney Morning Herald, **1987**: August 11, 15, 18, 22, December 9; **1988**: April 19, 20, June 2, 3, 14, August 5, October 15, 20, 29, November 1, 11, 12, 17, *The SMH Good Weekend magazine*, December 3; **1989**: January 14, 23; **1990**: June 11.
Julian Knight's legal challenges:
Knight vs *Sec to the Vic Dept of Employment, Education and Training*; *Lapidos* vs *Vic Dept of Justice*; *Knight* vs *Core [Public Correctional Enterprise]*; *Knight* vs *Wise and Spadano*; *Knight* vs *Core*; *Knight* vs *Vic Minister for Corrections & Ors*; *Knight* vs *Core*; *Knight* vs *Core*; *Knight* vs *Spadano & Anor*; *Knight* vs *Sec to the Vic Dept of Justice*; *Knight* vs *Vic Minister for Corrections & Ors*; *Knight* vs *Vic Minister for Corrections & Ors*; *Knight* vs *State of Vic & Wise*; *Knight* vs *Spadano & Ors*; *Knight* vs *Sec to the Vic Dept Justice*; *Attorney-General for the State of Vic* vs *Knight*.

6 Outback Rampage, 1973

Additional reporting by Norm Lipson
Court transcripts
The Nine Network
Network Ten
The Seven Network
ABC-TV
The Central Coast Herald, May 26, 28, 2001.
The Illawarra Mercury, June 15, 2002.
The Newcastle Herald, November 19, 2005.
The Sydney Morning Herald, **1973**: November 11, 12, 13, 14, 15, 17, 18, 19, 20, December 1; **1974**: January 9, 11, 12, February 19, 20, June 11, 12, 14, 15, 20, 21, 22, 25, 27, July 5, August 13, October 17; **1975**: February 8, May 23, October 8; **1981**: April 10; **1986**: March 16; **1987**: June 17, 21; **1988**: May 30, June 2; **1992**: December 11; **1993**: May 7, 11, April 5; **1997**: April 5, 6, 26, May 11; **2000**: July 1; **2001**: May 26, June 1; **2003**: January 29; **2006**: March 20.
The Sunday Telegraph, Sunday, February 29, 2004
www.abc.net.au/7.30/content/2004/s1037442.htm
www.crimelibrary.com/notorious_murders/mass/baker/1.html
www.federationpress.com.au/pdf/Fardon.pdf
www.hcourt.gov.au/media/Baer.pdf
www.parliament.nsw.gov.au
www.thecrimeweb.com/Crump%20and%20Baker.htm
www.theissue.com.au/www_root/pdf/ti020108.pdf

7 The Killing of Dr Victor Chang, 1991

Additional reporting by Norm Lipson
Court transcripts
The Nine Network
The Seven Network
SBS
ABC-TV
Network Ten
Police records of interview
Vanessa Chang, *Victor Chang: A Tribute to my Father,* Pan Macmillan, Sydney 2001.
Ron Stephenson, *Victor Chang: Murder of a Hero,* New Holland, Sydney 2004.
The Age, October 31, 1992.
The Daily Telegraph, June 30, 2001.
The Daily Telegraph Mirror, **1991**: July 5, 6, 8, 9, 10, 12, 13, 14, 15, 16, 17, 19, 20, 23, 27.
The Sunday Telegraph, July 7, 1991.
The Sydney Morning Herald, **1991**: August 9, September 30, October 1, 4, 21, November 14, December 13; 1992: October 19, 20, 27, 31, December 23; **2006**: June 29.
AAP General News Wire, July 3, 2006.

8 The Cross-dressing Killer, 1917

Court transcripts
Peter Doyle with Caleb Williams, *City of Shadows: Sydney Police Photographs 1912–1948,* Historic Houses Trust, 2005.
Suzanne Falkiner, *Eugenia: A Man,* Pan Books Australia, Sydney, 1988
Ruth Ford, '"The Man-Woman Murderer": sex, fraud, sexual inversion and the unmentionable "article" in 1920s Australia', *Gender & History,* vol 12, no. 1, April 2000, pp. 158–96.
'Woman who killed her "wife"', *People* (Sydney), 21 October 1953, pp. 32–3.
Lorae Parry, *Eugenia,* Victoria University Press, Wellington, NZ, 1996.
The Daily Telegraph, October 6, October 7, 1920.
The Forbes Flyer, Autumn 2006 (Issue 11): 'Eugenia Falleni: Harry Crawford'
The Sydney Morning Herald, **1917**: October 3; **1920**: October 7.
R. vs *Eugene Falleni,* depositions, 9/7250, and trial transcripts, 6/1007 (State Records New South Wales).

9 Expelling the Demons, 1993

Additional reporting by Norm Lipson
Court transcripts
The Nine Network
Network Ten

The Seven Network
ABC-TV
Dennis Passa, 'Of Good and Evil', *Who Weekly*, December 19, 1994.
Larry Writer, 'Death in the Name of God', *Who Weekly*, February 22, 1993.
Larry Writer, 'The Exorcists', *Who Weekly*, November 14, 1994.
The Herald-Sun, **1993**: February 3, 4, 5, 6, 7, April 10, 18, 23, July 22, September 14, 15, 17; **1994**: February 15, September 30, October 18, 19, 20, 21, 22, 25, 26, 27, 28, 29, November 3, 4, 10, 17, 18, 19, 22, 23, 24, 25, 26, 29, 30, December 1, 2, 3, 24; **1995**: May 12, September 7, 8.

10 Partners in Crime, 1986

Additional reporting by Norm Lipson
Court transcripts
The Advertiser, October 13, 2005.
The Australian, July 28, 2004.
The Daily Telegraph, **1986**: November 12, 13; **1987**: February 11, March 4; **2005**: November 30.
The Sunday Times, October 9, 2005.
The Sun-Herald, November 16, 1986.
The Sydney Morning Herald, **1986**: November 13, 15, 18, December 13; **1987**: February 11, March 4, September 15; **1988**: January 18.
AAP Wire, December 6, 2004; October 7, 2005; November 29, 2005.
ABC Premium News, **2005**: February 25, March 4, 30, October 8; **2006**: June 19; **2007**: May 19.
http://www.crimelibrary.com

11 The Night Stalker, 1988–91

Additional reporting by Norm Lipson
Court transcripts
ABC-TV
The Nine Network
The Age, **1991**: April 14, 15; **1992**: April 11, 12, 13; **1993**: February 6; **2003**: October 8.
The Herald (Melbourne), **1988**: December 28, 29, 30; **1989**: January 23; **1990**: July 5, 6, 11, 13, 20, September 3.
The Herald-Sun, **2001**: March 31, April 2, 4, December 31; **2003**: August 4, 7.
Mercury, August 4, 2003.
The Sunday Herald-Sun, November 14, 2004.
The Sun-Herald (Sydney), July 8, 1990.
The Sydney Morning Herald, **1988**: December 28; **1989**: January 2; **1990**: July 5, 7, 9, 12.
The Sunday Age, April 1, 2001.

12 The Acid Test, 1907–08

Court transcripts
Anna Haebich, 'Murdering Stepmothers: The Trial and Execution of Martha Rendall', *Journal of Australian Studies,* University of Queensland Press, 1998.
The Prison Telegraph: Crime and Punishment. Published by the Government of Western Australia [n.d.].
The West Australian, **1909**: August 11, 12, 13, 17, September 8, 9, 10, 11, 13, 14, October 4; **1910**: September 15, 24, 27, 28, 30, October 2, 5, 6, 7.
www.members.telocity.com/~snyderboy/femvio/serial_murder.htm
www.redbackwebs.com.au/cufflinks/police/serial.html#Rendall

13 The Slaughter of Anita Cobby, 1986

Additional reporting by Norm Lipson
The Nine Network
The Seven Network
ABC-TV
Network Ten
Julia Sheppard, *Someone Else's Daughter: The Life and Death of Anita Cobby* (edited by Larry Writer), Ironbark Press, Sydney, 1991.
The Daily Mirror, **1986**: February 3, 4, 5, 6, 7, 8, 9, 20, 23, March 17, June 11, 17.
The Daily Telegraph, **1986**: February 3, 4, 5, 6, 7, 8, 9, 20, 23, March 17, June 11, 17.
The Sun, **1986**: February 3, 4, 5, 6, 7, 8, 9, 20, 23, March 17, June 11, 17.
The Sydney Morning Herald, **1986**: February 3, 4, 5, 6, 7, 8, 9, 20, 23, March 17, June 11, 17.

14 Suffer the Children, 1989–1999

Additional reporting by Norm Lipson
Court transcripts
The Nine Network
The Seven Network
SBS
ABC-TV
Network Ten
Larry Writer, 'Courage of Conviction', *The Reader's Digest,* January 2004, based on interviews with Detective Sergeant Bernie Ryan.
The Daily Telegraph, **2001**: April 19, 20; **2003**: April 27, 28, 29, May 6, 7, 9, 11, 14, 15, 19, 20, 21, 24, October 25.
The Newcastle Herald, **2001**: April 19; **2003**: April 21, May 21, 24.
The Sydney Morning Herald, **2003**: April 24, 27, May 6, 9, 10, 16, 21, 20, 24, October 25.

15 The Brunswick Baby Farmer, 1892

Court transcripts

The Argus, **1893**: November 28, 29, 30, December 1, 2; **1894**: January 8, 15, 16.

The Australian Dictionary of Biography: Frances Knorr, entry by Kathy Laster. Melbourne University Press, 2005.

http://www.crimezzz.net/serialkillers/K/KNORR_frances.php

http://www.homes.vic.net.au/~pioneers/pppg5bp.htm

http://www.spondee.net/poets/RussonPenni.htm

16 The Disciple and the Devil – The Truro Murders, 1976–77

Larry Writer, 'The Killing Fields', *Who Weekly,* October 17, 1994.

The Advertiser, **1979**: April 18, 19, 20, 27, 29, May 2, 3; **1980**: February 23, March 11, 14, April 21, 23, May 16, June 20.

The Sydney Morning Herald, **1979**: April 18, 19, 20, 27, 28, 30, May 1, 3, 4, 5, 9, 10, 12, 24, 25, 26, 27, 29, 30, June 2, 8, July 5, September 4, 5, 6, 7, 8, 9, 12, 14, October 5; **1980**: February 23, March 11, 13, 14, April 22, May 16, June 20; **1981**: November 8; **1983**: July 31; **1985**: May 15; **1986**: July 16, November 15; **1987**: June 16; **1989**: May 31; **1990**: March 3; **2000**: February 8; **2002**: November 23.

'The Truro Serial Murders', Paul B. Kidd, www.crimelibrary.com/serial_killers/predators/worrell/index_1.html

17 Portrait of Evil, 1954–1961

Additional reporting by Norm Lipson

Court transcripts

Sally Davis, interview with author

The Daily Telegraph, January 26, April 5, 1962.

The Daily Mirror, **1954**: May 8, 18; **1961**: November 8, 9, 10, 16, 17, December 14, 22; **1962**: January 25.

The Sun-Herald, **1962**: April 8; **1978**: August 27; **1986**: June 8; **2003**: November 30.

The Sydney Morning Herald, **1962**: April 5, 7, 9; **1972**: July 22, December 16; **1976**: April 29; **1978**: July 18, August 5; **1979**: March 17; **2004**: February 22.

http://www.sa.liberal.org.au/chapman/content/files/documents/07%20Child%20Pornography.doc

18 Sins of the Son, 2001

Additional reporting by Norm Lipson

The Nine Network

The Seven Network

ABC-TV

Network Ten

The Age, September 17, 2004.
The Australian, **2001**: July 11, 12, 13, 21; **2002**: June 14.
Catholic News
The Daily Telegraph, **2001**: July 11, 12, 13, 21; **2002**: June 14; **2004**: May 21, August 22; **2005**: September 25; **2007**: August 24
The Sydney Morning Herald, **2001**: July 11, 12, 13, 21; **2002**: June 14; **2004**: May 21; **2007**: November 27.
ABC Online, May 20, 2004; September 17, 2004
NSW Supreme Court Regina vs *Gonzales* [2004] NSWSC 822 (September 17 2004)
www.austli.edu.au/au/cases/nsw/supreme_ct/2004/822.html
Rummage.com.au

19 The Kimberley Killer, 1987

'The Kimberley Killer', an episode in the Nine Network and Fox TV series *Crime Investigation Australia*, hosted by Steve Liebmann
Northern Territory News, **1987**: June 15, 16, 17, 18, 19, 22, 23, 24, 25; **2007**: March 17.
Sunday Territorian, June 19, 2005.
The Sun-Herald, June 21, 28, 1987.
The Sydney Morning Herald, **1987**: June 13, 17, 18, 19, 20, 22, 23.

20 The Port Arthur Massacre, 1996

Additional reporting by Norm Lipson
Transcripts of police interviews with Martin Bryant
Mike Bingham, *Suddenly One Sunday: The True Story of the Port Arthur Tragedy Based on Eyewitness Accounts*, HarperCollins, Sydney, 1996.
Psychiatric Report on Martin Bryant, Paul E Mullen, Professor of Forensic Psychiatry, Monash University, Director of Victorian Forensic Psychiatry Services.
Larry Writer, 'Prisoners for Life', *The Australian Women's Weekly*, February 2004.
Court TV's crime library, *The Port Arthur Massacre: A Killer Among Us*
Mercury, **1996**: April 29, 30, May 1, 2, 3, 4, November 8.
The Sydney Morning Herald, **1996**: April 29, 30, November 8; **2006**: March 29.
The Age, March 29, 2006.
Psychology in Action, March 28, 2006.
'Managing Martin: the Jailing of Martin Bryant', ABC Radio National, March 16, 1997.
Enough Rope with Andrew Denton, August 16, 2004, ABC-TV.

21 Gone to Gowings, 1940s–1980s

Court transcripts
The Daily Mirror, February 14, 1950.

The Sun-Herald, March 1, 1998.

The Sydney Morning Herald, **1955**: November 22; **1956**: December 30; **1958**: January 14, 15, 17, February 1; **1960**: March 20, May 9, 10, July 12, August 11, 18; **1961**: February 5, May 20; **1963**: January 20, July 13, 21; **1964**: February 9; **1965**: February 14, June 22, July 1, 14, 15, August 26, 27, 28, 29, September 12, October 2; **1967**: May 27, September 15, 17, 19, November 11, 12; **1968**: March 21, May 15, December 8; **1969**: September 15, 21, November 18, 19, 21, 26, 30, December 4, 7, 12, 13, 17, 20, 27, 30; **1970**: January 1, 3, 6, 7, 8, 9, 10, 14, 15, 16, 17, 28, 30, February 21, March 20, April 29, May 5, 12, 16, 23, June 13, October 3, 31, December 9; **1971**: March 1, May 18, 20, 21, 22, 25, 26, September 9, 11, 17; **1972**: September 4; **1974**: February 10; **1975**: November 5; **1976**: May 31, June 19; **1977**: February 5, 22, 23, March 31; **1978**: December 20, 21; **1980**: May 29, 30, July 13, October 26; **1981**: March 2, April 9, July 14, 19, 21, October 15, November 27; **1982**: October 19, 20, 23; **1984**: March 16; **1985**: February 3, August 4, November 8, 9; **1986**: May 3, September 12; **1987**: January 13, June 17; **1988**: February 24, May 8, July 17; **1990**: March 25; **1991**: August 24, 27.

First published in 2008 by Pier 9, an imprint of Murdoch Books Pty Limited

Murdoch Books Australia
Pier 8/9
23 Hickson Road
Millers Point NSW 2000
Phone: +61 (0) 2 8220 2000
Fax: +61 (0) 2 8220 2558
www.murdochbooks.com.au

Murdoch Books UK Limited
Erico House, 6th Floor
93–99 Upper Richmond Road
Putney, London SW15 2TG
Phone: +44 (0) 20 8785 5995
Fax: +44 (0) 20 8785 5985
www.murdochbooks.co.uk

Chief Executive: Juliet Rogers
Publishing Director: Kay Scarlett

Editorial Manager: Colette Vella
Editor: Anne Savage
Concept and Design: Joanna Byrne
Production: Kita George

National Library of Australia Cataloguing-in-Publication Data

Author: Writer, Larry.
Title: The Australian book of true crime / Larry Writer.
Publisher: Sydney, NSW: Murdoch Books, 2008.
ISBN: 9781 741962079 (pbk.)
Subjects: Crime—Australia. Criminals—Australia. Criminal investigation—Australia.
Dewey Number: 364.994

A catalogue record for this book is available from the British Library.

Printed by Imago in 2008. PRINTED IN CHINA.
Reprinted 2009.